Networks of Influence?

The Global Economic Governance Programme was established at University College in 2003 to foster research and debate into how global markets and institutions can better serve the needs of people in developing countries. The three core objectives of the programme are:

- to conduct and foster research into international organizations and markets as well as new public–private governance regimes;
- to create and maintain a network of scholars and policymakers working on these issues; and
- to influence debate and policy in both the public and the private sector in developed and developing countries.

The Programme is directly linked to Oxford University's *Department of Politics and International Relations* and *Centre for International Studies*. It serves as an interdisciplinary umbrella within Oxford, drawing together members of the Departments of Economics, Law, and Development Studies working on these issues and linking them to an international research network. The Programme has been made possible through the generous support of Old Members of University College. Its research projects are principally funded by the MacArthur Foundation (Chicago) and the International Development Research Centre (Ottawa).

Networks of Influence?

Developing Countries in a Networked Global Order

Edited by

Leonardo Martinez-Diaz and Ngaire Woods

OXFORD
UNIVERSITY PRESS

OXFORD

UNIVERSITY PRESS

Great Clarendon Street, Oxford OX2 6DP

Oxford University Press is a department of the University of Oxford.
It furthers the University's objective of excellence in research, scholarship,
and education by publishing worldwide in

Oxford New York

Auckland Cape Town Dar es Salaam Hong Kong Karachi
Kuala Lumpur Madrid Melbourne Mexico City Nairobi
New Delhi Shanghai Taipei Toronto

With offices in

Argentina Austria Brazil Chile Czech Republic France Greece
Guatemala Hungary Italy Japan Poland Portugal Singapore
South Korea Switzerland Thailand Turkey Ukraine Vietnam

Oxford is a registered trade mark of Oxford University Press
in the UK and in certain other countries

Published in the United States
by Oxford University Press Inc., New York

British Library Cataloguing in Publication Data

Data available

Library of Congress Cataloging-in-Publication Data

Networks of influence? : developing countries in a networked global
order/edited by Leonardo Martinez-Diaz and Ngaire Woods.
p. cm.
Includes index.
ISBN 978-0-19-956442-2
1. International finance. 2. Finance–Developing countries. 3. Developing
countries–Foreign economic relations. 4. Capitalists and financiers–Social
networks–Developing countries. I. Martinez-Diaz, Leonardo, 1976- II.
Woods, Ngaire.
HG3881.N48 2009
332'.042091724–dc22   2008049442

Typeset by SPI Publisher Services, Pondicherry, India
Printed in Great Britain by the
MPG Books Group, Bodmin and King's Lynn

ISBN 978–0–19–956442–2

1 3 5 7 9 10 8 6 4 2

Acknowledgements

We gratefully acknowledge the International Development Research Centre, Ottawa who sponsored this research, and in particular Rohinton Medhora who offered valuable advice and inspiration along the way. We would also like to acknowledge the valuable initial work done by Calum Miller in setting up this project, and the comments and suggestions made by Persio Arida, Atrayee Basu, Nicholas Bayne, Amar Bhattacharya, Tess Bridgeman, Christine Cheng, Soedradjad Djiwandono, Jose Maria Fanelli, Valpy Fitzgerald, Sara Fyson, He Fan, Richard Higgott, Clare Lockhart, Sarah Mulley, Kevin Watkins, and Lindsay Whitfield, all of whom participated in a workshop hosted in Oxford on 16–17 March 2006 to discuss early drafts of the papers. Our thanks go to Robert Keohane and Mayur Patel for their feedback, and to the OUP team for their excellent work.

Contents

Contents

List of Figures and Tables

Figure

Tables

Contributors

Khadija Bah currently serves as an Advisory Group Member for the Inter-Regional Facility for Inequality and the Millennium Development Goals (MDGs). She has previously served as the Programme Facilitator regarding the MDGs for NEPAD and has also worked in an advisory capacity for the UN Millennium Project and a UNAIDS Special Project on AIDS in Africa. Other organizations she has worked for include the UN World Food Programme and the World Bank Group. Her publications include 'Peace Through Agrarian Justice: The need to protect the labour, land, and property rights of rural women and youth in West African countries affected by war' (with P. Richards) and *Social Capital and Survival: Prospects for Community-Driven Development in Post-Conflict Sierra Leone* (with J. Vincent).

Sir Nicholas Bayne, KCMG, is a Fellow at the International Trade Policy Unit of the London School of Economics and Political Science. He also teaches at the School of Policy Studies at Queen's University. As a British diplomat, he was High Commissioner to Canada from 1992 to 1996, Economic Director at the Foreign and Commonwealth Office from 1988 to 1992, and Ambassador to the Organization for Economic Cooperation and Development from 1985 to 1988. His publications include *The New Economic Diplomacy: Decision Making and Negotiation in International Economic Relations* with Stephen Woolcock and *Hanging Together: Cooperation and Conflict in the Seven-Power Summits* with Robert D. Putnam.

Kenneth G. Coates has been the Director General of the Centre for Latin American Monetary Studies (CEMLA) since January 2001. He has previously served as Executive Director on the Board of the World Bank representing the Southern Cone countries, Uruguay's Financial Representative in Washington, and as an economist at the IMF. His academic appointments have included the Chair in Development Economics at the University of the Republic of Uruguay and the Chair in International Economics and Finance at ORT University. In the private sector, he has consulted for various international financial institutions and was a member of the Montevideo Stock Exchange. His most recent publications include 'A Strategic Approach to New Central Banking', *CEMLA Quarterly Bulletin*, vol. LIII, No. 2, April–June 2007 and 'Measurement Problems in Household International Remittances', Third Conference of the Irving Fisher Committee on Central Bank Statistics, Bank for International Settlements, Basel.

Gerry Helleiner is Professor Emeritus, Department of Economics, and Distinguished Research Fellow, Munk Centre for International Studies, University of Toronto. Professor Helleiner is an Officer of the Order of Canada and a Fellow of the Royal Society of Canada. From 1991 to 1999, Professor Helleiner was Research Director of the Group of 24 (the developing countries' caucus at the IMF and World Bank). He has been chairman of the Boards of the North–South Institute in Ottawa and the International Food Policy Research Institute (IFPRI) in Washington; member of the Board and Executive Committee of the International Development Research Centre (IDRC) in Ottawa, the Executive Board of the African Capacity-Building Foundation (ACBF) in Harare, and the UN Committee on Development Planning (CDP). Professor Helleiner is currently chairman of the Board of International Lawyers and Economists Against Poverty (ILEAP).

Alex Matheson is currently a New Zealand-based adviser on public governance and management. He was Division Chief of Budgeting and Management in the OECD, Paris (1999–2005) charged with providing analytical and advisory services on governance, budgeting, and management to the senior central agency officials of the 30 OECD member states, and the governments of major transitional economies. Previously he was senior public sector management adviser for the Commonwealth Secretariat, London (1997–1999). Prior to that he was a New Zealand public servant serving at Senior Executive levels in Foreign Affairs and Trade, Tourism, Justice, and the State Services Commission.

Matthew Martin is Director of Debt Relief International and Development Finance International, both non-profit organizations which build developing countries' capacities to design and implement strategies for managing external and domestic debt, and external official and private development financing. Previously he worked at the Overseas Development Institute in London, the International Development Centre in Oxford, and the World Bank, and as a consultant to many donors, African governments, international organizations, and NGOs. He has co-authored books and articles on debt and development financing.

Leonardo Martinez-Diaz is Political Economy Fellow in the Global Economy and Development Program at the Brookings Institution. He also serves as Deputy Director of Brookings' Partnership for the Americas Commission, a high-level advisory group on US policy toward Latin America, and is a consultant for the Independent Evaluation Office of the International Monetary Fund. Previously he was a Research Associate with the Global Economic Governance Programme at Oxford University. As a Luce Fellow in Indonesia, Martinez-Diaz worked as an academic, consultant, and freelance journalist. His recent publications include *Waiting for the Barbarians: the Politics of Banking-Sector Opening in the Emerging World* (Cornell University Press, 2009).

Helen E. S. Nesadurai is Senior Lecturer in the School of Arts and Sciences, Monash University, Malaysia. She has held previous appointments as Assistant Professor at the Institute of Defence and Strategic Studies, Nanyang Technological University, Singapore, and as Senior Analyst at the Institute of Strategic and International Studies, Kuala Lumpur, Malaysia. Her research explores the link between globalization and regionalism, focusing in particular on how this relationship plays out in the broad Asia-Pacific region through regional groupings such as ASEAN, APEC, and ASEAN Plus Three. She is currently researching 'bottom-up', transnational articulations of economic governance proposed by the region's civil society and labour groups and the prospects that such processes could lead to a more just and inclusive form of regional economic governance in Southeast Asia. She is the author of *Globalisation, Domestic Politics and Regionalism: The ASEAN Free Trade Area* (Routledge, 2003) and the editor of *Globalisation and Economic Security in East Asia: Governance and Institutions* (Routledge, 2006). She holds degrees in Biochemistry (BSc and MSc, Universiti Malaya), Development Economics (MSc, University of Oxford), and Politics and International Studies (PhD, University of Warwick).

Jochen Prantl is a Senior Research Fellow in International Relations at Oxford University and a Research Fellow of Nuffield College. He works in the field of International Relations, with a focus on international security (institutions), theories of global governance, risk and conflict management, and conflict transformation. Currently, Prantl is directing a major ESRC-funded project entitled 'Whither Multilateralism?' Prior to his academic career, he worked in financial services with Allianz SE. He is co-editing (with Dr. Amrita Narlikar, Cambridge) a recently launched book series of Martinus Nijhoff Publishers on *Studies in International Institutional Dynamics*. Recent publications include *The UN Security Council and Informal Groups of States: Complementing or Competing for Governance?* (Oxford: Oxford University Press, 2006); 'Informal Groups of States and the UN Security Council', *International Organization* 59:3 (2005); and co-authored with Jane Boulden, Neil MacFarlane, and David Williams, *The Consolidation of Peace in Africa* (Oxford: Centre for International Studies, 2005).

Vanessa Rubio-Marquez is Spokeswoman and Head of the Promotion and Institutional Relations Unit of the Mexican Pension System Regulator (CONSAR). Previously she was Deputy Director General of International Affairs at the Ministry of Finance and Public Credit of Mexico serving variously as their Secretary General of the Group of Twenty during 2003, lead negotiator for Mexico at the Monterrey Consensus on Financing and Development in 2002, Secretary General for Mexico in the APEC Finance Ministers' process during 2002, Director for Mexico on the Board of the Directors at the Caribbean Development Bank, Director for the OECD, Director for North America, Asia-Pacific and the Caribbean, and Professor of Foreign Economic Policy Analysis at the Technological Institute of Monterrey.

Richard Webb Duarte is an international consultant and Director of the Instituto del Peru at the University of San Martin de Porres. Previously he served as the President of the Central Bank of Peru (2001–2003), President of the Banco Latino (1999–2001), Advisor to the Superintendencia de Banca y Seguros (1998), Senior Fellow at the Brookings Institution in Washington DC (1990–1997), and President of the Instituto Cuanto (1988–2001 and 2003). He is a widely published scholar on public policy, income distribution, poverty and economic reform, and was a co-author of the seminal two-volume Brookings Institution history of the World Bank *The World Bank: Its First Half Century*.

Myles Wickstead was educated at St Andrew's University and New College Oxford. Most of his career has been spent in the Department for International Development and its predecessors and the Foreign and Commonwealth Office. He coordinated the 1997 White Paper 'Eliminating World Poverty: A Challenge for the 21st Century'; then represented the UK on the Board of the World Bank (and was simultaneously Counsellor,

International Development at the British Embassy in Washington); was British Ambassador to Ethiopia and Djibouti from 2000 to 2004; and was Head of Secretariat to the Commission for Africa from 2004 to 2005. He has been Visiting Professor (International Relations) at the Open University since the end of 2005.

Ngaire Woods is Professor of International Political Economy and Director of the Global Economic Governance Programme at University College, Oxford University. Her recent books include *The Globalizers: the IMF, the World Bank and their Borrowers* (Cornell University Press, 2006), *Exporting Good Governance: Temptations and Challenges in Canada's Aid Program* (with Jennifer Welsh, Laurier University Press, 2007), and *Making Self-Regulation Effective in Developing Countries* (with Dana Brown, Oxford University Press, 2007). She has previously published *The Political Economy of Globalization* (Macmillan, 2000), *Inequality, Globalization and World Politics* (with Andrew Hurrell, Oxford University Press, 1999), *Explaining International Relations since 1945* (Oxford University Press, 1986), and numerous articles on international institutions, globalization, and governance.

Abbreviation List

AAP	Africa Action Plan
ABF	Asian Bond Fund
ABMI	Asian Bond Market Initiative
ADB	Asian Development Bank
AIF	Agence intergouvernementale de la Francophonie
AMF	Asian Monetary Fund
APEC	Asia Pacific Economic Cooperation
APP	Africa Progress Panel
APRM	Africa Peer Review Mechanism
APRs	Africa Personal Representatives
ASA	ASEAN Swap Arrangement
ASEAN	Association of Southeast Asian Nations
ASEM	Asia-Europe Meeting
AU	African Union
BBC	British Broadcasting Corporation
BSA	bilateral swap arrangements
BWI	Bretton Woods Institutions
CABRI	Collaborative African Budget Reform Initiative
CAC	collective action clauses
CBP	capacity building programme
CEMLA	Centre for Latin American Monetary Studies
CFA	Commission for Africa
CIS	Commonwealth of Independent States
CMI	Chiang Mai Initiative
Comsec	Commonwealth Secretariat
CPLP	Community of Portuguese-Speaking Countries
CSO	civil society organizations

CSSDCA	Conference on Security, Stability, Development and Cooperation in Africa
DAC	Development Assistance Committee
DCI	Development Cooperation Ireland
DDA	Department for Disarmament Affairs
DDRR	demobilization, disarmament, rehabilitation, and reintegration
DESA	Department of Economic and Social Affairs
DFID	Department for International Development (UK)
DPA	Department of Political Affairs
DPI	Department of Public Information
DPKO	Department of Peacekeeping Operations
DRI	Debt Relief International
EC	European Commission
ECA	Economic Commission for Africa
ECLA	Economic Commission for Latin America
EEMF	Economic Emergency Management Fund
ERPD	economic review and policy dialogue process
ESA	Economic and Social Affairs
EU	European Union
EWS	Early Warning System
FAO	Food and Agriculture Organization
FATF	Financial Action Task Force
FDI	foreign direct investment
FLAR	Latin American Reserve Fund
FM	Finance Minister
FMN	Finance Ministers' Network
FONDAD	Forum on Debt and Development
FSF	Financial Stability Forum
GDP	gross domestic product
GEAR	Growth and Employment and Redistribution
GNI	gross national income
GTZ	Gesellschaft für Technische Zusammenarbeit
HIPC	heavily indebted poor countries
HSGIC	Heads of State and Government Implementing Committee
IADB	Inter-American Development Bank

IDA	International Development Agency
IFAD	International Fund for Agricultural Development
ILO	International Labour Organization
IMF	International Monetary Fund
IMFC	International Monetary and Financial Committee
INSTRAW	International Research and Training Institute for the Advancement of Women
LAC	Latin America and the Caribbean
LAIA	Latin American Integration Association
LTDS	long-term debt sustainability
MD	Ministerial Declaration
MFG	Manila Framework Group
MOU	Memorandum of Understanding
MPH	Make Poverty History
NAI	New African Initiative
NAM	Non-Aligned Movement
NEPAD	New Programme for Africa's Development
NGO	non-governmental organization
NPM	New Public Management
OAU	Organization of African Unity
OCHA	Office for the Coordination of Humanitarian Affairs
ODA	Official Development Assistance
ODCCP	Office of Drug Control and Crime Prevention
OECD	Organization for Economic Cooperation and Development
OED	Operations Evaluation Department
OHCHR	Office of the High Commissioner for Human Rights
OHRLLS	Office of the High Representative for the Least Developed Countries, Landlocked Developing Countries and Small Island Developing States
OLA	Office of Legal Affairs
OMB	Office of Management and Budget (USA)
ONUB	UN operation in Burundi
OSRSG	Office of the Special Representative of the Secretary-General
PCO	Privy Council Office
PECC	Pacific Economic Cooperation Conference
PEFA	Public Expenditure and Financial Accountability

PGC	Public Governance Committee
PRGF	Poverty Reduction and Growth Facility
PRSP	Poverty Reduction Strategy Paper
PUMA	Public Management Committee
RSA	Republic of South Africa
SADC	South African Development Community
SBO	Senior Budget Officials
SDRM	Sovereign Debt Restructuring Mechanism
SEACEN	Southeast Asian Central Banks forum
SEANZA	Southeast Asia, Australia and New Zealand forum
SIDA	Swedish International Development Agency
UK	United Kingdom
UN	United Nations
UNCTAD	United Nations Conference on Trade and Development
UNDCP	United Nations Drug Control Programme
UNDP	United Nations Development Programme
UNECA	United Nations Commission for Africa
UNEP	United Nations Environment Programme
UNESCO	United Nations Educational, Scientific and Cultural Organization
UNFPA	United Nations Population Fund
UNHCR	United Nations High Commissioner for Refugees
UNICEF	United Nations Children's Fund
UNIFEM	United Nations Fund for Women
UNITAR	United Nations Institute for Training and Research
UNOGBIS	UN Peacebuilding Support Office in Guinea-Bissau
UNOPS	United Nations Office for Project Services
UNRISD	United Nations Research Institute for Social Development
UNRWA	United Nations Relief and Work Agency for Palestine Refugees in Near East
US	United States
WB	World Bank
WEF	World Economic Forum
WFP	World Food Programme
WHO	World Health Organization
WTO	World Trade Organization

Introduction: Developing Countries in a Networked Global Order

Leonardo Martinez-Diaz and Ngaire Woods

1. Networks and Global Economic Governance

Networks have become a buzzword among academics and policymakers alike. Scholarship on networks has multiplied almost as fast as the networks of regulators, legislators, corporations, activists, criminals, technical experts, and lawyers described by the literature. Much of this research came initially from sociologists and anthropologists, as well as from scholars in the hard sciences.[1] More recently, economists and political scientists have turned their attention to networks, and today, the study of these informal institutions is seen as particularly promising among students of international relations and global governance.[2]

For our purposes, a 'network' is a non-hierarchical governance structure in which relations among actors are repeated and enduring, but where no

---

[1] For a review of the literature, see Duncan J. Watts, 'The "New" Science of Networks', *Annual Review of Sociology*, 30 (2004), pp. 243–70. See also Joel M. Podolny and Karen L. Page, 'Network Forms of Organization', *Annual Review of Sociology*, 24 (1998), pp. 57–76 and Walter W. Powell, 'Neither Market Nor Hierarchy: Network Forms of Organization', *Research in Organizational Behavior*, 12 (1990), pp. 295–336.

[2] For surveys of the economics literature, see Matthew O. Jackson, 'The Study of Social Networks in Economics', in Joel Podolny and James E. Rauch (eds.), *The Missing Links: Formation and Decay of Economic Networks* (London: Russell Sage, 2007); and Sanjeev Goyal, *Connections: An Introduction to the Economics of Networks* (Princeton: Princeton University Press, 2007). For examples of the political science literature, see R. A. W. Rhodes and D. Marsh, 'Policy Networks in British Politics', in Marsh and Rhodes (eds.), *Policy Networks in British Government* (Oxford: Clarendon Press, 1992); Sol Picciotto, 'Networks in International Economic Integration: Fragmented States and the Dilemmas of Neo-Liberalism', *Northwestern Journal of Law & Business*, 17:1014 (1996–97); and David Lake and Wendy Wong, 'The Politics of Networks: Interests, Power, and Human Rights Norms', paper presented at the 2006 Annual Meeting of the American Political Science Association, 30 August–3 September 2006.

one has the power to arbitrate and resolve disputes among the members.[3] We find this definition (borrowed from Podolny and Page) useful because it helps us distinguish networks from other forms of governance, such as markets and hierarchies. Like networks, markets are also non-hierarchical, but in a market with many buyers and sellers, a particular set of participants may transact once but never again. In a network, the same group of actors interacts repeatedly in an iterative process. As in networks, actors that are part of hierarchical institutions may interact regularly, but in a hierarchy, there is by definition someone with the authority to arbitrate and resolve disputes when conflicts arise. In networks, there is no such delegation of authority.

The literature has identified many different kinds of networks. In this book, we focus on a specific kind of network, namely, government (or, more accurately, 'inter-governmental') networks.[4] These are networks composed primarily, but not exclusively, of government officials from different countries. Though dominated by government figures, these networks often include representatives from non-governmental organizations, the private sector, civil society, and international organizations. From a substantive standpoint, we focus on networks concerned with financial matters, broadly defined, including monetary and financial policy, development finance, public-expenditure management, and external debt management.

Why have networks—and government networks, in particular—become the object of scholarly attention? First, government networks have become more prominent features of global governance. These forms of governance are not new, but in the past two decades government networks have proliferated in number, the scope of their activities has expanded, and the density of their connections has thickened. This has led some scholars to proclaim the birth of a 'new world order', one in which international relations are increasingly conducted through networks, and one in which international cooperation may eventually take place primarily through networks rather than through treaties or formal organizations.[5]

A second reason why scholars have turned their attention to networks has to do with normative implications of a networked world order. For

---

[3] Podolny and Page, 'Network Forms of Organization', p. 59.

[4] For an informative discussion of government networks, see Anne-Marie Slaughter, 'Governing the Global Economy through Government Networks', in Michael Byers (ed.), *The Rule of Law in International Politics* (Oxford: Oxford University Press, 2000).

[5] Anne-Marie Slaughter, *A New World Order* (Princeton: Princeton University Press, 2004).

some, government networks promise to make global governance more effective and efficient. Slaughter writes that networks are uniquely suited to deal with a 'tri-lemma' characteristic of our age: the need to produce more global rules without resorting to more centralized power, all while retaining the capacity to hold rule-makers to account.[6] For those sceptical of international organizations and their lumbering bureaucracies, flexible, adaptive, and lean network structures appear to be superior alternatives. And even those who would not replace international organizations with networks see networks as potentially useful complements to formal institutions.

On the other hand, critics worry about the difficulties of holding networks accountable.[7] Networks, they argue, are creating opaque new spaces in the interstices of the domestic and the international, spaces where unelected experts can exert influence over public policy but cannot easily be held responsible for their actions. Scholars also fret that decision-making in networks is more permeable to influence by narrow interests, leading to policy debates and outcomes that are unrepresentative, undemocratic, and possibly deleterious to the public welfare.[8] A recent study of global regulation underscores the risks of regulatory capture in networks.[9] Finally, some worry that networks may reinforce, or even exacerbate, the inequalities already present in the international system. As Toope argues, '[n]etworks... are sites of power, and potentially of exclusion and inequality.'[10]

2. Broadening the Debate: Networks and Developing Countries

So far, the discussion about the implications of network-based governance has focused almost exclusively on networks created and populated by developed-country governments. This is not surprising, as the

---

[6] Slaughter, *A New World Order*, p. 10.

[7] See, for example, Philip Alston, 'The Myopia of the Handmaidens: International Lawyers and Globalization', *European Journal of International Law*, 8 (1997).

[8] Martin Shapiro, 'Administrative Law Unbounded: Reflections on Government and Governance', *Indiana Journal of Global Legal Studies*, 8 (2001).

[9] Miles Kahler and David Lake, 'Economic Integration and Global Governance: Why So Little Supranationalism?', in Walter Mattli and Ngaire Woods (eds.), *The Politics of Global Regulation* (Princeton: Princeton University Press, forthcoming).

[10] Stephen Toope, 'Emerging Patterns of Governance and International Law', in Michael Byers (ed.), *The Rule of Law in International Politics*.

advanced economies have a longer history of using networks in economic policymaking than middle- and low-income countries. From the network of central bankers based at the Bank for International Settlements to the 'club model' used by the so-called Gs (G3, G6, G7, G8, and G10), the governments of the world's largest economies have been using networks at least since the 1920s.[11] The enlargement and deepening of the European Community and later the European Union also led to an explosion in inter-governmental networking among developed states.

Meanwhile, little attention has been paid to the role of developing countries in the construction of government networks and to the implications for these countries of the shift to a networked world order. At the end of her extensive study of government networks, for example, Slaughter asks whether weaker states might be better or worse off in a networked global order.[12] She does not try to answer the question empirically but speculates that weaker states might be better off if they can make networks work for them. It is with this question that the present book enters the debate.

The proliferation of government networks partly or exclusively composed of low- and middle-income countries is already well under way. The G20 network of finance ministers and central bank governors, established in 1999, brought together the G7, Australia, and South Korea with 10 middle- and low-income countries. In East Asia, emerging economies have come together with Japan and South Korea to form the ASEAN Plus Three (APT) network for monetary cooperation. At the United Nations, some of the richest and poorest states have formed networks to support reconstruction in war-ravaged African countries. Government networks composed exclusively of developing-country officials have also appeared. These are networks of African budget experts, Latin American central bankers, and finance ministers from highly indebted poor countries, to give a few examples.

2.1. Research Questions

Assessing whether developing countries are better or worse off in a networked world order requires the answering of two distinct sets of questions. The first set of questions concerns mixed networks—networks that

---

[11] For an analysis of the club model, see Robert O. Keohane and Joseph S. Nye Jr., 'Between Centralization and Fragmentation: The Club Model of Multilateral Cooperation and Problems of Democratic Legitimacy', KSG Working Paper No. 01–004, February 2001.

[12] Slaughter, *A New World Order*, p. 229.

bring together officials from developed and developing countries (and in political terms, from relatively stronger and relatively weaker states). Are these networks exacerbating the inequalities of power already present with international politics by giving the most powerful states another vehicle to exert their influence? Or are they helping relatively weak states exert more influence of their own and to build more capacity than would otherwise be the case?

If we found that mixed networks are being used by strong states to marginalize international institutions—where weak states are somewhat protected by formal rules and procedures against abuses of the powerful— then we would conclude that these networks are exacerbating inequality in world politics. We would arrive at the same conclusion if we found that the most powerful states are using mixed government networks to write rules and standards designed primarily for their benefit, to build a consensus around these rules, and to promote their adoption and enforcement by weaker countries. Sometimes, these rules may even run against the interests of developing countries.

On the other hand, we might conclude that developing countries are benefiting from inclusion in some of these networks, even if they do not control or fully participate in them. Despite the lack of protection afforded by formal institutions, relatively weak countries may gain information, prestige, voice, and possibly influence by participating in these government networks. Whether or not this is the case depends on the dynamics, structure, rules, and practices of the network in question, and on the attitude of developing countries regarding their participation in the network.

The second set of questions relates to whether inter-governmental networks offer a relevant and useful model for developing countries, countries that often have little domestic capacity to channel into network-building and maintenance. Can and should developing countries emulate the example of the most advanced economies and build networks of their own? Networks might simply dissipate scarce resources and negotiating capacity. Alternatively, networking could allow developing countries to build their own capacity in key sectors through information exchange, policy coordination and cooperation, and mutual learning. Networks could also enhance the influence of relatively weak states in formal international organizations, where voting and procedural rules are not in their favour. The present study will address both sets of questions, examining the evidence of how networks have worked in practice.

3. The Functions of Networks

What do networks actually do? And how do they do it differently than other governance structures, especially formal international organizations? We identify five main functions networks may play: (1) agenda-setting, (2) consensus-building, (3) policy coordination, (4) knowledge exchange and production, and (5) norm-setting and diffusion.[13] We argue that, from the point of view of government policymakers, the distinctive characteristics of networks make them attractive vehicles for undertaking each of the five functions.

3.1. Agenda-Setting

Networks can put neglected policy issues on the agendas of national governments or international organizations, and they can put pressure on policymakers to give issues already on the agenda a higher level of urgency and attention. This network function has been extensively documented in the case of transnational advocacy networks seeking to foster action on human rights and environmental issues.[14] Networks can use a variety of strategies to influence the agenda of the powerful and galvanize previously indifferent social groups into action. According to Keck and Sikkink, these include information politics (using information to mobilize political actors), symbolic politics (using symbolic events to raise awareness), leverage politics (linking issues of concern to the network to the issues that governments and international organizations care about), and accountability politics (pressuring governments to uphold principles they have previously endorsed).

What makes networks effective at agenda-setting? Unlike international organizations, networks are not hostage to a bureaucracy with interests of its own.[15] Formal organizations as diverse as the IMF and the United Nations Population Fund have been depicted as 'runaway agencies' setting agendas on the basis of ideology or bureaucratic imperatives,

---

[13] On the functions of networks, see Wolfgang H. Reinicke and Francis Deng, *Critical Choices: The United Nations, Networks, and the Future of Global Governance* (Ottawa: IDRC, 2000), chapter 3.

[14] See, for example, Margaret E. Keck and Kathryn Sikkink, *Activists Beyond Borders: Advocacy Networks in International Politics* (Ithaca: Cornell University Press, 1998).

[15] David Epstein and Sharyn O'Halloran, *Delegating Powers: A Transaction Cost Politics Approach to Policy Making Under Separate Powers* (Cambridge: Cambridge University Press, 1999); Michael N. Barnett and Martha Finnemore, *Rules for the World. International Organizations in Global Politics* (Ithaca: Cornell University Press, 2004).

independently of their political masters.[16] By contrast, the members of a network forge an agenda without interference from a third party. Networks tend not to have secretariats, and where they do, the secretariats are not delegated power or authority. The influence of a network in agenda-setting stems not from formal authority. Rather, their collective voice depends on their numbers and their outreach capabilities. For example, one network we examine in this collection, the Commission for Africa, was successful in agenda-setting in part because it brought together a powerfully networked group of leaders who were able to transmit their shared message and priorities using their own networks.

3.2. Consensus-Building

A second function networks can play is building consensus on controversial issues, particularly when this consensus cannot be reached in other, more formal, forums. In international organizations, decision-making rules must be heeded, formal voting power must be respected, and everything takes place under some degree of public scrutiny, even if it is just the scrutiny of many other governments. By contrast, networks offer a more flexible and private environment for discussion, which gives policymakers more room to speak frankly and to shift positions. Indeed, there is evidence to suggest that less-politicized, and relatively insulated, private settings are more conducive to persuasion and consensus.[17]

Consensus can develop in different ways within a network. Powerful states, unwilling to use their dominant position in formal institutions to force through unpopular decisions, may instead prefer to build consensus in a more participatory and inclusive way through networks. This can give developing countries a greater voice than would otherwise be the case. Once consensus has been reached within the network, its members can then turn to formal institutions to translate consensus into policy.

On the other hand, networks can be used as vehicles for the cooption or subtle coercion of relatively weak states. Indeed, networks are sometimes preferred by powerful states precisely because there are no

---

[16] Nicholas Eberstadt, 'UNFPA: A Runaway Agency', *PRI Review* 12:3 (May–June 2002), p. 8. 10; David E. Sanger, 'The IMF: Runaway Agency or U.S. Pawn?', 2 October (Hoover Institution, Public Policy Critiques, 1998).

[17] Jeffrey Checkel, 'Social Learning and Identity Change', *International Organization*, 55(3) (2001), pp. 553–88.

constraints imposed by formal rights of representation or mechanisms to protect minorities or small shareholders. This can allow relatively strong states to bully or pressure other states into endorsing a common policy position. How consensus develops ultimately depends on who created the network, how membership was determined, and how the network's agenda was set.

3.3. Policy Coordination

Governments may also find networks useful to coordinate policy and implement policies requiring concerted action. The same qualities of networks that are useful for consensus-building—informality, flexibility, and confidentiality—also help harmonize policies, especially during crises, when rapid coordination is required and where governments cannot afford the delays imposed by operating through large bureaucracies and ordinary government-to-government channels.

For example, an informal network directly linking the IMF's Management and the G7 finance ministers and their deputies proved instrumental during the emerging-market crises of the 1990s for keeping open bank credit lines and mobilizing rescue packages. Another example comes from the area of international public health. Here, the Global Outbreak Alert and Response Network (GOARN)—a global network of government agencies, non-governmental organizations, and UN bodies—has helped coordinate policy to prevent the spread of infectious disease, most notably the spread of Severe Acute Respiratory Syndrome in Asia.

3.4. Knowledge Production and Exchange

Networks can facilitate the exchange of policy-relevant knowledge among participants, sometimes leading to mutual learning. This can happen in two ways.[18] First, a network can provide channels for the transmission of knowledge that resides in each of the network's nodes. In the case of government networks, this typically takes the form of officials sharing their personal or national views on problems and solutions of common interest to the participants, providing members with potentially valuable knowledge they would not otherwise have. Second, networks can facilitate the synthesis of information in novel ways, producing knowledge that is qualitatively different from that residing in the nodes. For example,

---

[18] See Podolny and Page, 'Network Forms of Organization', pp. 62–3.

government officials may work together through the network to generate new solutions to policy problems, solutions that were not previously available to any of the individual members.[19]

As was the case with agenda-setting, networks may offer a superior alternative to formal organizations for knowledge production and exchange because networks can avoid a host of unwanted political pressures. In international organizations, knowledge production and exchange is inevitably shaped by political factors, such as the preferences of powerful states within the organization, and the way the agency is organized and managed. For example, the World Bank describes itself in part as a 'Knowledge Bank' with a mission to collect, pool, and share information.[20] Endowed with expertise, staff, and data, the Bank is well-placed to do this, but knowledge production and exchange has often failed to reflect the priorities of borrowing members and has come to reflect instead a very particular mixture of political priorities and bureaucratic imperatives.[21] Free from large bureaucracies and their agendas, networks should be able to avoid these pitfalls in knowledge production and exchange.

3.5. Norm-Setting and Diffusion

Networks of policymakers can diffuse norms—standards of appropriate behaviour—among members, offering a direct peer-to-peer forum in which norms can be debated, shaped, and monitored. This is distinct from the way international organizations function. Scholars of international relations have pointed to the role of international organizations as 'teachers' of norms, developing standards of behaviour or institutional design and then persuading states to adopt them.[22] However, as discussed above, norm diffusion by international agencies can be strongly shaped (some

[19] In international relations, learning through network-like structures has been most extensively discussed in the literature on 'epistemic communities'. See, for example, Peter Haas (ed.), *International Organization*: Special Issue on Epistemic Communities, 46 (Winter 1992).

[20] Robert Axelrod and Robert Keohane, 'Achieving Cooperation under Anarchy: Strategies and Institutions', *World Politics*, 38:1 (October 1985), pp. 226–54.

[21] Ngaire Woods, *The Globalizers: the IMF, the World Bank, and their Borrowers* (Ithaca: Cornell University Press, 2006), chapter 2. A recent high-level independent evaluation of the World Bank's research found that the research was being used to proselytize on behalf of Bank policy, often without taking a balanced view of the evidence, and without expressing appropriate scepticism. Internal research that was favourable to Bank positions was given great prominence, and unfavourable research ignored. Abhijit Banerjee et al., 'An Evaluation of World Bank Research, 1998–2005' (24 September 2006).

[22] Martha Finnemore, 'International Organizations as Teachers of Norms: The United Nations Education, Scientific, and Cultural Organization and Science Policy', *International Organization*, 47:4 (Autumn 1993), pp. 565–97.

would say distorted) by political and bureaucratic imperatives within the organization.

By contrast, networks have a very thin structure and few resources. The necessary expertise for norm-setting resides within the network itself, and their role in diffusing norms is executed through a mix of knowledge exchange and peer pressure. Through their peers, policymakers might be exposed to new policy initiatives or entirely new 'policy models'—novel paradigms or principles for policymaking in an issue area.[23] Over time, policymakers may choose to emulate these models. In addition, networks can put informal pressure on their members to adopt certain norms, particularly if members value their affiliation with the network and wish to remain in good standing with their peers.

Based on these functions, we draw a broad distinction between two categories of networks. 'Advocacy' networks aim to mobilize support for a certain cause, policy, or standard of behaviour, within but also outside the network—they are primarily involved in agenda-setting, norm-setting and diffusion, and consensus-building. 'Self-help' or 'problem-sharing' networks, on the other hand, focus on improving the capacity of the network's member governments to make policy and address problems. These networks are primarily engaged in knowledge production, knowledge exchange, and policy coordination.

4. When Do Networks Emerge and Work for Developing Countries?

In this study, whether a network is deemed to 'work' for developing countries depends on whether the network plays its functions effectively and in a way that reflects at least some of the stated preferences of the participating developing-country officials. In other words, we want to know if these networks are providing developing countries with more knowledge, capacity, and influence over financial affairs. To guide the empirical analysis in this book, we developed the following conjectures about the conditions under which government networks emerge and work best for developing-country members.

---

[23] Kurt G. Weyland (ed.), *Learning from Foreign Models in Latin American Policy Reform* (Baltimore: Johns Hopkins University Press, 2004). See also Beth A. Simmons, Frank Dobbin, and Geoffrey Garrett, 'Introduction: The International Diffusion of Liberalism', *International Organization*, 60 (Fall 2006), pp. 781–810 and related articles in the same issue.

4.1. The Origins of Networks

Our first conjecture concerns why networks emerge in the first place. *We posit that networks emerge as a reaction to real and perceived failings of formal institutions, and of international organizations in particular.* Where international organizations fail to produce public or club goods, we might expect to see a network emerge in an attempt to replace the organization.[24] Networks might also appear in response to countries' dissatisfaction with the agenda-setting process of international organizations or with the degree to which the agenda reflects (or does not) the priorities of developing-country policymakers. To foreshadow one of our conclusions, we find robust evidence that networks do emerge as a response to real or perceived shortcomings of international organizations, either because those organizations are attempting to provide a public or club good and doing so ineffectively or because they are not in the business of providing those goods at all.

4.2. The Role of Dominant States within Networks

While relatively inexpensive to set up and run compared to international organizations, government networks are not costless. Their creation and management entails non-trivial expenditures of financial, human, and intellectual resources. International organizations have devised ways to apportion those costs among the membership based on each country's ability to contribute. For example, member contributions to international organizations are often calculated with respect to the size of the member country's economy. The burden-sharing formula is often formalized, and formal voting power and informal influence are attached to the relative size of members' contributions. Countries that do not pay their dues in international organizations can have their voting rights suspended and can be expelled.

Networks must also devise ways to apportion costs, but the method is informal, and there are no sanctions to force members to contribute because no one has the authority to levy them. Instead, costs are more often allocated in an improvised manner, with countries volunteering resources on an ad hoc basis. Because networks have no formal voting

---

[24] Club goods are non-rivalrous but excludable—while one person or group's consumption of the good does not prevent consumption by another (as long as there is no congestion), users of the good can form a collective and control the number of consumers at the margin. For the classic treatment of club goods see James M. Buchanan, 'An Economic Theory of Clubs', *Economica*, 32:125 (February 1965), pp. 1–14.

mechanisms, resource contributions do not entitle members to voting power, but they invariably endow the largest donors with a degree of informal influence. *Our conjecture is that the largest contributors of resources to a network use the influence they derive from their contributions to 'capture' the network and steer its activities towards their own interests, possibly at the expense of those of other members.*

Our studies confirm this conjecture but also suggest a more nuanced finding. We found that members that provide the bulk of the network's resources do derive informal influence and are often tempted to capture the network. But they also make considerable efforts to avoid dominating (or appearing to dominate) the network. The leading contributors are kept in check by the low barriers to exit—if they alienate the network's members, these will walk away, dissolving the network. Large contributors must therefore find the right balance between exercising influence and leadership over the network and preserving a sense of ownership—real or perceived—among all members.

4.3. *Networks and Hierarchy*

Our third conjecture is that even with unequal resource contributions, networks provide developing countries with greater voice and influence than international organizations. The reason is that networks are non-hierarchical in structure; they have no weighted voting systems or special privileges that entrench the influence of major shareholders, such as veto powers or the power to name political appointees. Members interact largely as equals and can walk away if they feel unfairly treated. In a network, relatively weak or poor countries can sit at the same table with heavyweights and participate in agenda-setting or knowledge production or policy coordination to a greater extent than in international organizations, where the powerful have a lock on resources, procedures, agendas, and bureaucracies. All this makes networks more attractive to developing countries than international organizations.

The case studies showed mixed results on this conjecture, but the exercise allowed us to identify conditions under which developing countries were empowered through their participation in the network. Developing countries faced best in networks where adequate resources were made available to the network, but where the members providing the bulk of resources did not attempt to capture the network out of fear of alienating the membership. Also critical was an environment in which developing-country members felt they could talk freely and challenge viewpoints without fear of negative repercussions from donors or developed countries in other forums.

4.4. Networks and International Organizations

Our final conjecture echoes those who envision a 'new world order' in which international relations is carried out through networks, not formal institutions. *We posit that networks will replace international organizations because they are much less resource-intensive, more flexible, and more egalitarian.* These qualities allow networks to perform many functions of international organizations more rapidly, more efficiently, and more effectively. In a world where the value of international organizations is increasingly being questioned, and where politicians are increasingly loath to spend taxpayer funds to sustain what are perceived to be white elephants, networks will become the preferred means for global governance, at least in finance.

The cases in this study will highlight many of these advantages of networks, but they will also demonstrate that networks complement, rather than replace international organizations. The two forms of governance perform distinct but complementary functions. Networks are rarely effective on their own—they need to form a symbiotic relationship with international organizations. The emerging world order is one in which networks, rather than operating alone, come to incorporate and work hand in hand with international organizations.

5. Method and Cases

This book breaks new ground by offering thick descriptions of eight government networks that include developing-country officials. The cases explore the networks' origins, evolution, impact, and limitations. Four of the cases are 'mixed' networks of developing and industrialized country officials. The other four comprise only developing-country officials. Unlike much of the existing literature, this study goes beyond a functionalist interpretation (networks as 'problem-solving' vehicles) and explicitly considers the role of power and politics in the creation and evolution of government networks. It also pays close attention to the structure, practices, and formal and informal rules that shape interactions within the networks.

This book draws heavily on the 'insider accounts' of network participants. Involving network insiders in this project was essential to gain a clear understanding of how these structures operate because government networks are highly opaque entities that produce little publicly available documentation and keep most of their proceedings confidential. To balance the inevitable bias of these participant accounts, we paired them, when possible, with more critical commentaries from outsiders looking in.

All eight networks covered in this study are concerned with financial matters. Three are primarily concerned with development finance, one with public-expenditure management and budgeting, one with debt relief and debt management, two with monetary- and financial-policy cooperation, and one (the G20) that has been concerned with most of these issues at one time or another. We chose to focus on finance networks because in this policy sphere, power and knowledge are highly concentrated in the hands of a very few firms, governments, and regulatory and donor agencies, especially when compared to areas such as trade, antitrust regulation, and environmental policy, where regulatory and rule-making power is more diffuse.[25] For this reason, finance should be a 'least-likely case'—if networks of developing-country officials can be shown to enhance developing-country influence in finance, they may show even more promise in policy spheres where power is less concentrated.[26]

In selecting the cases, we employed three criteria. The first was geographic distribution: the networks are drawn from East Asia, Africa, and Latin America. Two of the networks (the G20 and the HIPC finance ministers) have global memberships. Africa has been the site of very active network-building recently and is therefore somewhat overrepresented. Second, we chose a group of networks at diverse stages of development. The network of Latin American central bankers, for example, is a mature network that started operating in the 1950s. By contrast, the network of African budget officials (CABRI) is a recent start-up. The rest of the

[25] On concentration of power in finance, see Beth A. Simmons, 'The International Politics of Harmonization: The Case of Capital Market Regulation', *International Organization*, 55:3 (2001), pp. 589–620. On concentration of power in competition and environmental policy, see Kal Raustiala, 'The Architecture of International Cooperation: Transgovernmental Networks and the Future of International Law', 43 *Virginia Journal of International Law*, 1 (Fall 2002).

[26] On the use of least likely cases, see Gary King, Robert O. Keohane, and Sidney Verba, *Designing Social Inquiry: Scientific Inference in Qualitative Research* (Princeton: Princeton University Press, 1994).

cases fall somewhere in between. Finally, the networks selected exhibit a wide diversity in membership, objectives, structure, rules, practices, and resources, and this variation allows us to probe some of the conjectures outlined above. Table 1 summarizes the cases examined, outlining their membership, origins, and scope.

This book begins with the Group of Twenty Finance Ministers and Central Bank Governors (G20), perhaps the highest-profile government network in finance that includes developing-country officials. Established in 1999, this network was designed to be an informal forum for discussion among officials from the G7 countries and from 'systemically significant' developing countries. Its remit is wide, though its initial focus was the international financial architecture. In two chapters, we present different perspectives of the G20. Vanessa Rubio-Marquez, from Mexico's Ministry of Finance, provides an informative, insider's analysis of the network, while Leonardo Martinez-Diaz takes a more critical view looking from the outside in. Central themes in both pieces are whether and how the G20 can reach consensus on key issues despite the diversity of its members' interests, as well as whether the consensus reflects the views of a few powerful countries or of the larger membership.

In Chapter 3, Helen Nesadurai examines two East Asian networks for financial cooperation, which we group here as a single case. These are the ASEAN Plus Three (APT) network and the Executives' Meeting of East Asian and Pacific Central Banks (EMEAP). The APT grouping has met annually since 1999, while the EMEAP dates back to 1991. Both networks are dedicated to financial cooperation through information exchange, dialogue, and consultation on financial and economic policy. Key themes in this chapter include the leadership roles of China, Japan, and Korea in building the network, as well as the impact of the Asian financial crisis in creating a unity of purpose among what is otherwise a very diverse group of states.

Chapter 4 presents a third case, described by its author Jochen Prantl as 'quasi-networks': the ECOSOC Ad Hoc Advisory Groups for African Countries Emerging from Conflict. These UN-based advisory groups are created upon request by any African country in a post-conflict scenario and seek to facilitate the integration of relief, rehabilitation, reconstruction, and development into a comprehensive approach. The two groups examined here deal with Guinea-Bissau and with Burundi. Admittedly, the ad hoc groups are an unusual choice for the study, as their remit goes beyond financial matters and its participants are United Nations diplomats rather than finance-ministry officials or central bankers. We included these

Table 1. Summary of networks examined

Case	Participants	Participants' countries of origin	Policy issues covered by the network
Group of Twenty Finance Ministers and Central Bank Governors (G20)	Ministers of finance and central bank governors	G7, Australia, South Korea, and 10 middle-income countries, the IMF, the World Bank, and the European Central Bank	Monetary- and financial-policy cooperation, global financial governance, debt relief and management, development finance
East Asian financial networks (APT and EMEAP)	Ministers of finance and central bank governors	APT: 10 ASEAN countries plus Japan, China, and Korea EMEAP: 5 ASEAN countries plus Japan, China, Korea, Australia, and New Zealand	Monetary- and financial-policy cooperation
ECOSOC ad hoc advisory groups on African countries emerging from conflict	UN Ambassadors	4–5 countries plus other UN officials	Development finance, among others
Commission for Africa	Heads of state, government ministers, civil society leaders, former international civil servants	G7 and African countries	Development finance
Africa's 'G4'	Heads of government	Nigeria, South Africa, Algeria, and Senegal	Development finance
HIPC Finance Ministers' Network	Ministers of finance	34 highly indebted poor countries	Debt relief and management
Senior budget officials' networks	Senior budget officials	OECD: OECD members CABRI: 12–17 sub-Saharan African countries CESEE: 19 Central and Eastern European countries	Public-expenditure management
CEMLA networks	Central bank governors	30 Latin American countries	Monetary- and financial-policy cooperation

networks because they display how innovative networking can help mobilize development financing for some of the most desperate countries in the world, countries that are too small and too poor to have much influence in networks dominated by 'systemically significant' countries.

Chapters 5 and 6 are also rooted in Africa but concern efforts to attract private investment and official development assistance to Africa. Chapter 5 explores the Commission for Africa (CfA) as seen by the former Head of its Secretariat Myles Wickstead, who provides an insider's view of the network. Now defunct, this eclectic network was composed of a mix of African and non-African leaders, including three heads of government and several ministers, senior officials, and representatives of the private sector and civil society. The network's main objective was to generate new ideas and action to support African economic growth. A key theme in this piece is how the CfA served as a 'network of networks' that combined the resources of both developed and developing countries. In his comments, Professor Nicholas Bayne of the London School of Economics provides a more sceptical view of this network.

Our fifth case is also an African network focused, among other issues, on promoting investment and development assistance for the continent. Chapter 6 presents this personality-driven network, which author Khadija Bah refers to as 'Africa's G4'. It is composed of the presidents of Nigeria, Senegal, Algeria, and South Africa. Acting informally and to a large extent independently of regional institutions, this network of Africa's most visible heads of state was instrumental in the creation of two major initiatives to attract development financing to Africa. The network also claimed to speak for the whole continent. Bah highlights the downsides of a personality-driven network, which—while effective at building consensus and influencing opinion—lacks legitimacy and is perceived as insufficiently representative.

Returning to a more traditional type of finance network, in Chapter 7, Matthew Martin examines the network of finance ministers from highly indebted poor countries (HIPCs). This network was established by Martin and others in 1999 as an informal forum for HIPC governments to press for greater debt relief. Like the ad hoc groups, this network includes some of the world's poorest countries. In this chapter, Martin highlights the tension between influence and ownership, particularly the difficulties of retaining developing-country ownership of the network while simultaneously accepting financial support from developed-country governments and international financial institutions. Professor Gerald Helleiner offers an outsider's commentary on Martin's analysis.

Chapter 8 takes a different approach. Insider Alex Matheson describes a highly successful network (the OECD Senior Budget Officials' Working Party, or SBO), which was formed 27 years ago to promote better budgeting and public-expenditure management practices among the industrialized economies of the OECD. This chapter then examines how two groups of developing and transition economies—one in Africa and another in Central and Eastern Europe—are trying to emulate this model by forming their own networks. The main theme here is the successes and the limits of learning from developed-country government networks and emulating them in a developing-country context.

The final case examines a mature and traditional finance network of central bankers, this one nested within the Centre for Latin American Monetary Studies (CEMLA), established in 1952. In his piece, CEMLA Director Kenneth Coates describes a group of networks of central bank governors that meet under the auspices of the CEMLA, and which have become particularly active during crisis periods. Former central bank governor Richard Webb provides more critical commentary. One important theme in this chapter is how a mature network can be marginalized when new networks materialize and fulfil policymakers' needs more effectively. Finally, in the concluding chapter to this book we describe the most striking theoretical and policy-relevant insights to emerge from this exercise.

1

The G20: A Practitioner's Perspective

Vanessa Rubio-Marquez

1.1. Introduction

This chapter focuses on one of the most visible networks of developing-country officials—the Group of 20 Finance Ministers and Central Bank Governors (G20). Drawing on my experience as both Director General of International Financial Affairs at Mexico's Ministry of Finance and as Secretary General of the G20 in 2003—positions that allowed me to experience the internal workings of the G20 first-hand—I examine the origins and achievements of the network. I conclude that the G20 has evolved into one of the most important bodies for ensuring international financial stability and argue that there are powerful reasons for keeping the network alive. To preserve its relevance over time, however, the network needs to have a clear mandate vis-à-vis other institutions, as well as a carefully designed agenda that promotes the interests of all its members and one that lends itself to the provision of concrete deliverables.

The chapter progresses in three sections. First, it examines the factors that led the Group of Seven (G7) to establish a vehicle for permanent dialogue with emerging-market countries through the G20, as well as the reasons why the latter embraced the proposal. It then offers an assessment of the political significance of the G20 by analysing its role and practices. Finally, it asks whether the G20 can maintain its relevance and vigour in the light of the challenges that lie ahead.

1.2. The Emergence of the G20

In the mid-1990s, crisis prevention and resolution were placed at the top of the international financial agenda, particularly after the systemic consequences of the so-called *tequila, dragon, samba,* and *vodka* effects demonstrated that financial crises in emerging markets could affect the entire international financial system. The emerging-market crises of the 1990s were different from those of the 1980s. The mix of domestic economic imbalances varied from case to case, but unlike the crises of previous decades, there were a number of new ingredients. These included vulnerabilities resulting from rushed or inadequately sequenced financial liberalization processes, magnified exposure to imbalances arising from the large stakes international economic agents had accumulated in emerging markets, contagion effects derived from greater interdependence, and inflexible exchange rate regimes. At the same time, the traditional indicators that had been used to anticipate a crisis (low growth, high fiscal deficits, high inflation, low savings, and investment rates) were not altogether present in the crisis countries of the 1990s.

In the immediate aftermath of these crises, policymakers began to think of ways to strengthen crisis prevention and resolution. The existing international infrastructure was speedily reoriented to address these objectives according to the comparative advantages of existing institutions. The International Monetary Fund (IMF) and the World Bank strengthened their traditional programmes and operations to assist members with economic restructuring and the adoption of institutional reforms. This occurred mainly through intensified consultations, financial and technical assistance, policy advice, and knowledge-sharing. The Bretton Woods institutions also developed ad hoc strategies to help countries cope with crises and build a more resilient infrastructure, stronger policies and institutions. Meanwhile, other international organizations, including the Bank for International Settlements (BIS), the Organization for Economic Cooperation and Development (OECD), and a variety of standard-setting bodies, allocated large amounts of resources to developing international codes and standards and evaluating countries' observance of them.

The creation of new forums was also encouraged. In the autumn of 1998, the G7 joined forces with Australia, Hong Kong, Singapore, the Netherlands, and a number of relevant international financial institutions to establish the Financial Stability Forum (FSF). The objective of the FSF was 'enhancing the exchange of information, cooperation and financial supervision and surveillance to promote international financial stability, improve the functioning of markets and reduce systemic risk'.[1]

In September 1999, Argentina, Australia, Brazil, China, India, Indonesia, Mexico, Russia, Saudi Arabia, South Africa, Korea, and Turkey were recognized by the G7 as 'systemically significant' countries and were offered the opportunity to engage in a preferential dialogue with G7 members. The logic behind this proposed dialogue was clear. Preventing and managing crises was a G7 priority, as financial crises could jeopardize the legitimacy and future of economic openness and globalization. The G7 understood that the crises originated in a group of middle-income countries, which had recently pursued liberalization processes and were thus more open and vulnerable to external imbalances. Therefore, the problem had to be tackled in cooperation with the representatives of these emerging economies. Yet, there was no exclusive forum where the financial authorities of emerging and developed countries could come together to share their perspectives and where consensus could be built around measures for crisis prevention and resolution.

To fill this gap, the G7 announced the creation of the G20 at its September 1999 meeting, and the inaugural gathering of the Group took place in Berlin three months later. The network's stated goal was to 'provide a new mechanism for informal dialogue in the framework of the Bretton Woods institutional system, to broaden the discussions on key economic and financial policy issues among systemically significant economies and promote cooperation to achieve stable and sustainable world economic growth that benefits all'.[2] The IMF's International Monetary and Financial Committee, the World Bank's Development Committee, and the European Central Bank were also invited to participate in the network.

The Group was implicitly given a mandate to do three things: (1) facilitate agreement on domestic and international action, institutional arrangements, and priorities to prevent and resolve crises; (2) provide legitimacy to the process of globalization, notably by promoting its benefits worldwide to prevent a backlash against it; and (3) build consensus around key international financial issues that would facilitate

---

[1] www.fsforum.org.
[2] Meeting of G20 Finance Ministers and Central Bank Governors, Communiqué, Berlin, 15–16 December 1999.

decision-making within other institutions, primarily the IMF and the World Bank.

1.3. The Workings of the G20

The G20 is not an international organization—it has neither a founding formal charter nor a formally constituted secretariat, nor does it create legally binding commitments. It is an informal gathering of countries with a common purpose based on dialogue and consensus. The real strength of the forum lies in its representativeness, its legitimacy, and the systemic influence its members wield abroad. The G20 operates through consensus, not voting. It is geared toward consensus-building through free-floating discussions. Discussions are always informal and no topic is dealt with conclusively. The only decisions made by members are of an operational nature, such as agreeing on the annual agenda, the chairmanship, and qualitative and quantitative features of the meetings. Members do not form blocs but try to understand the perspectives of other countries and, if necessary, seek to persuade sceptics rather than press forward with an alternative stance.

With the exception of the Communiqué, few G20 documents are publicly disclosed. Most of the working documents are kept as background material for the participants, and only in the case of selected policy dialogues, such as the one on 'Globalization and Institution Building', have the papers been published. This has allowed for an open and frank dialogue among members without the usual restrictions imposed by an environment where any comments are considered to be country positions and where policymakers' statements can affect public opinion and financial markets.

Under the leadership of its finance ministers, the G20 also brings together the heads of member states' central banks to strike a balance between financial and monetary authorities. Though G20 meetings are attended by public sector officials alone, representatives from the private sector have sometimes participated on an ad hoc basis, depending on the issues under discussion. On some occasions, selected academics or private sector representatives have been invited to express their views to deputies or ministers during a specific session. However, they were not permitted to attend the entire meeting.

In the case of seminars, where the participation of academics and technical experts may be necessary to help the discussion, outside participation has been much more common. For instance, the seminar convened in Banff, Canada in June 2006 on the topic of 'Energy and Resources' saw the largest attendance of experts, academics, and company representatives at a G20 event to date. This demonstrates the flexibility of the G20's working arrangements.

From a functional point of view, the G20 can be seen in three ways. First, it is a policymakers' think tank, where practitioners benefit from the input and perspectives of their peers, based on the assumption that they find themselves, or have previously found themselves, in similar circumstances or faced comparable challenges. Second, it is a space where systemically significant national policies can be reviewed by policymakers from other states, who may be affected by the consequences of such policies. And third, the group is a forum for consensus-building around key international issues that are afterwards discussed at and agreed to by other organizations and institutions.

The G20 is not really in the business of knowledge production. Compared with most academic research, studies carried out by the G20 are of a practical and policy-oriented nature. They do not seek to create new knowledge, and rarely go beyond the compilation of existing information and perspectives on a given topic. The purpose of these publications is to promote discussion, peer commitment, and consensus-building. Research per se is not an aim of the Group; this is left to other organizations that have both a mandate and the resources.

For example, a typical output of the G20 is a collection of case studies designed to compare and contrast country experiences and to generate policy lessons. While the case studies are prepared by member governments themselves, comparative studies have sometimes been developed with the assistance of international institutions. These results are then discussed by policymakers at different levels during ministerial- and deputy-level meetings and seminars.

1.3.1. The Mechanics of the G20

The G20 meets three times per year in two forms. There are two G20 deputies' meetings every year, whose task is to finalize the agenda and make preparations for the ministerial meeting. Held each autumn in October or November (shortly after the annual meetings of the World Bank and IMF), the ministerial meetings are the network's main event. At the conclusion of each meeting, the Group issues a communiqué outlining the consensus. The location of the ministerial meetings changes every year, depending on which country is entitled to chair the Group.

The country holding the presidency or chairmanship of the network plays a key role.[3] That country hosts the annual ministerial meeting and plays a central role in setting the agenda for the current year as well as the year ahead, including the agendas of the two deputies' events, the technical seminars, and the ministerial. In addition, officials from that country also chair the network's meetings, which involves chairing and moderating the deputies' and ministerial events. According to customary practice, the chair of the meeting directly issues the formal invitations, proposals, and communications.

Paul Martin, then Minister of Finance of Canada and the most enthusiastic leader behind the creation of the G20, was selected as the Group's first president (he faced no competition). However, little thought was given at this point to how the role of the president could be institutionalized. After two ministerial meetings chaired by Paul Martin, the network's members began to reflect on how the presidency could be institutionalized. To strike a balance between the G7 and developing countries, it was agreed after the second annual meeting that the chair would be selected from five groups of countries on a rotating basis. Though no mechanism was specified for selecting a country from within each group, an unwritten rule has prevailed whereby the members of the relevant group establish an initial consensus on who should be the next candidate for the chairmanship. The country is then presented to the other G20 members to be formally endorsed. So far, all the candidates for the chairmanship so proposed have been approved unanimously. Since the first two meetings of the G20 were chaired and hosted by a developed country (Canada), the next chair was selected from a group of developing countries (India).[4]

Finance ministers and central bankers have participated on an equal footing in the G20 meetings but not in the governing structure. To date, no central banker has chaired the Group; only the finance minister of the country holding the presidency has done so. For this reason, finance ministries have enjoyed more influence over the forum's workings. Not

---

[3] G20 communiqués refer interchangeably to the 'presidency' and 'chairmanship' of the network.

[4] However, India was unable to host the meeting in November 2001. Paul Martin stepped into the breach and offered to host the G20 meeting in Canada. The following year, India hosted the meeting as initially intended.

surprisingly, the topics on the agenda are more closely related to financial, rather than monetary, matters.

To provide continuity, a 'Troika' mechanism was devised during India's chairmanship in 2002. Under this system used by the European Union, the Group's agenda in any given year is set jointly by the country that filled the chair during the previous year, the country occupying the chair that year, and the country scheduled to occupy the chair the following year. The Troika is chaired by the country holding the presidency. The first G20 Troika was composed of Canada, India, and Mexico. Since then, the Troika has served as an executive body to discuss the working agenda before a broader discussion with the rest of the Group. The Troika has also functioned as a vehicle through which a chair can pass on his or her knowledge of organizational matters (such as the setting-up of the secretariat and the unwritten rules that govern the network) to succeeding chairs.

The G20 has no resources of its own. There is no membership fee and no permanent secretariat to arrange the meetings and logistics. The costs of travel and lodging are borne by the members' respective governments. Also, the G20 has no research capacity of its own, and any preparatory or analytical work related to the network draws on whatever resources members devote to the task from their own ministries and central banks. Neither is there a centrally managed, permanent website.[5]

The network has no permanent secretariat. Instead, a temporary secretariat office is established each year by the country holding the presidency to handle logistics and assist the delegates during deputy and ministerial meetings. The secretariat's activities include designing the annual agenda, processing member states' input to create the final work programme, proposing measures to advance each of the agenda topics, and preparing background material. The secretariat initiates and follows up all communication on logistics and organization matters. It organizes mid-term events, mainly seminars, either in the host country or elsewhere, in which case organizational duties are shared.[6] The secretariat is also in charge of

---

[5] Each country that holds the presidency of the G20 sets up its own ad hoc website for the duration of its presidency. A web-based Members' Forum is usually set up for the exclusive use of members and their deputies. The secretariat is also in charge of creating a webpage in which public documents are posted and where restricted documents are made available to members and participating institutions. These documents are password-protected. This webpage has served as an efficient way for members to consult available documents in preparation for the meetings. Since each chair defines the way in which it operates, the arrangements have varied from one secretariat to another, though many features have become permanent.

[6] It has been common practice for countries other than the chair to organize the technical seminars. This is mainly due to two reasons: strong interest on the part of a particular country

organizing the two deputies' meetings and the ministerial event. In most cases, the secretariat is comprised of the same officials and staff of the host state's ministry of finance, resulting in a heavy workload for the relevant officials. Occasionally, the chair is assisted by other members or institutions. The chair, through the secretariat, also generates the first draft of the communiqué and holds the pen during the course of the negotiations. Outside meetings, the network's participants communicate through e-mail and the webpage set up by the presidency. Troika members usually meet just before the deputies' and ministers' events in the same venue, as well as at special gatherings. To make the process more efficient, these meetings have been replaced by videoconferences since the German presidency in 2004.

The internal workings of the secretariat are left largely to the discretion of the country chairing the Group. For example, during Mexico's chairmanship in 2003, an organizational structure was established following Mexico's recent experience as chair of the APEC Finance Ministers' Process. An official from the Ministry of Finance acted as Secretary General of the forum during 2003, concentrating on both the substantive and the logistic preparatory work. Two different teams were established, one for the preparation of background documents and another for the organization of meetings. This approach proved to be a very effective way of using the human resources the Ministry allocated for dealing with the G20.

Over time, the G20 has enhanced its strategy for disseminating information, and the official websites of the respective chairs have been improving in quality, promoting wider public understanding of the objectives and activities of the Group. Today, basic background information as well as communiqués from previous years is easily available. As for working documents, there are links to previous official webpages that allow members to consult information that was prepared for previous years. Guidelines for designing the official webpage by the chairing country have never been formally discussed at the G20, but it might well be advisable to establish such guidelines. The Group may also want to tackle the issue of consistency and continuity sometime in the near future, given the fact that the webpage is the only place where information relating to the workings of the Group is made available.

in a specific topic, or the occurrence of international agenda restrictions that make a particular venue more convenient. (For instance, Mexico organized a deputies' meeting in London since officials were due to attend the IMF/World Bank Dubai meetings the following day.)

G20 meetings are typically divided into sessions, one for each topic of the agenda. Sessions are kicked off by selected discussants chosen among those members having the most representative positions on a specific issue. Following the overview, the floor is opened for a general discussion. The resulting consensus is contained in the communiqué or 'ministerial declaration' issued after each ministerial meeting. The communiqué results from a series of negotiations among the members and aims to provide a synthesis of the main activities of the year and of the main discussions and conclusions reached during the annual ministerial event. Other working documents are maintained as internal discussion papers and are usually prepared by the chair or other countries or institutions that volunteer to present background information. These documents are generally not made public.

Although there are two clear categories of countries within the G20—developed countries and emerging economies—the Group functions as a single but flexible entity. In the beginning, developed countries intended to gather informally before each meeting, but this was not well regarded by the rest of the membership. No exclusive gatherings of developing countries have been proposed since, except when a specific topic on the agenda called for such a gathering, as during discussions on the code of conduct for debt restructuring. In that case, parallel meetings of developing countries were held before the ministerial, with the full knowledge and understanding of the rest of the membership. In contrast to other organizations, where it is common practice to have constituencies or 'caucuses' of countries that share specific interests or memberships, the G20 does not promote these kinds of gatherings, aside from the Troika.[7] Nevertheless, as in any other network, the formal meetings create opportunities for bilateral encounters to discuss issues of common interest.

1.3.2. Strengths and Weaknesses

The G20's informal and confidential character is one of its most important strengths. Discussions are fluid, prepared speeches discouraged, and all

---

[7] In other organizations, whether universal, multilateral. or regional (such as the UN, the OECD, and the Caribbean Development Bank), it is common practice to have the 'developing countries', the G7, the NAFTA, or the OECD Caucuses. This is a generalized and well-regarded practice since there are specific interests/positions shared by a rather smaller group of countries where useful agreements take place prior to general meetings. This scheme can provide for easier consensus-building when the dynamics that arise due to the size of the group render the process of consensus-building at certain junctures more difficult.

meetings take place in a single working language (English). The G20's discussions are kept confidential. The network has been criticized for its lack of transparency, but it is precisely this culture of confidentiality that makes it a valuable vehicle to its members. Confidentiality allows ministers, governors, and their deputies to talk in a frank and open manner, without the need to police what they say, resulting in more intense and productive discussions. Moreover, since the spirit and substance of the discussions are reflected in the communiqué, and since the G20 does not make decisions or undertake binding commitments, there is no obvious reason for greater transparency, which could undermine the effectiveness of the network.

Another key strength is the network's seniority. While participants in many international forums are represented by officials two or three steps down from the top of the hierarchy, at the G20 only the most senior officials turn up. By convention, meetings are attended by officials of equal or similar rank, and the number of participants in the room is kept to a minimum.[8] These features have created an ambiance of camaraderie that enhances understanding and dialogue. The seniority of G20 participants ensures that they can speak with both knowledge and authority. It also affords them the freedom to express positions and opinions without having to seek clearance from their capitals.

The network has also benefited from able leadership. Leadership within the Group is usually provided by the president. In the early days, Paul Martin was the leading voice within the Group, and it was clear that Canada had not only a clear vision of how the Group should evolve but also the ability to persuade the rest of the members to support this vision. Since 2001, that leadership role has passed to other ministers of finance. Two activities in particular require leadership—setting the agenda and defining the network's deliverables.

Although both are based on a proposal set forth by the president, members ultimately seek to establish a consensus. Effective leadership in the G20 demands that the president propose an agenda that is relevant to the members and pertinent given the specific global juncture in which the meeting takes place. Also, the president has to persuade the rest of the members to embrace the proposal. Sometimes, individual members have specific agendas, as was the case when the US government put measures for combating the financing of terrorism on the table in November 2001.

---

[8] The deputies' meetings allow for the two deputies (one for the Ministry of Finance and one for the Central Bank) plus two aides, while the minister and governor have only one extra chair that is usually occupied by the Finance Deputy.

In these cases, the interested countries provide leadership to carry forward the issues under deliberation according to their own expectations and interests.

1.3.3. *The G20's Achievements*

The G20 has made several important contributions. From 1999 to 2000, the network focused on building consensus among its members on the importance of codes and standards for maintaining sound financial systems. At their first meeting, G20 members 'agreed that the widespread implementation of such codes and standards would contribute to more prosperous domestic economies and a more stable international financial system'.[9] To this effect, a matrix was created through which members would report regularly on their degree of compliance with the demands made by two surveillance programmes set up by the IMF and World Bank—the Reports on Observance of Standards and Codes (ROSCs) and Financial Sector Assessment Programmes (FSAPs). This matrix became a mechanism to exert peer pressure on members.

At the end of 2000, as part of a 'standing-by-globalization' commitment, the G20 focused on spreading a positive message regarding the benefits—both actual and potential—of a globalized world economy. This was a response to the emergence of various anti-globalization movements, which coloured the ambiance of the 2000 ministerial gathering. The network's activities throughout the year were used to communicate that globalization was not an option but a reality, and that the process came hand in hand with a wide array of opportunities to improve living standards around the world. The G20 recognized that the challenge was to reduce vulnerabilities and emphasized the need to improve international institutions and to implement what was called 'the emerging international consensus on policies to reduce countries' vulnerability to financial crises'. This consensus generated a checklist of policies that was put forth by the G20 a year later.[10]

In addition, the G20 ministers and governors committed themselves to a series of measures, which would define the future working agendas of the Group. The aim of these measures was to improve the effectiveness of

[9] G20 Communiqué, 1999.

[10] Meeting of the G20 Finance Ministers and Central Bank Governors, Communiqué, Montreal, 25 October 2000, p. 2. Sound national economic and financial policies, solid national balance sheets, appropriate debt management, government policies that positively affect the borrowing decisions of private firms, sustainable exchange rate regimes, and consistent monetary policies.

international institutions, implement policies to reduce vulnerability to financial crises, improve financial globalization, create more favourable conditions for heavily indebted poor countries, strengthen the combat of financial abuse, enhance the provision of global public goods, and further efforts for multilateral trade liberalization and the design and implementation of social safety nets.[11] This agenda established the priorities of the G20 members to promote financial stability as a prerequisite for long-term sustainable growth and highlighted the role of international institutions, domestic financial and social policies, international trade, and development, all of which permeated the subsequent work agendas.

The 2001 meeting was marked by the events of 11 September and the emerging financial crisis in Argentina. That year, G20 ministers and governors delivered a positive message to global financial markets, offering assurance that the economic turbulence would be overcome and growth would resume. A strong call was also made to develop a predictable and sound framework for crisis resolution, including improved communication between borrowers and creditors, who share the objective of 'reducing uncertainty and ensuring the sustainability of capital flows to emerging markets'.[12] Wider global acceptance of codes and standards also grew within and outside the G20 at this time. As a result, its members felt that with the crisis-prevention framework up and running, their future activities should focus on encouraging members to report on their degree of compliance with the agreed norms. Efforts were reoriented toward the development of a crisis-resolution framework that would be acceptable for emerging economies and market leaders.

Agreement on crisis-resolution measures was far more difficult to achieve than in the case of crisis prevention. The crisis-prevention framework had been built on the basis of codes and standards developed by specialized standard-setting bodies. Discussions were technical in nature and limited to specific sectors. The G20 served as a catalyst for the framework and contributed toward creating a sense of ownership around these standards. The network also emphasized their relevance in preventing crises and fostered a spirit of shared responsibility. By contrast, creating a crisis-resolution framework was more challenging since no general agreement

[11] G20 Communiqué, 2000.
[12] Meeting of the G20 Finance Ministers and Central Bank Governors, Communiqué, Ottawa, 16–17 November 2001, p. 2.

had been previously reached at the IMF, nor had any such agreement been reached between creditors and debtors. Previous crises had been dealt with on a case-by-case basis, and although some precedents existed, no pair of cases had been treated in quite the same way. In addition, crisis resolution generally involves a more complex set of actors and significant amounts of resources.

The 2002 Delhi Communiqué did not truly reflect the intense debate that was taking place behind the scenes on a crisis-resolution framework. Since no agreement was reached on this issue, the final communiqué focused instead on policies to promote economic growth and development. This was the first time that the United Nations' Millennium Development Goals were addressed by the network. The topic of financing for development, including Official Development Assistance (ODA), assumed a more prominent position in the agenda, complementing the discussions that were taking place elsewhere on innovative financing mechanisms to implement the Monterrey Consensus.

Nevertheless, pressure to reach agreement on a crisis-resolution framework grew. Parallel meetings took place on the IMF's role as lender of last resort, on collective action clauses for emerging-market bond contracts, on a sovereign debt restructuring mechanism, and on a code of conduct for debtors and creditors. These topics were the subject of passionate discussions, with members putting forward conflicting arguments based on their own experience, their evaluation of the costs of the proposals, and their respective relationships with international creditors.

The activities of the 2003 meeting chaired by Mexico dealt with two issues only: crisis prevention and resolution. The crisis-prevention framework was regarded as complete, so members limited themselves to reporting on systemically significant domestic policies and on the achievements of ROSCs and FSAPs. Most of that year's agenda was dedicated to trying to reconcile the diverging positions on crisis resolution.

During the first G20 deputies' meeting chaired by Mexico, the first element of the crisis-resolution framework was agreed. Emerging countries were fearful that the abrupt inclusion of Collective Action Clauses (CACs) in new bond contracts could be perceived by markets as a signal of vulnerability, and add a risk premium to the price of their sovereign bonds. To implement the CACs proposal in a generalized manner, emerging countries had to agree on a set of clauses acceptable to both issuers and investors, and the 'first mover problem' had to be resolved. Although the guidelines for the formulation of the CACs were established by the Group of Ten[13] in consultation with members of the Bank of International Settlements (BIS), the G20 facilitated discussions between bond issuers and private sector representatives in the context of the deputies' meetings and through ad hoc gatherings.

As a result, Mexico announced at the March 2003 G20 deputies' meeting that it had included CACs in its bonds for the first time in its history. The news was well received by markets, with investor demand outweighing the amount on offer. After Mexico, other G20 emerging economies such as Brazil, South Africa, and Korea followed this practice, as did other developing countries, including Belize, Guatemala, and Uruguay. Many of these issues were oversubscribed and showed no evidence of a premium associated with the use of CACs.[14]

Meanwhile, two other topics were discussed—the role of the Fund in sovereign debt restructuring and the code of conduct. The IMF first proposed a Sovereign Debt Restructuring Mechanism (SDRM) as a way to 'facilitate the orderly, predictable and rapid restructuring of unsustainable sovereign debt, while protecting a set of values and creditors' rights'.[15] Discussions at the G20 revolved around the designation of roles in crisis resolution (mainly with respect to the IMF, debtors and creditors) and the reform of those IMF articles that were needed to implement such a mechanism. The G20 served as a place where high-level representatives from key developed and emerging countries shared their views and learned about each other's points of view before a formal position had to be established at the Fund.

In the end, consensus moved toward a debtor–creditor-led approach for debt restructuring, rather than an IMF-led, statute-based approach such as the SDRM. The latter was seen by many as too rigid a response, since it was a solution that gave too great a role to an institution rather than to debtors and creditors. Moreover, the proposal would take a long time to implement because of its statutory nature. The SDRM proposal was

---

[13] The Group of Ten is a constituency of 11 industrialized nations within the BIS that comprises Belgium, Canada, France, Germany, Italy, Japan, the Netherlands, Sweden, Switzerland, the UK, and the USA. It gathers Finance Ministers and Central Bank Governors to discuss economic and monetary issues of common interest.

[14] International Monetary Fund, 'Progress Report of the International Monetary and Financial Committee on Crisis Resolution', 5 September 2003, p. 3.

[15] Anne O. Krueger, 'A New Approach to Sovereign Debt Restructuring', Address at the Indian Council for Research on International Economic Relations, Delhi, India, 20 December 2001.

therefore shelved, and a new impetus was given to the so-called voluntary code of conduct.

During the second deputies' meeting in 2003 and the ministerial gathering that year, the G20 entered into consultations with the Institute of International Finance (a global association of private financial institutions) to develop a voluntary set of principles that would facilitate dialogue between debtors and creditors. The idea was to promote crisis-prevention measures, corrective policy action to reduce the frequency and severity of crises, and a prompt resumption of capital flows to emerging markets. Emerging markets pushed for voluntary guidelines rather than a binding code, sufficient flexibility to adapt to different restructuring processes and circumstances, a market-based approach, and a focus not only on crisis resolution but also on the strengthening of debtor–creditor communication during 'normal' times as a pre-emptive measure.

During the first deputies' meeting in 2004, the G20 announced its 'Principles for Stable Capital Flows and Debt Restructuring in Emerging Markets'. These principles were based on previous efforts to strengthen crisis-prevention measures and enhance the predictability of crisis management. By securing agreement on these principles, the Group had achieved two important objectives: creating a framework for crisis prevention based on internationally agreed codes and standards and establishing a crisis-resolution framework, composed of the principles and the generalized use of Collective Action Clauses.

1.3.4. *In Search of a New Agenda*

The achievement of these two objectives made the agenda for the rest of 2004 more challenging. The topics that had captured the G20's attention for the entirety of its existence would, from now on, require little more than close monitoring. Thus, for the first time since its inception, G20 members began to think about a new agenda. Attention quickly turned to 'achieving stable and sustainable world economic growth that benefits all',[16] resulting in a proposal to focus discussion on growth-enhancing policies and strategies. For the rest of the year, members discussed and agreed on a set of requirements for long-lasting growth based on their individual experiences. These were compiled

---

[16] G20 Communiqué, Berlin, 1999.

in the 'G20 Accord for Sustained Growth'.[17] To implement its provisions, countries committed themselves to a set of actions relating to domestic reform measures, which were set out in the 'G20 Reform Agenda'.[18]

During its presidency in 2005, China put on the agenda issues most relevant to developing countries. These included demographic challenges, brain-drain, migration, and innovative financing mechanisms for development. Moreover, as part of the Xianghe Communiqué, Finance Ministers and Central Bank Governors made a statement on 'Reforming the Bretton Woods Institutions', which prepared the ground for the role played by the G20 the following year.[19] The document highlighted the need to improve both the governance and effectiveness of the IMF and the World Bank, while ensuring broad-based representation of members within these institutions. In October 2005, the presidency shifted to Australia, which tried to define an agenda that ensured the G20's continued relevance. Three issues dominated this time—reform of the Bretton Woods institutions, the problems associated with demographic change, and the issue of energy security. Of the three, it was the reform of the Bretton Woods institutions which guaranteed the G20 a place at the centre of events.

By the beginning of 2006, long-expected efforts to reform the IMF gained momentum. Calls for IMF reform were a response to a series of long-standing criticisms concerning its legitimacy, effectiveness, and, ultimately, the relevance of the institution. The consensus reached at the IMF Annual Meetings held in Singapore—a consensus which brought together members accounting for more than 90 per cent of the voting power in the institution—was made possible by a previous agreement that took place at the G20. Indeed, the G20 played the leading role throughout this process by making room for diverging expectations and proposals and generating a solid agreement between developed, emerging, and developing countries. This agreement was crucial for the wider acceptance of the two-stage IMF reform process that eventually emerged.

The first decision made in the G20 was to drop the fruitless discussion on the IMF's *raison d'être*. It was agreed that the Fund was and should

---

[17] G20 Meeting of Finance Ministers and Central Bank Governors, Communiqué, Berlin, 20–21 November 2004 (see Appendix 2.1).

[18] G20 Communiqué, Berlin, 2004 (see Appendix 3.1).

[19] 'G20 Statement on reforming the Bretton Woods Institutions', Xianghe, Hebei, China, October 2005.

remain one of the pillars of international financial stability, and that its original mandate was still relevant for addressing key issues of economic cooperation in the international system. At the meeting in Adelaide in March 2006, the G20 established a set of principles for IMF reform—credibility, effectiveness, and legitimacy. The first part of what would become a two-step approach was then devised—it called for an ad hoc increase in quotas and voting power for China, Mexico, Turkey, and Korea. The initial set of discussions revolved around how to identify the countries whose quotas should be increased and how to calculate the amount of the increase. Another point of contention was about which topics to include in the first stage of the reform process and which ones to leave for the second stage. These issues were debated not only at the Adelaide meeting, but also at an ad hoc meeting of the G20 deputies that took place before the IMF/World Bank annuals in Singapore.

1.4. Conclusions

This chapter has argued that the G20 is a forum that adds value by giving impetus to existing initiatives in other organizations or institutions, by creating consensus and drafting guidelines to address specific matters in other organizations, and by providing a space for national policies to receive attention from high-level policymakers. So far, the G20 has taken up existing initiatives under discussion elsewhere rather than introduced new issues to the international agenda. It has provided a space for thought and the exchange of views and perspectives for policymakers to streamline proposals, build consensus, and ensure that relevant ideas are embraced by key actors of the international financial system.

The G20 also provides a mechanism for emerging-market countries to increase their influence in the international financial architecture. International relations over the last 50 years have been divided into two distinct camps—developed economies on one hand and developing economies on the other. Globalization has created large differences within developing economies, effectively placing those that are larger and more dynamic into a separate group of so-called emerging markets. During the 1990s, some of these emerging economies started to participate in multilateral organizations and institutions on an individual basis (for instance, at the OECD and APEC), until some of them were identified as systemically significant and brought into contact with the G7. As a result, the influence of these countries in matters pertaining to the international financial architecture has grown.

Also, the network provides for a level playing field on which emerging economies can forge joint positions on relevant topics relating to the international financial agenda, positions which can then be considered together with the most advanced economies. The fact that the origins of the financial crises of the 1990s were mainly in emerging economies served as an incentive for the G7 to listen more carefully to these countries' positions, experiences, and concerns. Since future economic growth depends largely on the domestic reforms implemented by developed and emerging countries alike, incentives for maintaining a level playing field remain. Moreover, the success of the G20 in dealing with systemically significant topics such as crisis prevention and resolution and the reform of the Bretton Woods institutions provides yet another incentive for maintaining this dialogue.

So far, the Group can boast several significant achievements. It has provided for the first time a space in which developed and emerging countries alone can exchange views on the most relevant topics of the international financial agenda. Second, it has provided for a mechanism in which systemically significant countries can discuss potentially far-reaching initiatives proposed elsewhere. Third, the network has given participating states the opportunity to establish a framework for crisis prevention and resolution. Fourth, the Group has generated consensus among its members on the need to pursue and maintain liberalization and economic reforms in a context where protectionist measures could appear to offer answers to external shocks. And finally, it has given members the opportunity to reach consensus on the issue of IMF reform.

Today, however, the G20 is at a crossroads, and its future is uncertain. The Group's success in producing crisis-prevention and crisis-resolution frameworks left the network with an agenda vacuum. This vacuum was subsequently filled by the reform of the Bretton Woods institutions, an issue which will give the Group renewed relevance for the next few years. However, the informal character of the Group, whereby dialogue and discussion prevail, may not be the most efficient mechanism to pursue the reform agenda, since it might be necessary to consider stronger, more binding commitments to effect lasting IMF reform.

The future relevance and legitimacy of the G20 will depend largely on the ability of the network and its chairs to identify an agenda that captures the attention of the network's ministers and is sufficiently weighty to take the Group beyond its original objectives of crisis prevention and resolution. If the chairs are successful in generating a meaningful agenda, the G20 will continue to be one of the most influential networks on financial stability and sustainable growth. Otherwise, the network's future could be in danger.

2

The G20 After Eight Years: How Effective a Vehicle for Developing-country Influence?

Leonardo Martinez-Diaz[1]

2.1. Introduction

To many observers, the creation of the Group of 20 Finance Ministers and Central Bank Governors (G20) in 1999 marked a watershed in global governance. After decades in which the most important decisions in global financial and monetary management had been the exclusive province of a small club of the three, five, or at most seven richest nations, a ministerial-level network had emerged, bringing together the world's most advanced economies and some of the largest developing countries. Convened at the initiative of the USA and other industrialized countries, the network promised to be a powerful, yet inclusive forum for global economic management. For the most sanguine commentators, the emergence of the G20 heralded a new age of more inclusive economic governance.

After eight years of G20 meetings and communiqués, there is little consensus about what the G20 has actually meant for the voice of developing countries in global governance. Some scholars have embraced the network with optimism, arguing that the creation of the G20 has at least established a key institutional mechanism by which emerging market economies are able to affect the way in which the global financial

[1] This piece has benefited from the thoughtful feedback of Ngaire Woods, Amar Bhattacharya, Gerry Helleiner, Jeff Chelsky, Tom Bernes, Calum Miller, Brad Setser, and the participants of the 'Networks of Influence' workshop held in Oxford on 16–17 March 2006.

system is governed'.[2] Others have been less positive: 'The G20 is severely flawed . . . as at present constituted, it is unlikely to lead anywhere. Its very existence deflects energies from more appropriate and hopeful processes and agendas'.[3]

Which of these views is right? Has the G20 made a real difference to the degree of voice and influence developing countries enjoy in global economic governance? The existing academic and policy literature has mostly described the G20 in the context of efforts to build a new international financial architecture,[4] tried to explain the network's genesis,[5] analysed its impact in global governance,[6] or prescribed ways to reform the G20.[7] However, the influence of developing countries in the G20 has been neglected by scholars.

This piece complements Rubio-Marquez's 'insider's view' of the G20 by taking a critical look at the network from the perspective of an outsider looking in. It tries to assess whether participation in the G20 network has enabled developing countries to exercise greater voice and influence in global economic governance. The paper does this by evaluating the degree to which the G20's annual communiqués reflect the policy preferences of the G20's developed and developing-country members. Nine

[2] Randall D. Germain, 'Global Financial Governance and the Problem of Inclusion', *Global Governance*, 4:7 (October 2001), p. 411.

[3] Gerry Helleiner, 'Developing Countries, Global Financial Governance, and the Group of Twenty: A Note', paper prepared for the Governance Working Group of the Global Financial Governance Initiative, March 2001, p. 5.

[4] Roy Culpeper, 'Systemic Reform at a Standstill: A Flock of "Gs" in Search of Global Financial Stability', North-South Institute, June 2000; and Randall D. Germain, 'Reforming the International Financial Architecture: The New Political Agenda', paper presented at the International Studies Association, Chicago, 24 February 2001.

[5] Tony Porter, 'The G7, the Financial Stability Forum, the G20, and the Politics of International Financial Regulation', paper prepared for the International Studies Association Annual Meeting, Los Angeles, California, 15 March 2000.

[6] John Kirton, 'Guiding Global Economic Governance: The G20, the G7, and the International Monetary Fund at Century's Dawn', in John Kirton and George von Furstenberg (eds.), *New Directions in Global Economic Governance: Managing Globalization in the Twenty-First Century* (Ashgate: Aldershot, 2001), pp. 143–67; John Kirton, 'The G20: Representativeness, Effectiveness and Leadership in Global Governance', in John J. Kirton, Joseph P. Daniels, and Andreas Freytag (eds.), *Guiding Global Order: G8 Governance in the Twenty-First Century* (Ashgate: Aldershot, 2001), pp. 143–72; and John Kirton, 'From G7 to G20: Capacity, Leadership, and Normative Diffusion in Global Financial Governance', paper presented at the International Studies Association Annual Convention, 20 February 2005.

[7] See, for example, Anne-Marie Slaughter, 'Government Networks, World Order, and the G20', paper prepared for the project 'The G20 Architecture in 2020—Securing a Legitimate Role for the G20', IDRC, 29 February 2004; Barry Carin and Gordon Smith, 'Making Change Happen at the Global Level', paper prepared for the project 'The G20 Architecture in 2020— Securing a Legitimate Role for the G20', IDRC, 29 February 2004; and Colin I. Bradford, Jr. and Johannes F. Linn, 'Global Economic Governance at a Crossroads: Replacing the G7 with the G20', Brookings Institution Policy Brief No. 131, April 2004.

policy issues are selected in which developed and developing countries have expressed significant differences of opinion in forums outside the G20. Then, consensus on those issues is compared systematically across the communiqués of the G20, the G7, and the G24. The G7 and the G24 communiqués are used as proxies for the policy preferences of the developed and developing countries of the G20, respectively.

I use the term 'developing countries' in this paper to refer to G20 members other than the G7 (USA, United Kingdom, France, Germany, Italy, Canada, and Japan) and Australia. This category includes low-income India and middle-income Argentina, Brazil, China, South Africa, Turkey, Mexico, Indonesia, and Russia. Two high-income countries—Saudi Arabia and Korea—are also included in this category because they have tended to identify with other middle-income countries and because they face social and political problems more characteristic of developing countries than of mature economies.

The paper proceeds in two sections. First, I explore the degree of influence developing countries enjoy within the network by evaluating the degree to which G7 and G24 positions on nine key issues are reflected in G20 communiqués. The second section draws some conclusions from this comparative exercise and discusses scenarios for the G20's future. Appendix 2.1 contains the detailed comparison of the G7, G20, and G24 communiqués. Before assessing the G20, however, a brief comment on the origins of the G20 is in order to supplement the material in the preceding chapter.

2.2. Why the G20?

As Vanessa Rubio-Marquez has already explained, the G20 was a child of the Asian financial crisis of 1997–98, and its creation was largely driven by the realization that financial crisis prevention and resolution could not be addressed by the G7 governments acting alone—they required the active participation of and 'buy in' from the largest, systemically significant developing countries. But why resort to a network rather than using existing formal institutions or creating new ones?

From the beginning, the G7—and the US government, in particular—sought a structure that would disturb as little as possible the existing institutional architecture. Therefore, the creation of new international organizations was quickly ruled out. In a June 1999 report to their heads of state, the G7 finance ministers explicitly rejected the creation of new international organizations and instead endorsed efforts 'to widen the ongoing dialogue on the international financial system to a broader range of countries...'[8] Proposals for an Asian Monetary Fund were famously buried by strong US Treasury opposition.

At least two existing organizations could have been used to 'broaden the ongoing dialogue'. The Bank for International Settlements (BIS)—the Basel-based 'central bankers' bank' and forum for bank regulators—might have been expanded to include the new systemically significant middle-income countries. However, the addition of up to 12 developing countries to the BIS roster would have changed the character of the organization, whose board of directors has been controlled since the 1930s by half a dozen industrialized countries, while its committees report directly to the G10.[9] In addition, the institutional culture of the BIS is dominated by central bankers and bank regulators, not by the broader-vision finance ministries. The relatively narrow and technical focus of BIS committees would have been too constraining for the type of dialogue required.

Another alternative would have been the International Monetary and Financial Committee (IMFC) of the IMF.[10] The Committee is charged with advising the Fund's Board of Governors on matters concerning the management of the international financial system. With a representation structure based on the constituency system of the executive boards of the IMF and World Bank, the 24-member IMFC was probably the other obvious alternative.

However, the US Treasury had misgivings.[11] The IMFC is not conducive to informal dialogue but lends itself to the reading of prepared, pre-negotiated statements. Also, IMF staff and management were seen as exercising too much control over the IMFC's agenda and communiqués, and the IMF as a whole was seen as underrepresenting Asia and overrepresenting Europe. Finally, the IMFC included a variety of countries beyond

[8] June 1999 report of the G7 finance ministers to their heads of state on 'Strengthening the International Financial Architecture'.

[9] The BIS Board of Directors is controlled by the founding members (the USA, United Kingdom, France, Germany, Italy, and Belgium), which are guaranteed a majority on the board (12 of 21 votes). The influential Basel Committee on Banking Supervision reports directly to the G10, which includes the founding members plus Canada, Japan, the Netherlands, Sweden, and Switzerland. Developing countries would eventually be invited to sit on the BIS's various committees, but only as observers with no voting power. The BIS and the G20 would eventually be linked indirectly through the Financial Stability Forum, as I discuss below.

[10] Originally the Interim Committee, the ministerial-level body was re-launched as the IMFC in September 1999.

[11] Correspondence with Brad Setser, former acting director of the US Treasury's Office of International Monetary and Financial Policy, 24 February 2006.

the handful of systemically significant economies the G7 was interested in engaging directly.

Soon, the need for a new forum—an inter-governmental network—became clear. Financial crises were to be prevented through enhanced surveillance undertaken jointly by the Bank and Fund, complemented by a loose structure of standard-setting bodies, financial regulators, private-sector actors, and developed- and developing-country governments. The IMF would remain the lender of last resort. This structure would be loosely tied together by a network of government officials from the G7, systemically significant countries, and the Bretton Woods institutions. After a few preliminary incarnations (the G22 and the G33), the G20 network finally came into existence.

2.3. Assessing Developing-Country Influence in the G20

Has the G20 enhanced developing-country voice and influence in global economic governance, or is it better described as a vehicle for mobilizing developing-country support for a G7-driven policy agenda? Several characteristics of the network affect the ability of the G20's developing countries to exert influence within the network. In theory, the G20's membership structure should benefit developing countries. 'Emerging markets' outnumber the G7 and Australia by a margin of 11 to 8, if one puts Russia in the developing-country camp (not an unreasonable assumption given that Russia's economic structure and policy dilemmas have more in common with those of other developing countries than with the G7 members). In addition, the exclusion of least-developed countries means that the G20 developing countries can avoid some of the damaging policy splits that divide middle- and low-income countries in other forums, such as the World Trade Organization and United Nations. Finally, the chair of the G20, first held by a G7 country (Canada) for three consecutive ministerial meetings, now rotates regularly among the membership.[12]

Yet, other features of the network undermine developing-country influence. Since the G20 is a consensus-based forum for discussion rather than a voting-based, decision-making entity, the developing countries' numerical advantage does not necessarily translate into greater influence. In addition, the G7 countries have more resources at their central

---

[12] The chair has rotated from Canada (1999–2001) to India (2002), Mexico (2003), Germany (2004), China (2005), Australia (2006), South Africa (2007), and Brazil (2008).

banks and finance ministries to devote to G20 matters and therefore may enjoy an advantage in terms of shaping the agenda, conducting research, and developing positions. For example, Australia and Canada have taken the leadership in hosting G20 workshops and preparing position papers.

Another important factor is the existence of multiple points for G7 influence over the G20's agenda and workplan. The G7 wields considerable influence in the networks and organizations that surround the G20, particularly the International Monetary and Financial Committee (IMFC), the executive boards of the World Bank and IMF, the Bank for International Settlements (BIS), and the Financial Stability Forum (FSF). This means that the G20 must react and engage with issues and positions in a heavily G7-dominated institutional environment. The G7's influence is further enhanced by the fact that G7 finance ministers—by virtue of holding their own ministerial and head-of-state meetings before the G20 ministerial each year—are more likely than developing-country ministers to arrive with a common agenda and a set of well-articulated positions. The G7 finance deputies meet six times a year and communicate regularly via conference call, compared with the G20's semi-annual deputies' meetings.

What does the record tell us about the relative influence of developed and developing countries in the G20? When the preferences of the G7 and the G20 developing countries differ on a certain issue, are the latter able to qualify, moderate, or shift the view of the leading industrialized states? Or does the network act mainly as a vehicle for legitimizing the G7's policy preferences? Although the G20's internal documents and proceedings remain confidential, it is possible to take a first cut at this question by examining the public record.

My approach is to first identify the preferences of the G7 and the G20's developing countries in key policy areas by looking at the positions the two groups have taken independently in forums other than the G20. The position of the G7 finance ministers, I take from the group's annual communiqués and the reports to their heads of government from 1999 to 2007. The positions of the G20 developing countries, I infer from the semi-annual communiqués and related documents of the G24 over the same period.

Established in 1971 to coordinate the positions of developing countries on international financial issues, the G24 meets twice a year before the spring and annual meetings of the IMF and World Bank governors. Using G24 communiqués for this comparative exercise has three advantages.

First, the G24 includes seven of the 11 'developing-country' members of the G20 (China and Saudi Arabia are regular participants, even though they are not in the original membership), so the group's statements can provide us with a reasonable proxy for these countries' preferences.[13] Second, G24 meetings are highly attuned to the discussions at the G7, IMFC, and G20, so G24 communiqués address the same issues and debates as these other groupings. And third, the G24's broader developing-country membership can help us detect differences in the interests of the middle-income countries of the G20 and low-income countries.

After examining the G7 and G24 positions on key issues, I then compare them with the positions articulated in the G20's annual communiqués for the same years. If the G20's position is indistinguishable from the G7's on issues on which the G24 and the G7 disagree, we can conclude one of two things. Either the G7 is coaxing or coercing at least some of the membership of the G20 into agreement, or the split is within the G24 itself—the middle-income countries which sit on both networks may actually have more in common with their G7 counterparts than with low-income countries. If, on the other hand, we find that the G20 position reflects a compromise between the G7 and G24 view, or if the G20 position largely reflects the G24's preferences, then this would suggest that the G20 really is a forum where developing countries are changing the views of the most powerful states.

For this comparative exercise, I look at nine policy issues that have been discussed by all three country groupings and which are of special relevance to developing countries. In all nine issues chosen, the G24 stance differed in some significant respect from the G7 position. The areas selected were (1) capital account liberalization and capital controls, (2) the formulation and adoption of standards and codes, (3) developing-country representation in new international forums, (4) the formulation and implementation of anti-money-laundering measures and measures to combat the financing of terrorism (AML-CFT), (5) IMF and World Bank conditionality, (6) reforming the governance of the Bretton Woods institutions, (7) rules and practices in international trade, (8) debt relief and poverty reduction, and (9) sovereign debt restructuring. The full comparative exercise is detailed in Appendix 2.1.

---

[13] The G24 is currently composed of Algeria, Argentina, Brazil, Colombia, Cote d'Ivoire, Democratic Republic of Congo, Egypt, Ethiopia, Gabon, Ghana, Guatemala, India, Iran, Lebanon, Mexico, Nigeria, Pakistan, Peru, the Philippines, South Africa, Sri Lanka, Syria, Trinidad and Tobago, and Venezuela. However, all members of the G77 are welcome to attend G24 meetings.

Table 2.1. Classification of G20 positions

← More developed-country influence		More developing-country influence →	
G20 endorses G7 position and expands on it	G20 endorses G7 position	G20 remains silent or neutral	G20 builds on the G24 position
AML-CFT	Standards and codes	Conditionality	Sovereign-debt restructuring
	Representation in new forums	Capital controls	Reform of the BWIs
	Debt relief	Trade	

The result of this exercise is four categories of G20 positions, sorted according to how they relate to their G7 counterparts. In the first category, the G20 stance not only drops all significant G24 objections and embraces the G7 posture but also expands upon it. This 'G7 plus' position adds to the original number of policy commitments, makes them more detailed, or provides mechanisms or timelines that might make them 'harder' and more enforceable. Issues in the second category are those in which the G20 dropped the G24's objections and endorsed the G7 position without adding new commitments or refinements. The third category includes issues in which the G20 simply chose to remain silent, making only a very general statement without siding with either the G7 or G24. Finally, issues that fall in the fourth category are those in which the G20 adopted elements of the G24 position, elements that do not appear in G7 communiqués. Table 2.1 above shows the categorization of the nine selected issues. The categories on the left suggest greater developed-country influence, while the categories on the right suggest that developing countries may have a greater capacity to shape the consensus.

2.3.1. 'G7 Plus'

The most extreme example of the G20 adopting a G7 position is in the area of measures to combat money laundering and the financing of terrorism. The G20 not only endorsed the G7's position, but adopted a more detailed and extensive version of the G7's own 'Action Plan to Combat the Financing of Terrorism'. The 'G20 Action Plan on Terrorist Financing' is three times as long as the G7 plan, and includes more numerous and more detailed commitments in the areas of freezing terrorist assets, implementation of international standards, information sharing, technical assistance, and compliance and reporting. At the same time, the G24's concerns about the G7's Financial Action Task Force (FATF) framework were all dropped in the G20 communiqués, including concerns about the 'non-voluntary' and 'non-cooperative' ways in which FATF recommendations were applied to non-FATF members.

This outcome is not surprising, as the US government made AML-CFT measures a top national security priority and was prepared to pressure other countries into accepting and implementing them. Also, the G20's annual meeting in 2001 took place only weeks after the 11 September attacks, in an environment that made it difficult and unpopular to challenge the US-proposed measures. Finally, the G7 countries had started developing an AML-CFT framework several years before 2001, so that by the time the terrorist attacks took place, there was already a set of detailed initiatives that could be tabled at the G20 in short order.

2.3.2. Endorsing the G7 Position

Three issues fall into the second category, where the G20 communiqués endorsed the G7 position without additions or refinements. The first issue is standards and codes, where the lines between the G7 and the G24 were clearly drawn. The G7 wanted compliance with the new standards to be part of regular IMF surveillance under Article IV, and it wanted standards and codes incorporated into Fund conditionality.[14] The G24, on the other hand, argued that the scope of IMF surveillance should not be extended to include observance of standards and codes, and that such observance should not be a consideration in Fund conditionality. In addition, the G24 demanded that pressure to observe transparency standards also be put on hedge funds and other private financial institutions. It also called for a more inclusive process for developing standards and codes, one that gave developing countries a greater voice.

The G20's position aligned solidly with the G7's. The G20 agreed that 'IMF surveillance should be the principal mechanism for monitoring countries' progress in implementing standards and codes...'[15] G20 members committed to undertaking Reports on the Observance of Standards and Codes (ROSCs) and Financial-Sector Assessments Programmes (FSAPs)—the joint IMF and World Bank surveillance programmes created

[14] Communiqué of G7 Finance Ministers and Central Bank Governors to the Köln Economic Summit, 18–20 June 1999, 21(c).
[15] Communiqué of the G20 Finance Ministers and Central Bank Governors, 25 October 2000, Appendix, section 4.

to monitor the observance of codes and standards. G24 calls for a more inclusive standard-setting process and for applying standards to hedge funds were dropped, and the G20 stayed silent on whether observance of standards and codes should be a consideration in the design of conditionality.

A second issue in this category is developing-country representation in new forums. The G24 repeatedly voiced concerns about the lack of developing-country participation in the Financial Stability Forum and expressed alarm at the growing role of international forums in which developing countries had little voice, such as the BIS. Yet, the G20 did not raise these concerns in its communiqués and instead endorsed the work of the FSF and its affiliated bodies.

Third is the case of debt relief. In its 2000 and 2002 communiqués, the G24 expressed 'deep concern' about the under-funding of the HIPC Initiative and Trust Fund and the slow implementation of the debt relief initiative.[16] It also noted that the HIPC Initiative's funding arrangements shifted a disproportionate burden of the cost of the initiative on other developing countries. However, the G20 chose not to voice these concerns or to convey a sense of urgency about the funds shortage. Instead, it echoed the G7's call on countries to commit to a 100 per cent reduction of ODA claims and eligible commercial claims. It also welcomed donors' commitments to increase aid.

2.3.3. *Silence and Neutrality*

The third category of issues includes those in which the G20 preferred to sidestep a controversy by saying little about it and declining to take sides. This was the case with IMF and World Bank conditionality. On this critical issue for developing countries, the G7 and G24 positions clashed, especially in 1999–2000. G7 documents from this period staked out specific policy areas where conditionality should remain in place, even though some of these areas were not considered core competences of the Bretton Woods institutions. These included trade liberalization, the creation of non-discriminatory insolvency regimes, and the elimination of state-directed lending on non-commercial terms.[17] At the same time,

---

[16] Intergovernmental Group of Twenty-Four on International Monetary Affairs Communiqué, 15 April 2000 and Intergovernmental Group of Twenty-Four on International Monetary Affairs Communiqué, 27 September 2002.

[17] Communiqué of G7 Finance Ministers and Central Bank Governors, 20 February 1999, Appendix, section XXVI.

the G24 was condemning the intrusiveness of conditionality and its expansion beyond the mandate of the Bretton Woods institutions. The G24 also called for streamlining conditionality.

Over time, the G7 and G24 found common ground in supporting IMF efforts to review and streamline conditionality. By contrast, the G20 stayed out of this debate entirely, at least in public. G20 communiqués made no direct mention of conditionality, and the group's 2005 'Statement on Reforming the Bretton Woods Institutions' contained only a very general declaration about the appropriate roles of the IMF and World Bank.

Another case in this category is capital account liberalization. Capital controls were an issue of considerable interest to the middle-income countries of the G20 (at least six of which suffered a financial crisis triggered by capital outflows between 1999 and 2005). In its June 1999 communiqué, the G7 discouraged in somewhat tortured language the use of capital controls, declaring that 'controls on capital inflows may be justified for a transitional period, but more comprehensive controls carry costs and should not be a substitute for reform; controls on capital outflows carry greater long-term costs, are not effective policy instruments, and should not be a substitute for reform, though they may be necessary in exceptional circumstances'.[18] Instead of discouraging the use of capital controls, the G24 called for further analysis on the use and effectiveness of specific capital controls, especially those on derivatives trading.

The G20's communiqués made no mention of capital controls—they neither echoed the G7 stance discouraging most controls, nor did they affirm the G24's call for further analysis. The G20 ministers limited themselves to a general and anodyne statement—that capital account liberalization can be a good thing, as long as it is implemented carefully, with the right sequencing, with effective regulation and supervision, and supported by technical assistance.

Finally, on trade, the G7 and G24 communiqués were quite diverse and emphasized different policies. The G7 called for more trade-related technical assistance, the incorporation of trade liberalization measures in Fund and Bank programmes and operations, the reduction of trade-distorting support and subsidies, and increasing market access for developing countries, among other things. The G24 condemned protectionist measures

---

[18] Communiqué of G7 Finance Ministers and Central Bank Governors to the Köln Economic Summit, 18–20 June 1999, 50(g).

in developed countries, called on stronger IMF surveillance on the trade practices of industrialized countries, urged the Bank and Fund to publicize the development impact of trade restrictions, and blamed industrialized countries for the failure of the Doha round.

The G20 did not take sides in this debate and instead opted for general language on the need to reduce trade-distorting support and export subsidies. It omitted the G24's calls for ending industrialized-country agricultural tariffs and subsidies and for intensified IMF surveillance of industrialized-country trade policies. At the same time, it dropped G7 demands that trade liberalization be part of Bank and Fund programmes. The G20 did diverge from the G7 by highlighting the need for special and differential treatment for developing countries.

2.3.4. Building on the G24 Agenda

The fourth and final category includes issues in which the G20 adopted and sometimes expanded on elements that were part of the G24's agenda (but not of the G7's). Two issues fall into this category. The first is debt restructuring, where the G20 picked up on the G24's proposal for a voluntary code of conduct for sovereign debt restructuring that was agreed by both private creditors and sovereign issuers. Using its unique position as a forum that brought together the home countries of major private creditors and top issuers of sovereign bonds, the G20 played a proactive role by actively encouraging and later endorsing the 'Principles for Stable Capital Flows and Fair Debt Restructuring in Emerging Markets', as Rubio-Marquez details in this volume. This was a unique G20 contribution, as the G7 was simply not the right venue to endorse principles requiring the agreement of both creditor and debtor countries.

The other issue on which the G20 diverged from the G7's line and built on the G24 position was the reform of the Bretton Woods institutions. Since 2000, the G24 had been pushing for governance reform at the BWIs, including a more transparent process for the selection of the heads of the World Bank and IMF and streamlined formulas for calculating quotas and voting power at both institutions. Starting in 2005, the G20 took up that cause, echoing virtually all of the G24's concerns and proposals (the one exception was the G24's call for a formula using GDP in purchasing-power-adjusted terms). This pressure seems to have helped persuade the IMF and World Bank governors to approve an ad hoc quota increase for China, Mexico, Turkey, and Korea in September 2006. The G20's demands for reform went beyond the G7's more modest proposals, which focused on getting the BWIs to make more documents public and to establish an evaluation body at the IMF. The G7 did recognize in 2005 the need 'to review the Fund's governance and quotas to reflect developments in the world economy', but the G20 was more detailed and insistent than the G7 in calling for major reform at the BWIs.[19]

To summarize, in four of the nine issues studied, the G20 endorsed and elaborated on the G7's position (one case) and endorsed the G7's position with no elaboration (three cases). In three cases, the G20 remained silent or neutral on the issue, and only in two cases did the G20 incorporate and build on G24 concerns. In other words, the G7's position was reflected in the G20 communiqués twice as frequently as the G24's, and in a third of the cases, countries exercised a 'veto' that prevented the group from issuing anything more than a neutral statement.

Crucially, it should be noted that the distribution of burdens imposed on countries was *not* the same across issues. Those issues in which the G7 position prevailed over the G24's involved relatively high costs for developing countries, whether in the form of adaptation costs (as in the implementation of AML-CFT measures and standards and codes) or in terms of forgone resources (as in under-funded debt relief commitments). Those issues in which silence and neutrality predominated included those in which G7 consumers, firms, and governments would have had to bear much of the cost had the G24 position prevailed (as in the imposition of capital controls by emerging economies or the removal of tariffs and subsidies in agriculture).

And third, those issues in which the G24 position won the day promised modest benefits for developing countries but did not seriously challenge G7 interests. For example, the principles on debt restructuring promoted and endorsed by the G20 were prepared with extensive input from the International Institute of Finance, which represents the interests of leading US financial institutions. Also, the principles were consistent with the preferences of the US and UK governments, which favoured a flexible, case-by-case approach to debt restructurings.[20] In the case of BWI reform, the G20's pressure has so far led only to small ad hoc quota increases

---

[19] Statement by G7 Finance Ministers and Central Bank Governors, London, 2–3 December 2005.

[20] John Kirton, 'The G20: Representativeness, Effectiveness and Leadership in Global Governance', in John J. Kirton, Joseph P. Daniels, and Andreas Freytag (eds.), *Guiding Global Order: G8 Governance in the Twenty-First Century* (Ashgate: Aldershot, 2001), p. 152.

for four countries, a measure which has not meaningfully disturbed the balance of power in either institution. In short, the victories the G7 appears to have won at the G20 are not only more numerous—they have been of much greater consequence than those won by developing countries.

2.3.5. Two Hypotheses

How can we account for this pattern of declarations in G20 communiqués? And what does it tell us about developing-country influence in the network? A conclusive explanation would require a detailed study of the G20's internal dynamics and negotiations, which is beyond the scope of this paper. However, we can at least ponder two hypotheses. The first, mentioned earlier, is that the real split is within the G24, between the emerging-market economies and the rest of the developing world. If this hypothesis is correct, then the G24's quarrels with the G7 were primarily fuelled by the group's poor countries, countries such as Ethiopia, Guatemala, and Sri Lanka. Meanwhile, the G20's developing countries— large 'emerging markets' like China, India, or Brazil—did not have to be bullied or coaxed into agreement by the G7; they had already embraced that position freely, and this is why the G20's stance was in harmony with the G7's on key issues.

There are grounds to be sceptical of this hypothesis. There is no doubt that the large emerging economies have interests that differ from those of least-developed countries. Yet, on most of the issues selected for this comparative exercise, those differences proved small, or at least, they were set aside for the sake of consensus at the G24. Indeed, the G24's objections to the G7 agenda seem to be coming from middle-income countries as much as from low-income countries. This becomes clear when we examine the positions some of the G20's developing countries have taken at IMFC meetings. For example, Brazil has charged at the IMFC that 'exaggerated expansion of [IMF and World Bank] conditionality has become dysfunctional, detrimental to the Fund's effectiveness, and has made programme implementation unnecessarily more complicated'.[21] Chinese officials have declared in the same forum that on standards and codes 'we favour voluntary participation as opposed to forced

---

[21] Statement by Pedro Malan, Minister of Finance, Brazil, Meeting of the International Monetary and Financial Committee, 29 April 2001.

implementation...'[22] On anti-money laundering issues, China has also declared that 'While the FATF is invited to participate in the assessments, it should forgo its "name and shame" practice... The Fund/Bank-led assessments should not include aspects of law enforcement.'[23] Also, India has openly advocated the use of GDP on a purchasing-power-parity basis in a revised formula for calculating IMF and World Bank quotas.[24] All of these positions are echoed, sometimes verbatim, in G24 communiqués. In other words, the reason we often see convergence between the G7 and the G20 on key issues may not be because the G20's developing countries agree with everything their advanced-economy peers have to say.

An alternative hypothesis is that the non-G7 members of the G20 simply do not find it worthwhile to expend much political capital in the network, choosing instead to fight policy battles in formal institutional organs—such as the executive boards of the IMF and World Bank—where decisions have real implications. A central reality of the G20 is that an enormous wealth and power gap exists between the G7 countries (or, more accurately, the G3 or G5) and the rest of the countries sitting around the G20 table. For most developing-country officials, picking a fight with powerful G7 ministers on sensitive issues for the sake of a more balanced G20 communiqué that few will read is simply not worth the political cost, particularly if they fear potential G7 retribution in other venues. Thus, there may be a 'chilling effect' that biases the contents of G20 communiqués in the direction of the G7 position, particularly when G7 officials put their full weight behind a position, thereby raising the political cost to non-G7 members of opposing it.

If this hypothesis is correct, then it would provide a better explanation of why G7 and G20 positions converged on certain issues in G20 communiqués but diverged elsewhere. Telling is the declaration of a US Treasury official, who made the following remark in an interview, apparently in genuine puzzlement: 'I don't understand. In the G20, the [developing-country] governors had no problems with standards and codes. But then, in the executive board [of the IMF], they raised all kinds of problems. There seems to be a disconnect between the governors and

---

[22] Statement by Li Ruogu, Assistant Governor, People's Bank of China, Meeting of the International Monetary and Financial Committee, 29 April 2001.

[23] Statement by Dai Xianglong, Governor, People's Bank of China, Meeting of the International Monetary and Financial Committee, 28 September 2002.

[24] Statement by Palaniappan Chidambaram, Minister of Finance, India, Meeting of the International Monetary and Financial Committee, 17 September 2006.

their executive directors.'[25] There may very well be method to this apparent madness: the 'disconnect' does not reflect a breakdown of communication within national governments or bureaucratic insubordination. Rather, it may reflect a deliberate choice by governments to fight policy battles only in forums where they can reap tangible benefits for fighting them.

Finally, one important nuance is worth noting. The G20's dynamics have not remained static over time. The willingness of developing countries to challenge the G7 and to add new issues to the agenda appears to have grown over time. Developing countries were least active in the first three years of the G20, when a G7 country hosted the G20 meetings and occupied the chair. Developing-country officials were probably muted during this period by a mix of awe at the opportunity to sit in such an intimate setting with the world's great powers and mistrust about the G7's motivations for creating the forum.

But over time, developing-country officials have grown comfortable with the network and have learned how to make it work for them. Developing countries have started using their role as chairs to introduce into the agenda issues of special interest to them and to pursue initiatives they feel strongly about, such as the governance reform in the Bretton Woods institutions. Whether this greater assertiveness by developing countries will translate into a distinctly alternative policy agenda in G20 communiqués remains to be seen.

2.4. Conclusions

This paper has tried to assess whether the network has enhanced the influence of its low- and middle-income countries in global governance. To do so, it analysed the substance of the G20's public consensus on nine policy issues. Industrialized and developing countries expressed significant differences of opinion on these issues in other forums, namely, the G7 and the G24. Using G24 communiqués as a proxy for the views of non-G7 members of the G20, I found that in four of the nine cases studied, the G20 endorsed without qualification the G7 position. In another three cases, the G20 remained silent or neutral. Only in two of the nine cases did the G20 incorporate significant elements of the G24's alternative agenda into its public declarations. Notably, the distribution

---

[25] Confidential interview with senior US Treasury official.

of costs varied across issues. On those issues on which the G7 stance prevailed, the costs fell most heavily on developing countries, while the issues on which the G20 stayed neutral would have imposed the heavier costs on G7 firms and governments. Finally, the G24 viewpoint prevailed on issues that promised relatively modest benefits for developing countries without imposing significant costs on the most powerful states.

The comparative exercise suggests that the G20 has primarily served as a vehicle for mobilizing support for G7 policies, especially on issues about which the G7 cared most strongly, such as measures to fight money laundering, combat the financing of terrorism, and promote the adoption and implementation of standards and codes. Endorsement by the G20 has given these G7-driven policies a broader base of legitimacy and support. At the same time, positions favoured by developing countries—especially those that would have imposed large costs on G7 firms and governments but could have produced large benefits for developing countries—have made little headway in the group. Developing countries have become more active and assertive in the G20 as the network has matured, and in two instances they made original contributions to the global policy agenda. But so far the benefits of these initiatives have been modest. In sum, after eight years, the G20 has only modestly enhanced developing-country influence in global financial governance.

In view of all this, should developing countries give up on the G20? Not quite yet. Politics inside the G20 network have proven to be dynamic, and participation in the group may yet help developing countries influence the global agenda on key issues. Whether the G20 becomes a more effective vehicle for developing-country influence, however, will depend on how the network evolves over the next phase of its history. As Rubio-Marquez made clear in the previous chapter, the group has exhausted its initial mandate on financial crisis prevention and resolution and is struggling to recapture its sense of purpose and direction. The G7 has lost much of the interest it initially had in the G20, and the developing countries that have chaired the group in recent years have been struggling to design agendas that are at once urgent, relevant to the whole membership, and tractable. Thus, the G20 has reached an important juncture.

There are three possible scenarios for the next stage of the G20's evolution. One scenario is that G20 governors and ministers will continue to meet regularly, organizing seminars and producing occasional papers, exchanging country experiences, and producing uncontroversial and little-noted communiqués that mostly adhere to G7 declarations or remain neutral on controversial issues. Because the G20 is the only ministerial-level network that brings together the G7 and large emerging economies, its developing-country members will continue to attend, if for no other reason than because they value the prestige of sitting at the same table with the world's heavyweights. In this scenario, the network will remain a largely weak vehicle for developing-country influence.

The second scenario is that the G20 will give way to an 'L20' or similar incarnation, a grouping that brings together advanced economies and large developing countries at the head-of-state and head-of-government level.[26] In November 2008 such a G20 leaders' meeting was held in Washington DC. If the Heads of Government G20 continues, the G20 finance ministers will have served a crucial role as a stepping stone to a more inclusive form of global governance.

The third scenario is that the G20 will come of age. This is an optimistic possibility, but the G20's recent history suggests that it is not implausible. In this scenario, the non-G7 members of the network—emboldened by their growing weight in the global economy and led by China, India, and Brazil—begin to engage the G7 in a serious debate about key issues in global economic governance. With increasing frequency, they put issues on the G20 agenda that are not being discussed elsewhere, issues that would not be discussed otherwise, and issues extending well beyond the G20's traditionally narrow focus on financial and monetary issues. G20 communiqués begin to reflect a more substantive dialogue and to offer a genuine synthesis of developed- and developing-country prescriptions on global issues. Over time, the network could become the central locus for meaningful, high-level debate on economic matters among the world's key players, one that would influence the agendas of other governments, networks, and institutions. Whether or not this scenario comes to pass will depend on whether the G7 comes to appreciate the value of such a debate, and whether the non-G7 countries find it worthwhile to pursue it through a network such as the G20, rather than through formal international organizations.

---

[26] On this point, see Johannes F. Linn and Colin I. Bradford Jr., 'Summit Reform: Toward an L-20', in Johannes F. Linn and Colin I. Bradford Jr. (eds.), *Global Governance Reform: Breaking the Stalemate?* (Washington, DC: The Brookings Institution, 2007), pp. 77–87.

Appendix 2.1: Comparing G7, G24, and G20 Positions on Nine Key Issues

Issue area	G7 position	G24 position	G20 position
Capital account liberalization and capital controls	International capital flows enable a better allocation of capital and foster economic development; the opening of capital markets must be carried out in a well-sequenced manner, accompanied by well-regulated financial sector and consistent macroeconomic policy (1998–99); controls on capital inflows may be justified for a transitional period, but more comprehensive controls carry long-term costs and should not be a substitute for reform; controls on capital outflows carry greater long-term costs, are not effective policy instruments, and should not be a substitute for reform, though they may be necessary in exceptional circumstances (1999)	The benefits of further capital account liberalization depend on the prevailing circumstances of each country; the IMF can play a leading role in promoting an orderly and gradual liberalization as long as it is sensitive to local conditions and technical assistance (TA) is provided where needed (1998); further analysis of the use and effectiveness of specific capital controls is needed, especially in relation to derivatives trading (1999)	G20 ministers agree to advance global financial integration with TA and advice from the international financial community (2000); capital account liberalization should proceed in an appropriately sequenced manner (2001); increased financial liberalization, integration, and effective regulatory policies and supervision, with due regard to timing and sequencing, are means to enhance the development of the financial system (2003)
Standards and codes	Cornerstone of enhanced transparency in the financial system is internationally agreed standards and codes; BIS, IASC, IAS, and OECD should prepare new standards and codes (1999); IMF should monitor compliance with standards as part of regular surveillance under Article IV; IMF should publicize failures to meet standards, and adherence to standards should be used in determining Fund conditionality (1998); TA should be provided where needed; development of ROSCs and FSAPs applauded (2000)	Increased attention to standards and codes as part of Fund surveillance is acceptable, but it must remain within the core competences of the Fund and compliance should remain voluntary; compliance assessments should take into account countries' institutional capacities and level of development; TA should be provided (1998); participation of developing countries in development of standards and codes has been limited and a more inclusive process is needed; the scope of IMF surveillance should not be extended to cover the observance of standards and codes; transparency should apply to all players in the international financial system, including highly leveraged institutions (2000); observance of standards and codes should not be incorporated into programme conditionality (2001)	G20 ministers welcome the work of the BWIs and other bodies toward the establishment of standards and codes; more widespread implementation of these codes is desirable; members agree to undertake the completion of ROSCs and FSAPs (1999); G20 endorses FSF's recommendations and encourages continued work on incentives to foster implementation in a manner and at a pace that reflects each country's unique development, reform priorities, and institutional structure; IMF surveillance should be the principal mechanism for monitoring countries' progress in implementing standards and codes; governments should be encouraged to participate in IMF-led assessment programmes and conduct ongoing self-assessments of progress in observance of standards; TA should be available to assist countries with implementation (2000)

(cont.)

Appendix 2.1: (cont.)

Issue area	G7 position	G24 position	G20 position
Developing-country representation in new forums	Promoting financial stability does not require new international organizations; the G7 will convene the Financial Stability Forum (FSF); it will initially be a G7 initiative only, but more national authorities will be invited to join over time; new mechanism for informal dialogue (G20) proposed to complement and reinforce the role of the governing bodies of the Bretton Woods institutions (1999)	To have legitimacy and ownership, the choice of participants for the proposed forum (G20) should take into account the constituency structure of the Bretton Woods institutions and should not undermine their role; the creation of the FSF is welcomed, but there should be appropriate developing-country representation (1999); there is concern about the growing role played by international fora (other than the Bretton Woods institutions) where developing-country representation is limited (2000)	No explicit references to new forums and institutions; endorsement of the work of the FSF (2000)
AML/CFT	Support the efforts of the Financial Action Task Force (FATF); urge it to identify countries and territories that fail to cooperate in the fight against money laundering, consult with them, and if consultations are not productive, recommend action designed to convince them to modify their laws and practices (1999); encourage non-cooperative jurisdictions to demonstrate their willingness and ability to implement reforms so they can be de-listed from the non-cooperative countries list at the earliest possible time; G7 Action Plan to Combat Financing of Terrorism prepared (2001)	Anti-money laundering should be a cooperative venture between developed and developing countries; should include large financial centres as well as off-shore centres; there is concern about the non-cooperative and non-voluntary manner in which FATF recommendations are being applied to non-members; application of standards should take into account countries' capabilities and level of development; IMF should not become involved in law enforcement (2001); regrets that FATF has not totally abolished its non-cooperative approach and concern that many countries have been unfairly put in non-cooperative countries list (2002)	G20 ministers are committed to combating terrorism by cutting off its financial sources; endorsed a G20 Action Plan on Terrorist Financing which closely follows the G7 Action Plan to Combat the Financing of Terrorism (2001); support surveillance and voluntary self-assessment through the FATF and other bodies; agree to participate in self-assessment of eight special recommendations on terrorist financing (2001); committed to implementing revised FATF Forty Recommendations and the FATF Special Recommendations (2004); call on FATF and FATF-style regional bodies to broaden the support base for their work (2006)

	G7	G24	G20
IMF/WB conditionality	The IMF should continue to include in its conditionality policies on trade liberalization, elimination of state-directed lending on non-commercial terms, and provision of non-discriminatory insolvency regimes (1999); country adherence to standards and codes should be used in determining Fund conditionality (1999); G7 looks forward to upcoming review of conditionality by IMF (2000); G7 pleased with recent reforms on streamlined conditionality (2004)	The G24 is concerned about the intrusiveness of BWI conditionality into socio-political matters stretching beyond the mandate of the BWIs (1999); encourage IMF to streamline conditionality immediately for all new PGRF-supported programmes; conditionality has become excessive in magnitude and scope; need to take into account institutional capacity and domestic legislative processes when implementing conditionality; too much conditionality undermines ownership; welcomes review of IMF conditionality (2000); streamlining IMF conditionality should not result in shifting conditionalities to World Bank or others; need more Bank-Fund collaboration to reduce cross-conditionality (2002)	G20 ministers affirm that the IMF should primarily focus on national and international macroeconomic and financial stability, exercising enhanced surveillance, and strengthening crisis prevention and resolution; the World Bank should keep its focus on development, sharpening its financial and technical assistance roles for both least-developed countries and emerging markets (2005)
Reform of the Bretton Woods Institutions	Asian financial crisis has confirmed central role of IMF and World Bank in international financial system; quota increase and New Arrangements to Borrow will give IMF more resources to do its job; BWIs should become more transparent and publish more information, including PINS and Article IV consultations; IMF should develop a formal mechanism for systematic evaluation; creation of Contingent Credit Line welcomed (1998); Interim Committee should be given permanent standing as the IMFC; the G7 'takes note' of discussions to change the formula for calculating quotas at the BWIs (2000, 2001); the G7 countries 'stress the need to review the Fund's governance and quotas to reflect developments in the world economy' (2005)	Call for a modified Contingent Credit Line; call for design of a transparent and inclusive process for the selection of the IMF managing director and World Bank president (2000); quota formula should eliminate existing bias that underestimates size of developing economies; basic votes should be substantially increased (2002); call for timetable for enhancing voting power, voice, and participation of developing countries in BWIs (2003); strong disappointment that little has been done in this area or in the selection process; call for quota formula to incorporate GDP in purchasing-power-party adjusted terms (2004); welcome ad hoc quota increase for Mexico, China, Turkey, and Korea, but the Singapore reform package does not adequately address the fundamental issue of under-representation (2006); welcome agreement to amend Articles to keep basic votes at constant share of voting power (2007)	The governance structure of the BWIs (quotas and representation) should reflect changes in economic weight; call for achieving concrete progress on quota reform by Singapore meetings of IMF and World Bank in September 2006; selection of senior management of the IMF and World Bank should be based on merit and ensure broad representation of all member countries (2005); G20 welcomes the support given by IMF Governors in Singapore to quota and governance reform aimed at reflecting members' relative positions in the world economy and enhancing the voice of low-income countries at the Fund (2006)

(cont.)

Appendix 2.1: (cont.)

Issue area	G7 position	G24 position	G20 position
Trade	Strong commitment to open, fair, competitive and dynamic international trade (1999); urge BWIs to work with the WTO to improve effectiveness of trade-related technical assistance and to more fully incorporate policies promoting international trade into Fund programmes and Bank operations (2000); welcome industrialized country initiatives which, providing improved market access for exports from poorest countries, will facilitate their integration into the world economy (2001); more needs to be done to enhance South–South trade (2003); urge speedy resumption of Doha round (2004); call on all countries to substantially increase market access in agriculture, industrial products, and services, especially for developing countries; significantly reduce trade-distorting support; eliminate all forms of export subsidies in agriculture (2005); urge members to address the concerns of developing countries in trade negotiations (2006)	Protectionist measures employed by industrial countries impede global employment growth and poverty reduction (2000); urges developed countries to liberalize trade in areas of particular importance to developing countries (2002); blames for the failure of the WTO Cancun ministerial the unwillingness of major industrialized countries to remove barriers to agricultural imports (2003); IMF surveillance should focus on implementation of trade policies in industrialized as well as developing countries; urges World Bank and IMF to publicize the impact of trade restrictions and sanctions (2005); disappointment over suspension of Doha round; observes that current trading system is heavily biased against developing countries (2006)	Support efforts by the WTO to build consensus toward further multilateral trade liberalization; agree to promote domestic policies that help spread the benefits of integration to all members of society (2000); call on all WTO members to re-energize the Doha negotiation process (2003); committed to significantly increasing market access for goods and services, reducing trade-distorting domestic support, eliminating all forms of export subsidies in agriculture, providing effective special and differential treatment for developing countries, and increasing aid for trade (2005)

Debt relief and poverty reduction	G7 agrees that HIPC Debt Initiative is the appropriate framework for addressing debt problems of poorest countries (1999); strong support for efforts of HIPCs to develop PRSPs; note that some bilateral contributions have been made to HIPC Initiative, including Trust Fund, but some require legislative approval; emphasize importance of country-owned PRSPs; emphasize commitment to 100% debt relief on ODA and eligible commercial claims (2000); commitment to promote the participation of all creditors in financing the HIPC Trust Fund (2002); commitment to full implementation of HIPC Initiative, including topping up relief where appropriate (2003)	HIPC countries should be allowed to use Interim PRSPs to avoid delays in provision of debt relief while PRSPs are being finalized; deep concern about the insufficiency of bilateral contributions to HIPC Trust Fund; HIPC Initiative's funding arrangements shift disproportionate burden of costs to other developing countries (2000); disappointment that after six years of operations, only 5 of 38 eligible countries requiring debt relief have reached the completion point; a number of creditors are not providing their share of debt relief (2002)	Call for those bilateral creditors to commit to 100% reduction of ODA claims and eligible commercial claims (2000); welcome increases in ODA (2002); welcome donors' commitments to significantly increase development assistance and the debt relief initiative launched at Gleneagles (2005)
Sovereign debt restructuring	G7 calls upon private sector to broaden use of collective action clauses (CACs) (1998); G7 Action Plan issued to include CACs in debt contracts; welcome private sector and issuing countries' support for placing CACs in sovereign bond issues (2002); welcome work on code of good conduct and on proposal on a sovereign debt restructuring mechanism (2003)	The IMF should deepen studies for engaging, on a case-by-case basis, the development at the international level of equitable procedures for debt settlement as exist at national levels (2000); G24 prefers voluntary, country-specific, and market-friendly approaches to sovereign debt restructuring; open-minded about proposals for incorporating CACs (2002); welcome increasing voluntary use of CACs; proposals for a voluntary code of conduct for sovereign debt restructuring should be agreed by both private creditors and sovereign issuers; debt sustainability analyses should be based on country-specific circumstances (2003)	Support work on comprehensive and market-compatible approaches to crisis resolution, including CACs, a sovereign debt restructuring mechanism, and a code of good practices (2002); welcome increasingly widespread use of CACs, encourage discussions between issuers and market participants to develop workable code of conduct (2003)

3

Finance Ministers and Central Bankers in East Asian Financial Cooperation

Helen E. S. Nesadurai

3.1. Introduction

At least since the late 1950s, there have been networks of finance officials in the Asia-Pacific region. Nonetheless, the region has not had strong regional financial cooperation until the last decade.[1] The Asian financial crisis of 1997–98 catalysed a rapid deepening of regional monetary cooperation, undergirded by several key networks of officials. This chapter analyses the emergence and influence of these networks.

In the late 1950s, organizations such as the SEANZA (the Southeast Asia, New Zealand, and Australia forum) and SEACEN (the Southeast Asian Central Banks forum) were set up to provide training to regional central bank officials and have continued to do so.[2] In 1991, central bankers began to meet under the framework of EMEAP, the Executives' Meeting of East Asian and Pacific Central Banks. Since 1994, finance ministers have been meeting in the framework of the Asia Pacific Economic Cooperation (APEC) forum, while finance ministers from the Association of Southeast Asian Nations (ASEAN) began meeting in March 1997 just before the Asian financial crisis broke out in July of that year. Since 2000, a wider group of finance ministers—the ASEAN Plus Three group—has been meeting annually, and finance ministers also meet regularly as part of the Asia–Europe Meeting (ASEM). Thus, at least seven distinct but overlapping networks of finance ministers, central bankers, and their officials operate in the

---

[1] On this last point, see Hamilton-Hart (2003).

[2] For details, see www.seacen.org/training/Archive-Schedule.

Table 3.1. Key Asia-Pacific/East Asian finance networks

Network members	Central bank forums			Finance ministers' meetings			
	SEANZA Est 1956	SEACEN Est 1966	EMEAP Est 1991	APEC Est 1994	ASEM Est 1996	ASEAN Est 1997	ASEAN+3 Est 2000
China	X		X	X(MFG)	X		X
Japan	X		X	X(MFG)	X		X
South Korea	X	X	X	X(MFG)	X		X
Hong Kong	X		X	X(MFG)			
Taiwan		X		X			
Indonesia	X	X	X	X(MFG)	X	X	X
Malaysia	X	X	X	X(MFG)	X	X	X
Philippines	X	X	X	X(MFG)	X	X	X
Singapore	X	X	X	X(MFG)	X	X	X
Thailand	X	X	X	X(MFG)	X	X	X
Brunei		X		X(MFG)	X	X	X
Vietnam		X		X	X	X	X
Cambodia		X			X	X	X
Laos					X	X	X
Myanmar		X			X	X	X
Mongolia	X	X					
Macao	X						
Papua New Guinea	X	X		X			
Australia	X		X	X(MFG)			
New Zealand	X		X	X(MFG)			
USA				X(MFG)			
Canada				X(MFG)			
Mexico				X			
Chile				X			
Peru				X			
Russia				X			
Fiji		X					
Nepal	X	X					
India	X						
Sri Lanka	X	X					
Pakistan	X						
Bangladesh	X						
Iran	X						
European Union					X		

Notes: MFG refers to membership in the Manila Framework Group.

Sources: Wang (2002); SEACEN website (www.seacen.org).

Asia-Pacific. All seven are dedicated to cooperation through exchanging information as well as dialogue and consultation on financial and monetary policy matters. Table 3.1 provides details of membership in these networks and the dates that they were established.

Two networks were created in the wake of the Asian financial crisis: the ASEAN+3 finance ministers' network and the Manila Framework Group (MFG), an offshoot of APEC. The most successful and powerful of these, the ASEAN+3, has subsequently initiated two projects: the Chiang Mai

Initiative (CMI) and the Asian Bond Market Initiative (ABMI). These projects have been lauded as key mechanisms targeted at crisis management and crisis prevention, respectively. The CMI pools a proportion of members' foreign exchange reserves in order to provide liquidity support to members facing currency crises. This is seen as a way to minimize or avert the risk of a severe financial crisis in any one member or in the region.

At the time of writing, the CMI boasts a funding pool of US$ 77 billion. The ABMI, on the other hand, is a capacity-building project aimed at developing the institutional and regulatory infrastructure necessary to support national bond markets. This prompted one observer to note that ASEAN+3 'seems to be where the action is at present'.[3] Complementing these moves, EMEAP central bankers have launched two Asian bond funds that have the potential to catalyse the formation of a regional bond market which, if effective, could help channel the region's considerable savings for use within the region.

Compared to the other networks described in Table 3.1, ASEAN+3 and EMEAP clearly go much further in building regional capacity in crisis management and crisis prevention through the CMI and regional bond market projects. As this chapter shows, they are best viewed as self-help networks aimed at developing joint capabilities in regional financial governance.

Why was it deemed necessary by the members of ASEAN+3 and EMEAP to develop such capabilities? Why did the East Asian-centric networks— ASEAN+3 and EMEAP—emerge as the site for these key projects in regional financial governance if other networks in the Asia-Pacific already existed?.[4] What tangible benefits have emerged from ASEAN+3 and EMEAP cooperation in finance and what factors account for these outcomes? This is an important question given that economic cooperation in East Asia has long faced a number of hurdles stemming from divergent national interests that mirror the considerable economic diversity in the region; political rivalries, especially in Northeast Asia; and weak domestic

---

[3] Grenville, Stephen (2004), 'Policy Dialogue in East Asia: Principles for Success', in Gordon de Brouwer and Yunjong Wang (eds.), *Financial Governance in East Asia: Policy Dialogue, Surveillance and Cooperation*, London and New York: RoutledgeCurzon, pp. 16–37, 27.

[4] ASEAN+3 and EMEAP are best regarded as 'East Asian' networks given their inclusion of what are regarded as the core countries of 'East Asia'—Japan, China, South Korea, Indonesia, Malaysia, Philippines, Singapore, and Thailand. These countries are also APEC members.

regulatory capacity in a number of states that scholars argue precludes successful cooperation, especially in finance.[5]

The rest of this chapter explores these questions in detail, beginning with a brief description of the various finance and central bank networks currently operating in the region, particularly EMEAP and the ASEAN+3 finance network. The second section examines why East Asian states were driven to develop regional capabilities in crisis management and prevention, as well as the choice of ASEAN+3 and EMEAP as the site for the CMI, ABMI, and the two Asian bond funds. The analysis explores the extent to which the network features of these groups—such as the opportunities offered for learning among peers through the production and exchange of information and knowledge based on frank dialogue—have helped advance East Asian financial cooperation. Overall, the chapter assesses how effectively the ASEAN+3 and EMEAP groupings have fared in terms of the key functions commonly performed by networks: the production and exchange of information and knowledge, agenda setting, building consensus among network members, norm adoption and diffusion, and policy coordination and implementation.

3.2. The Emergence of Networks of Finance Officials in the Asia-Pacific

The primary motivating factor for financial cooperation among the East Asian governments was the 1997–98 Asian financial crisis.[6] What was crucial, however, was how the crisis was interpreted by these governments. While not discounting the role of domestic weaknesses, the East Asian governments identified poorly regulated global financial markets as a major contributing cause of the crisis. This shared perception of the cause of the crisis defined the response taken by the region to prevent future crises.

The shock of the financial crisis revealed to regional policymakers the importance of having some form of regional capacity to provide timely

---

[5] On this point, see Hamilton-Hart, Natasha (2003), 'Asia's New Regionalism: Government Capacity and Cooperation in the Western Pacific', *Review of International Political Economy*, vol. 10, no. 2 (May 2003), pp. 222–45.

[6] Hamilton-Hart, Natasha (2004), 'Cooperation on Money and Finance: How Important? How Likely?', in Kanishka Jayasuriya (ed.), *Asian Regional Governance: Crisis and Change* (London and New York: Routledge), pp. 173–88, 176–80.

and adequate financing to support currencies during crises.[7] It also led to discussions among East Asian policymakers and central bankers about ways to facilitate more efficient intermediation of the region's considerable savings.[8] Although East Asian governments could have chosen to address these problems individually or rely on global cooperation to do so, policymakers chose the *regional* route as the most viable option for East Asia. The crisis had revealed the futility of individual national efforts in dealing with speculative currency attacks in the absence of enormous financial reserves. The possibility of contagion, experienced during the Asian crisis, also revealed the need for coordinated solutions.

The lack of effective mechanisms in East Asia for preventing and managing financial crises had led to over-reliance on the IMF and external parties like the USA, which left the East Asian countries vulnerable to unwelcome external influence and conditionality.[9] The USA blocked Japan's proposal for the Asian Monetary Fund that many regional policymakers believed could have helped stem the sharp fall in currency levels by providing emergency financing.[10] The East Asian governments were also aware that another crisis cum contagion would need resources beyond the IMF's limited pool, further strengthening their interest in developing a regional capacity to deal with future emergencies.[11] Although the IMF had created the Credit Contingency Line in 1999, there were doubts as to its effectiveness as a source of emergency financing for countries facing an imminent crisis.

There was also little faith in East Asia that global reform efforts would provide any effective remedy to the systemic problems that the East Asian governments had identified as having played a major role in causing the crisis. In particular, governments called for the direct regulation of the highly leveraged hedge funds that had engaged in currency manipulation.[12] Although the near failure of the US-based hedge fund Long Term Capital Management in 1998 convinced developed-country officials that

---

[7] Wang, Yunjong (2002), 'Korea's Perspective on Regional Financial Cooperation', paper presented to the PECC Finance Forum Conference on Issues and Prospects for Regional Cooperation for Financial Stability and Development, 11–13 August 2002, Honolulu (www.pecc.org/finance/forum2002.htm, accessed 30 September 2005).

[8] Dobson (2001: 1005).

[9] See Grenville (2001) and Hall, Rodney Bruce (2003), 'The Discursive Demolition of the Asian Development Model', *International Studies Quarterly*, 47 (1): 71–99.

[10] Chang and Rajan (2001: 103).

[11] Grenville (2001); Wang (2002: 5).

[12] See, for instance, the views of Joseph Yam, Chief Executive of the Hong Kong Monetary Authority. Yam, Joseph (1999), 'Causes and solutions to the recent financial turmoil in the Asian region', 5 January 1999 (www.info.gov.hk/hkma/eng/speeches/speechs/joseph/speech_050199b.htm, accessed 13 August 2005).

hedge funds needed regulation, a position they had rejected until that point, the developed countries chose to leave hedge fund regulation to individual national authorities,[13] a disappointing outcome for governments in East Asia.[14] These governments were also increasingly sceptical that their interests would be addressed by the G7 despite the launch of new, supposedly inclusive forums such as the Financial Stability Forum (FSF) and the G20.[15]

East Asian governments turned to regional solutions which they discussed in forums such as that convened under the auspices of the Pacific Economic Cooperation Conference (PECC), the only 'track two' network of experts that is afforded observer status at APEC meetings. The PECC Finance Forum provided academic support for the establishment of a regional liquidity fund and a regional bond fund, two projects that had been proposed by EMEAP well before the Asian crisis. Surprisingly for a forum closely associated with APEC, many of the papers tabled at the PECC Finance Forum implicitly endorsed East Asia (and not APEC or the Asia-Pacific) as the appropriate regional unit to engage in financial cooperation.[16] While the Southeast Asian countries saw ASEAN as a possible site for regional financial cooperation, they conceded that developing a credible and effective capacity to respond to future currency attacks required resources beyond those available in Southeast Asia.[17] Several networks existed or emerged which could be used as forums for greater cooperation.

3.2.1. EMEAP: Stepping up Regional Central Bank Cooperation

EMEAP, a network of 11 central banks from East Asia, Australia, and New Zealand, was established in 1991 following a proposal by the Bank of Japan for a cooperative framework to undertake more intensive

---

[13] Eichengreen, Barry (2003), 'Governing Global Markets: International Responses to the Hedge Fund Problem', in Miles Kahler and David A. Lake (eds.), *Governance in a Global Economy: Political Authority in Transition*, Princeton, New Jersey: Princeton University Press, pp. 168–98.

[14] BNM (2000), *Annual Report 2000*, Kuala Lumpur: Bank Negara Malaysia (Central Bank of Malaysia). BNM (2002), *Annual Report 2002*, Kuala Lumpur: Bank Negara Malaysia (Central Bank of Malaysia). Costello, Peter (1999), 'Opening Address: Manila Framework Group Meeting', 26 March 1999 (www.treasurer.gov.au/tsr/content/speeches/1999/002.asp?pf=1).

[15] Sohn, Injoo (2005), 'Asian Financial Cooperation: The Problem of Legitimacy in Global Financial Governance', *Global Governance*, 11: 487–504 (495–6).

[16] These studies are available on the PECC website, www.pecc.org/finance/resources.htm, accessed 30 September 2005.

[17] Syed Hamid Albar (2000).

central bank cooperation beyond training activities.[18] However, little was achieved in this area of cooperation until 1996 when the first of the annual governors' meetings was held.[19] The reinvigoration of EMEAP was a direct result of the efforts of Bernie Fraser, the then Governor of the Reserve Bank of Australia, who in 1995 challenged EMEAP to take on more policy development and operational functions.[20] Fraser suggested that a renewed EMEAP take on at least three specific tasks: (a) facilitate the sharing of information and country experiences in macroeconomic management and banking supervision in the midst of rising and volatile capital flows; (b) develop a crisis management capacity through bilateral swap arrangements and regional liquidity support facilities; and (c) provide reserve management and other central banking services in line with those offered by the Bank of International Settlements (BIS).[21] Fraser, in short, envisaged EMEAP as an Asian BIS.

While a few EMEAP members were sceptical of the need for a regional body along these lines, others were more enthusiastic, although most urged a gradual expansion of tasks rather than rushing to establish a new regional body. Nevertheless, three concrete outcomes resulted from Fraser's suggestions. First, bilateral repurchase agreements of US treasuries were signed between five EMEAP central banks while the Hong Kong and Singapore monetary authorities agreed to intervene in foreign currency markets on behalf of the Bank of Japan. EMEAP countries had attempted to defend the Thai baht from speculative attacks for some time before the Bank of Thailand gave up and allowed the baht to float in July 1997, sparking the Asian financial crisis.[22] Second, annual central bank governors' meetings were inaugurated, with the first held in Tokyo in 1996. Third, three permanent working groups were established on payments and settlement systems, financial markets, and banking supervision.[23]

The positive and rapid response to Fraser's suggestions demonstrated that the EMEAP members, as central bankers, faced a common and rapidly changing global environment within which they had to perform

---

[18] See www.emeap.org for details of EMEAP.

[19] Chang, Li-Lin and Rajan, Ramkishen (2001), 'The Economics and Politics of Monetary Regionalism in Asia', *ASEAN Economic Bulletin*, 18 (1): 103–18.

[20] Fraser, Bernie (1995), 'Central Bank Cooperation in the Asian Region', *Reserve Bank of Australia Bulletin*, October 1995, pp. 21–8; Fraser, Bernie (1996), 'Central Bank Cooperation in Asia', *Reserve Bank of Australia Bulletin*, September 1996, pp. 21–6.

[21] Fraser (1996: 23–4).   [22] See Chang and Rajan (2001: 105).

[23] EMEAP (1998), 'The Third EMEAP Governors Meeting', *EMEAP Press Release*, 14 July 1998 (www.emeap.org/press/14jul98.htm, accessed 12 August 2005).

similar operational tasks. The EMEAP network's collegial, technically oriented working style, and 'stock of goodwill' (as Fraser described it), has helped it move forward to accomplish increasingly complex cooperative tasks that go beyond information exchange.[24] This helped EMEAP design and launch two regional bond funds—the first Asian Bond Fund in 2003 followed a year later by the second Asian Bond Fund. As a result, EMEAP has emerged as a key player in the regional financial architecture.

EMEAP has displayed a 'solid record of . . . central bank cooperation in the region' despite the absence of a central secretariat and a marked informality in the way in which its members engage with each other.[25] Secretariat functions for EMEAP are undertaken by the central bank designated as the host for that year's meetings. A virtual secretariat, first proposed in July 1997, is now in place so EMEAP members are connected electronically. This has facilitated the exchange of information, market intelligence, and experiences in central banking activities.[26] While confidentiality provisions in domestic legislation initially prevented the free exchange of financial information, this is now less of a problem as public disclosure of economic/financial information has increased following the Asian financial crisis.[27] Funding for EMEAP comes from Japan as well as from governments hosting EMEAP meetings.[28]

3.2.2. The APEC Finance Ministers' Process

During the mid-1990s, regional inter-governmental organizations such as APEC and ASEAN initiated regular meetings of their respective finance ministers, finance deputies, and central bankers. Commencing with their

---

[24] This point was confirmed by Dr. Boediono, a former Indonesian finance minister (from 2001 to 2004) who currently serves as Coordinating Minister for the Economy (appointed December 2005). He had participated in EMEAP in a previous capacity as a senior official of the Indonesian central bank. Author's interview, Jakarta, 11 October 2005.

[25] See Dobson, Wendy (2001), 'Deeper Integration in East Asia: Regional Institutions and the International Economic System', *The World Economy*, 24 (8): 995–1017, 1008. This point was also confirmed by central bank officials from the Philippines and Singapore interviewed by the author in September and October 2005.

[26] EMEAP (1997), 'Closer cooperation and coordination among EMEAP members', *EMEAP Press Release*, 25 July 1997 (www.emeap.org/press/25jul97.htm, accessed 12 August 2005).

[27] Interview with Professor Soedradjad Djiwandono, former governor of Bank Indonesia, the Indonesian central bank, conducted in Singapore in September 2005. See also Yam, Joseph (1997), 'Asian monetary cooperation', *The 1997 Per Jacobsson Lecture*, 21 September 1997 (www.info.gov.hk/hkma/eng/speeches/speechs/joseph/speech_210997b.htm, accessed 13 August 2005).

[28] Ibid.

inaugural meeting in 1994, APEC finance ministers now routinely engage each other through what is termed the 'APEC Finance Ministers' Process', which is primarily aimed at capacity building through information exchange and training programmes on issues ranging from corporate governance, banking supervision, securitization, and credit guarantee systems, to ensuring stable capital flows in a world of large and rising capital movements.[29]

In November 1997, the Manila Framework Group (MFG) was established under the auspices of APEC, although it involved only 14 APEC members: the six 'original' members of ASEAN (Brunei, Indonesia, Malaysia, Philippines, Singapore, and Thailand), four Northeast Asian economies (China, Japan, Hong Kong, South Korea), Australia, New Zealand, Canada, and the USA (Table 3.1). The MFG was initiated as a substitute for the Asian Monetary Fund (AMF). The latter had been proposed by Japan to provide countries with emergency financing to support currencies coming under speculative attack during the 1997 Asian financial crisis. Fearing that the AMF would supplant the IMF and allow countries to avoid painful domestic economic reforms, the USA and the IMF roundly rejected Japan's proposal, supporting instead the establishment of the MFG. The MFG was expected to support the work of the IMF in restoring the region's financial stability, principally by conducting regional surveillance and establishing a cooperative financing mechanism to supplement IMF resources. Facing numerous criticisms, the MFG was finally dissolved in November 2004.

3.2.3. *The ASEAN Finance Ministers' Network*

ASEAN was keen to institute regular meetings of its finance ministers to support plans to expand regional economic integration beyond trade liberalization.[30] Exchange of information and policy dialogue was expected to be the main focus of the annual finance ministers' meetings, first initiated in March 1997. The onset of the Asian financial crisis in July 1997, however, led finance ministers to explore ways in which they might cooperate to help address the crisis. As a result of these consultations, a regional surveillance mechanism was launched with the aim of warning members of impending crisis points in member economies. A second

---

[29] See www.apecsec.org.sg/apec/apec_groups/other_apec_groups/finance_ministers_process.html (accessed 30 August 2005).
[30] ASEAN (1997), 'First ASEAN Finance Ministers Meeting', *Joint Press Communiqué*, Phuket, Thailand, 1 March 1997 (www.aseansec.org/2457.htm) (accessed 1 June 2005).

move was to expand the ASEAN Swap Arrangement (ASA) first set up in 1976 to provide members with emergency funds to support currencies in crisis (although ASA funds were never used during the 1997 crisis). In 2000, the ASA was incorporated into the Chiang Mai Initiative.

Although ASEAN, unlike APEC, was keen to develop regional mechanisms to help prevent a recurrence of the financial crisis, it was constrained by a lack of financial resources and an absence of effective leadership that could identify relevant projects and persuade members of their utility. It is not surprising, therefore, that additional projects aimed at strengthening regional financial stability have been undertaken not by ASEAN alone but in collaboration with ASEAN's three Northeast Asian neighbours through the ASEAN+3 finance network.[31] This network launched both the CMI and the ABMI. Although the region cannot yet boast of a well-functioning regional financial architecture, some very concrete measures are already in place. The ASEAN+3 finance network is a core component of the region's financial architecture.

3.2.4. The ASEAN+3 Finance Ministers' Network

The ASEAN+3 regional grouping emerged gradually out of a series of ad hoc meetings held between the ASEAN governments and Japan, China, and South Korea to prepare the Asian agenda for the newly formed Asia–Europe Meeting (ASEM) in 1996. With growing interest on the part of China and Japan for regular summit meetings with ASEAN, it was only a matter of time before a dedicated summit of ASEAN+3 leaders was convened.[32] Following the first ASEAN+3 Summit held in 1997, annual ASEAN+3 Summits have been held following the annual ASEAN Summits. Alongside these events, a variety of ASEAN+3 ministerial meetings, including meetings of finance ministers, finance deputies, and central bank deputies, are now held regularly. The institutionalization of ASEAN+3 meetings and activities demonstrates that the ASEAN governments have recognized that their own prosperity and fortunes are tied closely to those

---

[31] All the ministerial statements issued by the ASEAN finance ministers following their annual meetings have, since 2000, devoted substantial attention to ASEAN+3 financial cooperation. These statements are available on the ASEAN website (www.aseansec.org).

[32] Stubbs, Richard (2002), 'ASEAN Plus Three: Emerging East Asian Regionalism?', *Asian Survey*, 42 (3): 440–55.

of Northeast Asia.[33] While ASEAN+3 aspires to have a fairly comprehensive cooperation agenda, it is in the financial realm that this grouping has displayed its most concrete cooperative outcomes to date, principally through the ASEAN+3 finance ministers' meetings.

An integral part of ASEAN+3, the ASEAN+3 finance ministers' network focuses on four specific projects: (a) developing the CMI as a regional liquidity facility; (b) establishing a regional bond market through the ABMI; (c) furthering the economic review and policy dialogue process (ERPD), or regional surveillance; and (d) supporting the ASEAN+3 Research Group. The latter two activities operate to provide support for the former two projects. Funding for the work of the ASEAN+3 finance network comes from the ASEAN+3 Finance Cooperation Fund. The Fund is maintained by the ASEAN Secretariat, which also acts as the Secretariat for ASEAN+3.[34] Annual contributions from ASEAN+3 members fund the organization, although the bulk of the money comes from the three Northeast Asian members, while the balance is provided through equal contributions from the 10 ASEAN states.[35]

Among the groups described above, the ASEAN+3 (including the ASEAN+3 finance ministers' forum) and EMEAP have been particularly influential. Both display key features of government networks. Although they are both in some sense 'official' inter-governmental forums in which government ministers and senior officials interact, they are non-hierarchical. They link a group of actors who share similar interests with respect to a policy issue and who are prepared to cooperate with each other to reach shared goals.[36] ASEAN+3 is backed by a secretariat and has a budget, while members are subject to some rules in its flagship project, the CMI, which is governed by a series of formal bilateral swap agreements between participating members. Nevertheless, these networks are generally unable to compel participation by their members in network activities and projects. Nor are they able to adjudicate in disputes between members. This is because each individual member government lies outside the hierarchical control of the other members. Put simply,

---

[33] Syed Hamid Albar (2000), Speech at the opening of the 33rd ASEAN Ministerial Meeting, July 2000 (www.aseansec.org/4086.htm, accessed 13 August 2005).

[34] ASEAN+3 (2003), 'Joint Ministerial Statement of the ASEAN+3 Finance Ministers Meeting', 7 August 2003, Makati, Philippines (www.aseansec.org/15033.htm, accessed 1 June 2005).

[35] Interview, 14 September 2005 with Philippine central bank officials involved in ASEAN+3 activities.

[36] Borzel, Tanja A. (1998), 'Organising Babylon: On the Different Conceptions of Policy Networks', *Public Administration*, 76 (Summer): 253–73.

consistent with the definition of networks used in this book, these groups do not have formal authority to make or implement decisions or to adjudicate disputes. Members choose to participate in network activities (and to subject themselves to some rules in the CMI) because they have accepted the goals of the joint enterprise and see merit in the shared undertaking. This enables network members to pool their competences and collaborate on solving the problems they face collectively. In the language of those who write about networks, officials 'pursue repeated, enduring exchange relations with one another'.[37] Finally, it is worth noting that there is a 'spirit of goodwill' that characterizes relations between network members who engage in dialogue and deliberation as a way to achieve common goals rather than through negotiations or strategic bargaining.[38]

The discussion to follow shows how the non-hierarchical nature of network forms of organizations has enabled the network's members to close gaps in information and knowledge that hampered the development of regional capabilities in financial crisis management and prevention.

3.3. The Workings of the Regional Networks

Although discussions on the future of regional financial cooperation had taken place within all the major finance networks described above (see Table 3.3), it was only at the ASEAN+3 and EMEAP levels that substantive proposals for managing and preventing future financial crises were put forward.[39] Although ASEAN was willing to act on these matters, the grouping lacked the necessary financial resources. APEC, which had the necessary funds, was unwilling to provide assistance to crisis-affected countries beyond reiterating the importance of continued capital liberalization. Even when the Hong Kong Monetary Authority first suggested that APEC develop an Asian bond fund, there was little interest in the idea.[40] It would be left to EMEAP to take up this initiative.

---

[37] Podolny, Joel M. and Page, Karen L. (1998), 'Network Forms of Organisation', *Annual Review of Sociology*, 24: 57–76.

[38] Podolny and Page (1998: 60–1).

[39] Author's interviews with senior officials from the ADB and the Philippine central bank.

[40] Amyx, Jennifer (2004), 'A Regional Bond Market for East Asia? The Evolving Political Dynamics of Regional Financial Cooperation', *Pacific Economic Papers*, No. 342, Canberra: Australia–Japan Research Centre, Australian National University. p. 11.

3.3.1. *The Failure of the Manila Framework Group*

APEC was also not able to take up this initiative because the USA was a key member country and was pushing (including in the IMF) for a non-regional perspective on the causes of and solution to the crisis. That explanation emphasized domestic policy mistakes and dysfunctional practices and institutional arrangements—crony capitalism—in the crisis-affected East Asian economies. These sentiments dominated APEC statements released during the crisis, reiterating the American line that the root causes of the conflict were domestic while remaining silent on possible systemic causes.[41] Key APEC members like the USA were not keen on developing *regional* institutional mechanisms for crisis prevention and management, perceiving these as a distraction from their central diagnosis of the problem.[42] It was for this reason that the Manila Framework Group (MFG) was conceived as a mechanism to support the work of the IMF in restoring the region to financial stability, principally by conducting regional surveillance and establishing a cooperative financing mechanism to supplement IMF resources.[43]

The Manila Framework Group was formed by APEC finance ministers in November 1997 and comprised 14 out of the 21 APEC members. The IMF was also a key participant. However, the MFG did not live up to expectations, failing to establish a regional financing facility, which was one of its goals.[44] There was only a vague commitment to lend financial support if the need arose, rather than any formal agreement that specified that a pre-determined quantum of funding would be provided (such as was provided for in the CMI).[45] Instead, regional surveillance became the

---

[41] APEC (1998), The Fifth APEC Finance Ministers Meeting, *Joint Ministerial Statement*, Kananaskis, Alberta, Canada, 23–24 May 1998 (www.apecsec.org.sg/apec/ministerial_statements/sectoral_ministerial/finance/1998_finance.html, accessed 24 August 2005).

[42] See the various statements issued by the APEC finance ministers and leaders, available from www.apec.org.

[43] On the suitability of the MFG as a framework for the CMI, see Grenville, Stephen (2001), 'Policy Dialogue in East Asia', Speech to the Australian National University Conference on Regional Financial Arrangements in East Asia, 12–13 November 2001. www.rba.gov.au/Speeches/2001/sp_dg_121101.html (accessed 3 June 2005).

[44] Wang, Yunjong (2000), 'The Asian financial crisis and its aftermath: Do we need a regional financial arrangement?', *ASEAN Economic Bulletin*, 17 (2): 205–17, p. 208.

[45] Cheong, Latifah Merican (2002), 'Country Paper: The Malaysian Perspective and Views of ASEAN Countries', paper presented to the PECC Finance Forum Conference on Issues and Prospects for Regional Cooperation for Financial Stability and Development, 11–13 August 2002, Honolulu (www.pecc.org/finance/forum2002.htm, accessed 30 September 2005).

'overriding purpose' of the MFG.[46] However, MFG surveillance has been criticized for not going much beyond the economic policy reviews and surveillance already conducted by the IMF. Moreover, many East Asian governments were uncomfortable with the way MFG surveillance was conducted; they tended to be one-way discussions in which the countries were subject to scrutiny and censure by the USA and the IMF and during which they had to defend their policy practices.[47] Despite attempts by East Asia in 2003 (led by South Korea) to reform the workings of the MFG,[48] the MFG was dissolved in November 2004.[49]

The absence of a shared definition of what caused the crisis among MFG members meant there was little agreement on how to prevent or manage crises, hindering the MFG from assuming a significant role in regional financial cooperation. As Martinez-Diaz and Woods note in this volume, when dominant members of a network wish to use it to push particular solutions, the network can rapidly lose its capacity to be a forum within which other members share their own concerns about the problem at hand. The MFG responded to the financial crisis in ways that reflected how the USA and the IMF, soon perceived as outsiders by East Asian states,[50] interpreted the crisis—as the outcome of domestic weaknesses that thus required far-reaching *domestic* reforms. The possibility that the crisis was also caused by systemic weaknesses was never seriously considered. The MFG soon came to be seen by its East Asian members as a 'forum for the IMF and the USA to pursue economic reform in East Asian countries rather than a forum for genuine dialogue between countries in East Asia and North America'.[51]

Despite resistance from the USA and the IMF to establishing a regional financing mechanism, governments from Malaysia, the Philippines, and Thailand that had been sympathetic to the AMF proposal continued, along with Japan, to explore other options.[52] China had also opposed the AMF proposal, as it was concerned that a functioning AMF would

---

[46] Rana, Pradumna (2002), 'Monetary and Financial Cooperation in East Asia: The Chiang Mai Initiative and Beyond', *ERD Working Paper Series*, No. 6 (Manila: Asian Development Bank, February), pp. 5–6.

[47] Author's interview at the Monetary Authority of Singapore. Also see Takahashi, W., quoted in De Brouwer, Gordon (2004), 'IMF and ADB Perspectives on Regional Surveillance in East Asia', in Gordon de Brouwer and Yunjong Wang (eds.), *Financial Governance in East Asia: Policy Dialogue, Surveillance and Cooperation*, London and New York: RoutledgeCurzon, pp. 38–49, 47.

[48] De Brouwer (2004: 47).   [49] Kawai and Motonishi (2005: 256), fn 16.

[50] De Brouwer (2004: 46).   [51] De Brouwer (2004: 47).

[52] Chang and Rajan (2001: 105).

accord Japan a central leadership role in the region.[53] Nevertheless, Chinese Premier Zhu Rongji declared in November 2000 that China was willing to engage in regional financial cooperation through the ASEAN+3 framework.[54] Although the USA was not keen on the idea of a permanent regional financing arrangement in East Asia, Washington did not attempt to block the CMI as it had the AMF.[55]

3.3.2. The Success of the ASEAN+3 Chiang Mai Initiative

One of the most successful initiatives in Asian financial cooperation has been the Chiang Mai Initiative (CMI) taken by ASEAN+3. The CMI consists of two components. The pre-existing ASEAN Swap Arrangement (ASA) provided the CMI with an initial funding pool of US$ 1 billion at the inception of the project in May 2000. However, the bulk of the CMI's funds come from its second component, the network of bilateral swap arrangements (BSA) negotiated between different pairs of ASEAN+3 countries. By December 2004, the funds available from 16 bilateral swaps totalled US$ 36.5 billion. From this pool, individual countries were able to draw on between US$ 1 billion and US$ 3 billion for up to 90 days, renewable for two years.[56] Until May 2005, countries could only access 90 per cent of the available funds if they adopted IMF conditionality criteria, while only 10 per cent of the fund was available immediately for emergency assistance.[57]

Despite the headway made on the CMI within four years of its launch, many shortcomings remained. Aside from the small amounts available to individual countries, the essentially *bilateral* nature of the CMI undermined its effectiveness since each bilateral swap had to be activated individually.[58] The surveillance mechanism linked to the CMI was rudimentary. For a few years it was based on the voluntary exchange of information between the parties involved in each bilateral swap agreement,

[53] Amyx, Jennifer (2005), 'What Motivates Regional Financial Cooperation in East Asia Today?' *East-West Center Analysis*, no. 76 (February), Honolulu: East-West Center, p. 7.
[54] Sohn (2005: 495).   [55] Amyx (2004 & 2005).
[56] ASEAN+3 (2004), 'Joint Ministerial Statement of the ASEAN+3 Finance Ministers Meeting', Jeju, Korea, 15 May 2004 (www.aseansec.org/16116.htm, accessed 1 June 2005).
[57] Kawai, Masahiro (2004), 'Regional Economic Integration and Cooperation in East Asia', paper prepared for the *Experts' Seminar on Impact and Coherence of OECD Country Policies on Asian Developing Economies*, Paris: Organization for Economic Cooperation and Development (OECD) (www.oecd.org/dataoecd/43/7/33628756.pdf).
[58] Comments by Haruhiko Kuroda, President of the ADB at the launch of the ADB book, *Asian Economic Cooperation and Integration: Progress, Prospects and Challenges*, in Singapore, 2 September 2005.

making the IMF link crucial to the CMI's credibility, ensuring it was not seen as a moral hazard inducing automatic bail-out. The IMF link, however, limited the CMI's effectiveness as an *emergency* liquidity support facility that could be mobilized rapidly in the event of a crisis.[59] The major creditor states of China and Japan had insisted on the IMF link to prevent their contributions to the CMI from being misused by countries in crisis.[60]

In May 2005, ASEAN+3 finance ministers announced a series of measures to address these shortcomings.[61] New swap arrangements were to be negotiated, especially among ASEAN states, as a way to expand the available funding pool, while current swap amounts would be doubled and all one-way swaps converted into two-way swaps. To this end, the ASEAN members doubled the ASA to US$ 2 billion in May 2005. The first BSA doubling took place in August 2005 between Japan and Indonesia, an extremely significant event since it took place at a time when the Indonesian Rupiah was under severe strain.[62] Plans were also announced to shift to a *collective* or synchronized activation of bilateral swaps based on a prototype framework for collective activation developed by the ADB.[63] Finance ministers also agreed to increase to 20 per cent the amount that may be drawn without IMF conditions to permit a more effective and speedy response to emergencies, with plans to increase this to 30 per cent.[64] Finally, finance ministers agreed to institute a more comprehensive surveillance mechanism.

If fully implemented, these proposed measures have the potential to ensure the CMI becomes an effective regional liquidity facility. By May 2006, the CMI funding pool had reached a substantial US$ 77 billion even though bilateral swap deals among ASEAN states have yet to be negotiated and some one-way swaps have not been converted to two-way deals. The state of play is depicted in Table 3.2 below. Surveillance now involves all the members of ASEAN+3 despite the fact that four of them (Cambodia, Laos, Myanmar, and Vietnam) do not participate in any bilateral swap

---

[59] Wang (2002); Park, Yung-Chul and Wang, Yunjong (2005), 'The Chiang Mai Initiative and Beyond', *The World Economy,* 28 (1): 91–101.

[60] Rana (2002).

[61] ASEAN+3 (2005), 'Joint Ministerial Statement of the 8th ASEAN+3 Finance Ministers' Meeting', Istanbul, Turkey, 4 May 2005 (www.aseansec.org/17449.htm, accessed 1 June 2005).

[62] *Agence France Presse,* 'Japan doubles currency swap with Indonesia as Rupiah plunges', 31 August 2005.

[63] Comments by the ADB President in Singapore, 2 September 2005.

[64] According to Pradumna Rana, Senior Director of the ADB's Office for Regional Economic Integration, quoted in the Manila Bulletin Online, 'ADB sees more FX deals', 6 September 2005, www.mb.com.ph/issues/2005/09/07/BSNS2005090743775_print.html, accessed 30 September 2005.

Table 3.2. The Chiang Mai initiative (as on 4 May 2006)

BSAs	Swap size (US$ billion)	Total funds available (billion)
Japan–Korea (1)	3.0 (two-way swap)	US$ 6.0
Japan–Korea (2a)	10.0 (one-way swap)	US$ 10.0
Korea–Japan (2b)	5.0 (one-way swap)	US$ 5.0
Japan–China	3.0 (two-way swap)	US$ 6.0
Japan–Thailand	3.0 (two-way swap)	US$ 6.0
Japan–Philippines	6.0 (one-way swap)	US$ 6.0
Philippines–Japan	0.5 (one-way swap)	US$ 0.5
Japan–Malaysia	1.0 (one-way swap)	US$ 1.0
Japan–Indonesia	6.0 (one-way swap)	US$ 6.0
Japan–Singapore	3.0 (one-way swap)	US$ 3.0
Singapore–Japan	1.0 (one-way swap)	US$ 1.0
China–Korea	4.0 (two-way swap)	US$ 8.0
China–Indonesia	2.0 (one-way swap)	US$ 2.0
China–Philippines	1.0 (one-way swap)	US$ 1.0
China–Malaysia[a]	1.5 (one-way swap)	US$ 1.5
China–Thailand[a]	2.0 (one-way swap)	US$ 2.0
Korea–Thailand	1.0 (two-way swap)	US$ 2.0
Korea–Malaysia	1.5 (two-way swap)	US$ 3.0
Korea–Philippines	1.5 (two-way swap)	US$ 3.0
Korea–Indonesia	1.0 (two-way swap)	US$ 2.0
Total BSA		US$ 75.0
ASEAN Swap Arrangement (ASA)	Among ASEAN-10	US$ 2.0
Total funds		US$ 77.0

Notes: BSAs are bilateral swap arrangements concluded between the ASEAN+3 countries.

[a] These swaps have expired and will be extended.

Source: Table compiled from information from the Bank of Japan (www.boj.or.jp/en/type/release/zuji_news/data/un0605a.pdf, accessed 23 November 2006).

arrangements. Although ASEAN+3 surveillance is voluntary, once a government has chosen to participate in surveillance it must comply with all surveillance requirements. Moreover, access to emergency funding from the bilateral swaps is now conditional on participation in surveillance.[65]

3.3.3. The Success of EMEAP in Developing Regional Bond Markets

The CMI is primarily a facility that helps alleviate currency crises. It does not directly address the *sources* of such crises, which stem from structural weaknesses in countries' financial systems. One of the more significant of these structural problems has been the heavy reliance on short-term foreign currency denominated bank loans for financing long-term

[65] Information on the conditions attached to recent bilateral swap agreements is available from the Bank of Japan website (www.boj.or.jp/en/type/release/zuji_news/data/un0605a.pdf and www.boj.or.jp/en/type/release/zuji_news/data/un0602a.pdf, both accessed 22 November 2006).

projects. This can create a double mismatch, in debt maturity structure and in currency mismatch, with the potential to precipitate a currency and financial crisis if market sentiments deteriorate, as happened during the Asian crisis. National bond markets offer better financing options in this regard. Regional central bankers believe, however, that a *regional* bond market could help overcome the deficiencies of smaller, national markets through consolidating risks and expanding liquidity conditions.[66]

The Hong Kong Monetary Authority first proposed the idea of an Asian bond fund to APEC. As already noted, the suggestion elicited little interest, and the idea was later taken up by EMEAP. In June 2003, EMEAP launched a US$ 1 billion Asian bond fund (ABF, later termed ABF-1) to which all 11 members contributed. The ABF would invest in a basket of US$-denominated bonds issued by sovereign and quasi-sovereign issuers in eight EMEAP countries (excluding Japan, Australia, and New Zealand).[67] Unfortunately, the ABF did not adequately address the currency mismatch problem as it was limited to investing in US$-denominated securities. However, the second Asian Bond Fund (ABF-2) established in December 2004 aimed at investing the US$ 2 billion contributed by EMEAP members in *domestic* currency bonds issued in the region.[68] Since its launch, the second bond fund has successfully raised US$ 400 million (as of the end of April 2006) from public, non-EMEAP sources, signalling its attractiveness as a fund, while its growth rate has been comparable to that of other bond funds in the region. ABF-2 has also gained acceptance among institutional investors, particularly from Japan.[69] In addition, the ABF-2 initiative has catalysed regulatory and tax reforms as well as improvements to the market infrastructure in various East Asian states, notably Malaysia, Thailand, the Philippines, and China.[70] The value of the ABF-2 clearly goes beyond its role as a financing instrument.

Complementing EMEAP's two Asian bond funds is the Asian Bond Market Initiative (ABMI) launched by ASEAN+3 in 2002.[71] Its objective

---

[66] Amyx (2005: 4).

[67] EMEAP (2003), 'EMEAP Central Banks to launch Asian Bond Fund', *EMEAP Press Statement*, 2 June 2003 (www.emeap.org/press/02june03.htm, accessed 12 August 2005).

[68] EMEAP (2004), 'EMEAP Central Banks Announce the Launch of the Asian Bond Fund 2', *EMEAP Press Statement*, 16 December 2004 (www.emeap.org/press/16dec04.htm, accessed 12 August 2005).

[69] Full details of the Asian Bond Fund 2 are found in EMEAP (2006), *Review of the Asian Bond Fund 2 Initiative*, A Report of the EMEAP Working Group on Financial Markets, June 2006. Available from the EMEAP website at www.emeap.org (accessed 23 November 2006).

[70] Ibid.   [71] See the AsianBondsOnline website at www.asianbondsonline.adb.org.

is to help members develop the national infrastructure needed to support efficient bond markets, particularly through its working groups on regulatory frameworks, new securitized debt instruments, credit guarantee mechanisms, foreign exchange transactions and settlement mechanisms, issuance of local currency denominated bonds, and enhanced rating systems.[72] All these elements are currently under-developed in the region, and the ABMI offers the chance for a region-wide, collective effort at building capacity in these areas.[73]

3.4. Conclusions

What factors have been central to the advances made in regional financial cooperation by the ASEAN+3 finance network and the EMEAP network of central bankers? The literature on networks emphasizes two features of networks that enhance their role in advancing cooperation: (a) the production and exchange of information and knowledge and (b) the centrality of dialogue and deliberation among members who regard themselves as equal.[74] Both these features facilitate learning, which in turn enhances the prospects for cooperation. While other governance structures such as hierarchies and markets are also capable of producing and exchanging knowledge, network forms of organization have been said to be better positioned to encourage learning because they maintain 'greater diversity of search routines than hierarchies' while providing more comprehensive and coherent information than markets.[75] There is not only greater diversity of knowledge produced within networks, especially in the form of the practical knowledge and real-world experiences of individual network members, but also a greater willingness to appreciate the importance of these diverse forms of knowledge.

Deliberative forms of interaction facilitate both the knowledge sharing function of networks and the search for consensus and compromise among members. Such interactions over a period of time may allow trust to be built up within the network. Trust, which is a social relation whereby network members come to believe that other members will not exploit their relationship through opportunistic actions or self-regarding behaviour, establishes a supportive environment wherein learning can

---

[72] Ibid.   [73] Amyx (2004: 16).   [74] Podolny and Page (1998).
[75] Podolny and Page (1998: 62).

occur.[76] As a result of learning, network members may redefine their interests in favour of group goals, discover new ways of achieving these goals and enhance their own capacity to meet group targets. When members share the same definition or interpretation of the problem at hand and are keen to avoid the losses associated with it, then problem-solving interactions are more likely to occur as opposed to negotiations and bargaining processes, which seek merely to reconcile members' self-interests.

In the case of ASEAN+3 and EMEAP, both networks promoted the generation and sharing of information and knowledge as well as the adoption of a deliberative style of interaction, which helped to advance the three major cooperative projects discussed above at crucial junctures. These successes are depicted in Table 3.3.

Another factor which is often omitted from the literature on networks was also critical to the success of the networks analysed in this chapter and that is leadership, or the ability of an actor (or group of actors) to influence and persuade others to take part in and contribute toward the effectiveness and success of some cooperative venture. In certain circumstances, leadership also involves the contribution of financial resources to support network activities, for example, funding knowledge production or, in the case of the CMI, building the funding pool. The non-hierarchical nature of networks may be undermined if leaders use their funds as tools of leverage to turn network interactions into negotiations and thereby push through decisions to achieve their preferred outcomes. How the leader chooses to behave and whether leadership is shared can reduce the potential for dominance of networks by one or another party. In ASEAN+3 and EMEAP, the discussion below describes how leadership was exercised by different actors (whether national governments, particular agencies, or individuals) on different network projects (the CMI, the ABMI, and the regional bond funds) using different resources (financial resources, knowledge resources, persuasion). Ultimately, the distribution of leadership minimized the possibility of dominance by any one party.

3.4.1. *Leadership*

Japan's leadership has been critical in the CMI. The Japanese finance ministry was responsible for initiating the proposal for a network of

---

[76] On different dimensions of trust, see Aykens, Peter (2005), '(Mis)trusting Authorities: A Social Theory of Currency Crises', *Review of International Political Economy*, 12 (2): 310–33.

Table 3.3. Assessing ASEAN+3 and EMEAP as networks of influence

Network function or outcome	Rating	Main achievement
Knowledge production	Strong	• Development of analytical tools, prototype models, and templates for surveillance activities, collective swap activation and bilateral swap agreements • Collection of new policy knowledge on a variety of issues • Role of ADB and large community of economists, consultants crucial to knowledge production, as is the growing involvement of private sector actors
Knowledge/ information exchange	Strong	• Greater willingness to exchange sensitive information • Frank discussions among network members • Networks emphasize the sharing of best practices in financial governance and on operational matters
Agenda expansion	Strong	• Adoption of the CMI as a regional liquidity facility • Adoption of the ABMI to support the development of diversified capital markets in the region • Launch of two regional bond funds • Currency coordination excluded although discussions on this are beginning to take place
Consensus building	Moderate	• Consensus reached on contentious items, for instance, on the need to strengthen regional surveillance and on its value to network members • Consensus achieved on the need to share information on sensitive data such as capital movements • No consensus as yet on third-party monitoring in regional surveillance or on currency and monetary coordination. Discussions on this are continuing
Norm diffusion	Moderate	• Efficiency and effectiveness promoted as goals of national banking and financial systems; norm of sound corporate governance emphasized • Within these broad principles, specific common standards slowly emerging
Policy coordination and implementation	Moderate	• Policy coordination limited although members increasingly undertake coordinated actions in the following areas: 　○ Bilateral swap agreements stipulate that surveillance is mandatory for disbursement of emergency swap funds 　○ Common template for bilateral swap agreements 　○ Common template for the coordinated activation of swaps now available 　○ Surveillance now involves all ASEAN+3 members who are required to submit data based on common data templates

swap arrangements that later became the CMI, and then designing and negotiating the general terms for these bilateral arrangements.[77] These formed the template (albeit with variations) for all other bilateral swaps. Japan learned from the failure of its first AMF proposal, which had been announced without much consultation with key parties. Subsequently, finance ministry officials devoted time to discussing ideas of a regional swap fund with their counterparts in the ASEAN+3 network.

Once the ASEAN+3 finance ministers adopted the idea in May 2000, Japan was instrumental in getting the CMI off the ground, using its large pool of foreign currency reserves quickly to bring to a close the first four of the CMI's bilateral swaps with Korea, Malaysia, the Philippines, and Thailand by the end of 2001. Over the next two years, swap arrangements with China, Singapore, and Indonesia were concluded.[78] Japan was also instrumental in persuading Singapore, which had been unenthusiastic about the CMI, to participate in the arrangement, initially as a recipient and later as a lender, though only to Japan.[79] Japan's 'New Miyazawa Initiative' of 1998 was also used to support two bilateral swaps with Malaysia and South Korea. Despite its limited capacity to take on the kind of leadership role assumed by Japan, China has also made significant contributions to the CMI, primarily as the second key lender after Japan during the project's early years.[80] By using its large pool of foreign reserves, China concluded five bilateral swap arrangements by the end of 2003 (compared to Japan's seven).

Initially, only Japan and China, given their vast foreign currency reserves (respectively totalling US$ 355 billion and US$ 168 billion in 2000), were in a position to take on a lending role in these bilateral swap arrangements. By 2004, Japan's foreign reserves would rise to US$ 820 billion while China's would total US$ 500 billion.[81] By this time, Korea's reserves had climbed to US$ 174 billion, and it had emerged as a key lending country in the CMI. Japan, China, and South Korea have taken part in 21 of the 28 individual bilateral swap deals concluded by May 2006, which collectively amounts to 85 per cent of the total funding pool (calculated from Table 3.2). Japan, however, is the primary lender in the CMI, currently accounting for about 46 per cent of the total funds available in the CMI, with South Korea in second place (22 per cent) and China third with an 18 per cent contribution (all figures calculated from

[77] Amyx (2005: 3).   [78] Kawai (2004: 22).   [79] Park and Wang (2005: 94).
[80] Amyx (2005: 7).   [81] Kawai and Motonishi (2005: 223).

Table 3.2). These three countries also underwrite much of the ASEAN+3 Finance Cooperation Fund that provides financial support for the activities of the ASEAN+3 finance network. The Japan-ASEAN Financial Technical Assistance Fund is also a key source of funding for ASEAN+3 finance network projects such as the scheme to monitor short-term capital movements in ASEAN+3.[82] Japan and China also fund the research work of the ASEAN+3 Research Group, which contributes to knowledge creation, a key factor in facilitating cooperation within these networks.[83] Without access to funding, cooperation would not have progressed to the extent it has in ASEAN+3.

Aside from providing funding, Japan and China shouldered much of the responsibility for negotiating the CMI's bilateral swaps during the project's first two years, which was crucial in sustaining the momentum of the project and in signalling the commitment of ASEAN+3 to the regional liquidity fund. The rudimentary surveillance mechanism that had been in place during the early years of the CMI did not mitigate the risks to which these countries exposed themselves as the CMI's principal creditors. Notwithstanding the requirement that 90 per cent of CMI funds could not be accessed without the recipient adopting an IMF programme, the willingness of Japan and China to accept the risks associated with their roles as creditors in the CMI highlights a key facet of their leadership and should not be disregarded. Of course, we should not discount the possibility that the competition between Japan and China for leadership in East Asia, particularly on the part of China, accounts for some of the notable commitments to the CMI made by these countries to date. This is one reason why Sino-Japanese rivalry has not derailed cooperation in the ASEAN+3 and EMEAP networks. It may also explain why we have yet to see dominating behaviour by Japan and China in these networks.

Some observers claim that China will be unwilling to continue to 'play second fiddle to Japan in any regional organisation in East Asia'.[84] In that case, how Japan responds to an assertive China could be key to the future of regional financial cooperation. A Philippine academic interviewed for this study observed that some members of the Japanese intelligentsia—notably a former Vice-Minister of Finance—supported the idea that China should take the lead in regional economic integration

[82] ASEAN+3 (2002), 'Joint Ministerial Statement of the ASEAN+3 Finance Ministers Meeting, 10 May 2002, Shanghai, People's Republic of China (www.aseansec.org/7924.htm, accessed 1 June 2005).
[83] Interview with senior ADB official.   [84] Wang (2002: 14).

and financial cooperation in East Asia.[85] It is unclear, however, whether this reflects the views of Japanese officials more generally. Although Sino-Japanese rivalry may have indirectly worked to the benefit of East Asian financial cooperation thus far, it is not guaranteed that tensions between the two might not derail cooperation in the future given the volatile state of relations between the two countries. However, an encouraging event was the May 2005 decision reached by ASEAN+3 members to advance the CMI, which took place during a time when relations between Japan and China were at their lowest in three decades. As Japanese finance minister, Sadakazu Tanigaki, noted, 'whatever happens, we need to promote financial cooperation even if there are [political] issues'.[86]

Although strategic rivalry and adversarial relations have the potential to undermine the workings of networks, networks can nevertheless provide settings in which necessary and mutually beneficial tasks are undertaken. This is important to note in the cases of ASEAN+3 and EMEAP. The strategic rivalry and tensions that normally exist between China and Japan are muted within these networks, at least for the present. One reason is that the kind of functional cooperation that takes place in these two networks largely involves officials of central banks and finance ministries who have maintained good working relations over a period of time and share common goals with respect to regional financial cooperation.[87] The economic benefits of cooperation are clearly perceived by all parties, including China, which stands to reap considerable gains from the CMI and the bond market initiatives. These projects allow China to tap into capacity-building initiatives, while also learning from the experiences other states have had in reforming their banking and financial systems.[88]

While Japan, China, and now South Korea are central actors in the CMI primarily because of the enormous economic resources they possess, other smaller countries possess other competences derived from their operational expertise that allows them to lead capacity-building activities in the bond market initiative.[89] No East Asian country is sufficiently strong in all aspects of bond market development, which requires the presence of sound regulatory frameworks, credit rating and guaranteeing agencies, and systems for advanced payments and settlements, among other features. The fact that these capabilities are diffused across the East

---

[85] Author's interview in Manila, 14 September 2005.
[86] *Straits Times* (2005), 'Three Asian giants join forces to fight currency attacks', 5 May.
[87] Author's interview with a senior ADB official in Singapore, 11 November 2005.
[88] Amyx (2005: 7).   [89] Amyx (2004: 15–17).

Asian countries (as well as in Australia and New Zealand in the case of EMEAP) has allowed the smaller members of ASEAN+3 and EMEAP to take the lead in areas in which they have expertise and operational experience. The opportunities for other members of the network to exercise leadership enhances the non-hierarchical nature of these networks, helps build levels of 'comfort' within them and offers a wider range of practical experiences to learn from.[90]

Aside from convergent interests and the exercise of financial leadership, the manner in which regional financial cooperation has unfolded from the time that the CMI, the ABMI, and the ABF were initiated reflects other dynamics at work. These are centred on the production and sharing of information and knowledge as well as the adoption of deliberative forms of interaction within these networks. In particular, the exchange of best economic and financial practices among network members and the development of analytical tools have helped overcome the barriers to regional financial cooperation stemming from informational and analytical gaps.

3.4.2. The Production and Exchange of Information and Knowledge

The pooling of information through the dialogue processes associated with the ASEAN+3 finance network and EMEAP has been important in underpinning some of the advances made on regional financial cooperation. To be sure, some of the progress seen to date is the result of growing macroeconomic interdependence and market-led financial integration in East Asia,[91] which has increased the incentives for governments to engage in regional financial cooperation. However, the role of deliberate knowledge sharing has also been instrumental as countries with very diverse economies have been able to learn from the experiences of other countries. While market interdependence creates incentives for cooperation, it does not necessarily provide clues as to *how* to cooperate. Officials, including a former Indonesian minister of finance interviewed for this study, have emphasized that sharing experiences with other countries in

[90] Interview with Philippine central bank officials, September 2005.
[91] Evidence for convergence is found in Kawai, Masahiro and Motonishi, Taizo (2005), 'Macroeconomic Interdependence in East Asia: Empirical Evidence and Issues', in ADB (ed.), *Asian Cooperation and Integration: Progress, Prospects, Challenges* (Manila: Asian Development Bank), pp. 213–68. This trend has been confirmed by recent ADB studies. See Rana, Pradumna (2005), 'Economic Integration in East Asia: Trends, Prospects and a Possible Roadmap', paper prepared for the *Third High-Level Conference on 'Building a New Asia: Towards an Asian Economic Community'*, Taiyuan, China, 15–16 September 2005.

governing financial markets is one of the most important functions of these networks, which allows members to know how others deal with similar situations.[92]

One instance in which a knowledge gap hampered progress was when EMEAP decided to launch ABF-2, the regional bond fund that was to invest in domestic currency-denominated bonds issued by East Asian states. This required the central bankers to come up with a range of standards for bonds to be issued in different local currencies. It was during this exercise that the barriers to cooperation posed by diversities in banking and financial systems, monetary policy regimes, and capital market development across East Asia became evident. By getting involved in designing, executing, and promoting the ABF-2, central bankers gained valuable knowledge about these market impediments which also enabled EMEAP to devise practical solutions to address these problems.[93] To accomplish these tasks, central bankers networked with experts from the BIS and the ADB as well as the private sector, including financial advisers and fund managers.[94] The difficulties posed by heterogeneous economies across East Asia also prompted research and studies on how to promote regional bond market development while maintaining market diversity. These studies, in turn, helped to get the ABF-2 off the ground.[95]

Monetary experts like Barry Eichengreen have argued that to deepen bond markets in East Asia requires addressing the inadequate supply of investment grade corporate securities and the limited demand for speculative grade issues.[96] He suggests that the region will need to 'upgrade accounting standards, corporate governance and local rating agencies to enhance the supply of higher-grade corporate securities and reforming tax and regulatory policies to broaden the demand for corporate issues'.[97] This is where the importance of the working groups set up under the ABMI becomes clear. These groups have developed shared expertise and have worked to provide technical advice to network members that can aid national authorities in establishing the infrastructure needed for efficient

[92] This point was confirmed by interviews with officials from Singapore and the Philippines, with Dr. Boediono, former Indonesian finance minister, as well as with officials from the ASEAN Secretariat and the ADB.

[93] EMEAP (2006: 5).

[94] Interviews with ADB and Philippine central bank officials. Also see EMEAP (2006: 32).

[95] Ibid.

[96] Eichengreen, Barry (2004), *Financial Development in Asia: The Way Forward* (Singapore: Institute of Southeast Asian Studies), pp. 26–7.

[97] Eichengreen (2004: 27).

bond markets.[98] As already noted, these regional efforts have already catalysed national-level reforms in some countries.

The development of trusted analytical tools has been essential to the workings of Asia's networks, especially in advancing ASEAN+3 surveillance and information-sharing. In this the Asian Development Bank (ADB) has been crucial. The region's finance ministers were reportedly concerned by the subjectivity involved in determining countries' economic and financial vulnerabilities through existing methods, and wanted more objective tools for detecting and assessing risks.[99] At their behest, the ADB has developed a prototype regional early warning system (EWS) for detecting emerging macroeconomic, financial, and corporate sector vulnerabilities with a greater degree of accuracy and objectivity within a 12–24 month period.[100] Although officials recognize that the EWS is not foolproof (in fact, the IMF does not employ EWS models in its surveillance exercises for precisely this reason[101]), officials from the region who were interviewed for this study believe that such models add to the arsenal of analytical tools available to support regional surveillance and national-level planning, especially when combined with other approaches which can monitor country risks and vulnerabilities.[102]

In addition to developing the EWS, the ADB has contributed to producing common data templates that ASEAN+3 members must use when submitting information for regional surveillance.[103] The ADB has also been responsible for developing the prototype model for the collective activation of bilateral swaps in the CMI, and for preliminary work on common currency arrangements.[104] The ADB has also been working on an East Asian currency index made up of ASEAN+3 currencies, which provides information on how these currencies as a group are moving against other currencies as well as showing how individual ASEAN+3 currencies are moving in relation to the ASEAN+3 grouping as a whole.

[98] Author's interviews with officials conducted in Manila, Indonesia, and Singapore, September–October 2005. Also see EMEAP (2006).

[99] Author's interview with senior officials from the ASEAN Secretariat.

[100] Interview with ADB senior official, 13 September 2005.

[101] Crow, John, Arriazu, Ricardo, and Thygesen, Niels (1999), *External Evaluation of IMF Surveillance* (Washington DC: International Monetary Fund). Available at www.imf.org/external/pubc/ft/extev/surv/index.htm.

[102] Author's interviews.

[103] Although there are still problems with the quality of information obtained from Cambodia, Laos, Myanmar, and Vietnam, all other members of ASEAN+3 now provide information based on a common data template, which facilitates comparison and further analysis. Interview with officials from the ADB and the ASEAN Secretariat.

[104] Interview with ADB official, 13 September 2005.

Despite some obstacles, there are plans for the index to be traded in the form of a currency unit or for regional bonds to be denominated in the currency unit.[105]

Overall Asia's networks have generated important policy knowledge for their members helping to build 'intellectual capital across the region'. The ASEAN+3 Research Group, funded by Japan, China, and the ADB, comprises a network of 30 think tanks from the region which support the ASEAN+3 surveillance process by providing technical assistance and research in areas including capital flow liberalization and institutional arrangements; capital market development; and prospects for regional policy coordination.[106] An important component of the research is its practical and policy content which identifies institutional arrangements and benchmark regulatory and supervisory practices that will enhance the management of capital flows in East Asia and the region's capacity to address whatever adverse consequences such flows might generate.[107] ASEAN+3 finance ministers have acknowledged the usefulness of the Group's studies to regional financial cooperation, while its research activities have also been important to EMEAP and its projects, especially in relation to developing regional bond funds.[108]

3.4.3. *Deliberative Forms of Interaction and the Search for Consensus*

To accommodate the diversity of member countries, discussions in ASEAN+3 and EMEAP networks and their associated working groups operate on the basis of deliberation/dialogue and the search for consensus. Although all discussions are reportedly very frank and open, no initiative or decision is taken unless each member is in agreement with whatever has been proposed. There may be implicit pressure on members holding back to cooperate, but no power is exerted, nor is there any attempt to coerce or cajole.[109] There is, however, open discussion of the problems or constraints that prevent a given member from supporting a project. Attempts are then made to find solutions to the problem,

---

[105] *New Straits Times* (2005), 'ADB to compile Asian currency index in 2006', 20 December.

[106] Rana (2005: 4). A list of past projects can be found on the website of the Ministry of Finance, Japan, www.mof.go.jp/english/if/regional_financial_cooperation.htm, accessed 3 October 2005.

[107] See the call for papers by the ASEAN+3 Research Group (www.aseansec.org/job25.htm, accessed 11 August 2005).

[108] Author's interview with officials from the Philippine and Singapore central banks, and with officials from the ASEAN Secretariat and the ADB.

[109] Ibid.

including through commissioning further study and consultation with outside experts as well as through learning from the experiences of other countries.[110] There is also no attempt by any one party or group of members to dominate the ASEAN+3 finance network or the EMEAP bankers' network, including the associated working groups. Negotiation and bargaining between members has not been a dominant feature of these networks.

Some governments do, however, take the lead on issues for which they possess the relevant technical and other capabilities, as noted above in the section on ASEAN+3. In EMEAP, for instance, all three working groups have rotating chairs who take the lead in tabling new initiatives for discussion. Often, it is officials from the more developed countries who assume the position of chair. Developing-country members do not see this as problematic; in fact, they have welcomed officials from countries with more developed banking and financial systems taking the lead and guiding working groups.[111] Again, this reflects the members' interest in learning from the practical experience of other countries on the policy and operational aspects of governing domestic banking and financial systems.

3.4.4. Lessons Learned

ASEAN+3 and EMEAP have been successful in each of the functions often attributed to networks: knowledge production, knowledge/information exchange, agenda expansion, consensus building, norm diffusion, and policy coordination (see Table 3.3 for a summary). They have generated and exchanged operational or practical knowledge on running effective banking and financial systems and on about how best to respond to environmental challenges associated with globalized financial markets. They have facilitated the production and sharing of comparable data and information on economic and financial indicators. They have developed analytical tools for regional surveillance, templates for bilateral swap agreements and models for the collective activation of bilateral swaps. Through these processes, network members have managed to overcome the technical and analytical barriers to advancing projects like the CMI, the ABMI, and the two regional bond funds. The role of the ADB has been particularly significant in this regard, as has the large regional epistemic community of economists and monetary economists from outside the

---

[110] Ibid.   [111] Ibid.

network. Private sector actors have also been consulted in these learning and knowledge exchange activities, thereby expanding the pool of knowledge on banking and financial sector governance.[112] Officials interviewed for this study found the sharing of knowledge and experiences among network members to be one of the most attractive features of these forms of cooperation.

The networks have also expanded the agenda of members, helping to enlarge the agenda for cooperation within the region in unexpected and significant ways. Regional financial cooperation is now a major area of activity with projects such as the CMI, the ABMI, and the two regional bond funds. These networks have not been successful, however, in placing the issues of currency regimes and currency coordination on the regional agenda, although there is now emerging discussion of these topics in both ASEAN+3 and EMEAP.

Both of these networks may provide channels for the diffusion of norms which help to establish and entrench sound economic, financial, and banking systems. However, so far the norms have been of a general rather than a specific and applied nature. Policy coordination has likewise been limited, although network members now coordinate their actions in a range of areas. A common template for the CMI's bilateral swap agreements is in place, which includes a clause that links disbursement of emergency swap funds to participation in ASEAN+3 surveillance.[113] ASEAN+3 surveillance also requires all members to submit comparable data based on a common data template. In addition, a template for the coordinated activation of bilateral swaps has been developed.

Part of the success of these networks lies with their consensus-based approach to decision-making. Consensus has been reached on contentious items such as the need to strengthen regional surveillance and the importance of all members participating in surveillance as well as sharing information on sensitive data such as capital movements. Governments were reportedly averse to making these commitments when regional financial cooperation first began.[114] However, the search for consensus does have its limitations. A case in point is the ASEAN+3 surveillance mechanism; finance officials and central bankers continue to debate the merits of third-party monitoring. According to one central

---

[112] EMEAP (2006: 32).

[113] Details of swap agreements are found on the website of the Bank of Japan (www.boj.or.jp/en/).

[114] Author's interview at the ADB.

bank official, this has 'derailed constructive discussions of an appropriate surveillance mechanism'.[115] There is clearly a trade-off between efficiency on the one hand and the need to include the views and priorities of all parties in these networks on the other. In this context, EMEAP fares better than the ASEAN+3 finance network, as its members share an inter-subjective framework based on their common roles and goals in running effective central banks. It is unlikely, however, that cooperation in ASEAN+3 and EMEAP would have advanced to the degree that we see today without the commitment to dialogue and consensus by network members, including by members who made substantial financial contributions to these networks. The fate of the MFG provides a persuasive counterfactual.

The Asian financial crisis of 1997–98 provided the primary impetus for East Asian financial cooperation. It prompted East Asian states to search for ways to prevent or minimize the occurrence of similar episodes in the future. These states opted to collaborate through two regional networks, ASEAN+3 and EMEAP. Crucial to these efforts has been the fact that network members shared similar understandings of the problem at hand. Their common interpretation of the cause of the financial crisis as a problem arising largely, though not solely, from poorly regulated global financial markets was also crucial in defining the partners required for cooperations and the types of policy responses to adopt. It is for this reason that ASEAN+3 and EMEAP emerged as key players in regional financial cooperation, while the Manila Framework Group failed. The latter had seemed, at its establishment, a likely site for East Asian countries to collaborate with other parties, notably the USA and the IMF, in responding to the financial crisis and in returning the region to financial stability. However, different understandings of the causes of the crisis held by MFG members—the USA and the IMF on the one hand and the East Asian states on the other—meant that the MFG could not work effectively. The interests and priorities of the two 'outsiders', the USA and the IMF, dominated the MFG agenda, and therefore the MFG emphasized domestic factors as the sole cause of the financial crisis, dismissing East Asian views and preferences for regional solutions that also acknowledged systemic causes of the crisis.

Because of shared understandings and interests within the ASEAN+3 finance network and EMEAP, network members could quickly begin devising ways to solve the problems they faced. Governments recognized the

---

[115] Cheong (2002: 12).

logic of developing regional capabilities in crisis management as well as the need to reform the financial and banking systems as a way to build longer-term resilience to market disequilibria. To the extent that weak regulatory capacity among regional states has hampered effective collaboration in the past, then the capacity-building activities that are now an integral part of these two networks are key to facilitating future cooperation.

Appendix 3.1

List of Abbreviations for Chapter 3

ABF	Asian Bond Fund
ABF-1	First Asian Bond Fund
ABF-2	Second Asian Bond Fund
ABMI	Asian Bond Market Initiative
ADB	Asian Development Bank
AMF	Asian Monetary Fund
APEC	Asia Pacific Economic Cooperation
ASA	ASEAN Swap Arrangement
ASEAN	Association of Southeast Asian Nations
ASEAN+3	ASEAN Plus Three
ASEM	Asia–Europe Meeting
BIS	Bank for International Settlements
BSA	Bilateral Swap Arrangements
CMI	Chiang Mai Initiative
EMEAP	Executives' Meeting of East Asian and Pacific Central Banks
ERPD	Economic Review and Policy Dialogue
EWS	Early Warning System
FSF	Financial Stability Forum
IMF	International Monetary Fund
MFG	Manila Framework Group
PECC	Pacific Economic Cooperation Conference
SEACEN	Southeast Asian Central Banks' forum
SEANZA	Southeast Asia, Australia, and New Zealand forum

4

Voice for the Weak: ECOSOC Ad Hoc Advisory Groups on African Countries Emerging from Conflict

Jochen Prantl

4.1. Introduction

In 2002, the United Nations created networked groups to strengthen the coherence of the organization's relations with countries emerging from conflict. The 'ad hoc advisory groups' were created by the Economic and Social Council of the United Nations—the principal organ for coordinating the economic, social, and related work of the 14 UN specialized agencies, functional commissions, and five regional commissions.

This chapter gives an assessment of the role and performance of the ECOSOC ad hoc advisory groups for African countries emerging from conflict.[1] It examines the potential and limits of these groups in providing conflict countries and other stakeholders with a greater voice in the transition process from war to peace. In this context, 'voice' includes the attainment of status and the mobilization of international (financial) support, as well as influencing decision-making at the UN Headquarters and the international financial institutions. ECOSOC ad hoc advisory groups are set up at the request of any African country emerging from conflict and seek to facilitate the integration of relief, rehabilitation, reconstruction, and development into a comprehensive approach to peace and stability.[2]

---

[1] This chapter draws on the findings of a report submitted to the Office of ECOSOC Support and Coordination, Department of Economic and Social Affairs, United Nations, New York. See Jochen Prantl, *ECOSOC Ad Hoc Advisory Groups on African Countries Emerging from Conflict: The Silent Avant-Garde* (New York: United Nations, 2006).

[2] See ECOSOC Resolution 2002/1, 15 July 2002.

Unlike networks more strictly defined, the ad hoc advisory groups operate within the mandates adopted by the ECOSOC and do have a degree of legitimate organizational authority. Nevertheless, ECOSOC ad hoc advisory groups display network-like functions, as this chapter will further illustrate; they are 'quasi-networks'.

With the goal of assessing the role and performance of the ECOSOC ad hoc advisory groups, the chapter is organized in three parts. The first part explains the rationale of the ad hoc mechanisms, addressing the question of why the groups have emerged. The second part assesses in detail the practice of the ad hoc advisory groups, focusing on four aspects: first, the composition of the groups, their meeting structure, and institutional back-up; second, the functions the advisory groups accumulated over time; third, the linkages with other formal and informal institutions; and fourth, shortcomings in the implementation of the advisory groups' mandate, including an assessment of the major successes and failures of these ad hoc groupings. The final section concludes with a comparative analysis of the advantages and disadvantages of (quasi-)networks vis-à-vis formal institutions such as the recently established Peacebuilding Commission.[3]

4.2. The Emergence of Ad Hoc Groups

The United Nations system is characterized by a lack of institutionalized relationships between its development and security agencies. At the same time, both the United Nations and the international financial institutions (IFIs) are state-centric organizations that do not have the institutional means to address civil conflict, which is transnational in character. Conflict settings frequently involve sub-national actors (rebel movements, civil society groups, criminal organizations, etc.). Prior to the establishment of the Peacebuilding Commission on 22 December 2005 there was no formal mechanism for sustained focus on the implementation of commitments by parties to the peace settlement. Nor was there any mechanism to keep track of the actual delivery of resources promised by international donors in support of negotiated agreements. Preventing a

---

[3] Answers to the question of how the outcomes achieved by the network differ from the outcomes achieved within formal organizations in the same area must therefore remain somewhat tentative, as any conclusions about the actual performance of the new Peacebuilding Commission are bound to be premature at this stage. Nevertheless, the design of the Commission will likely come under scrutiny.

reversion to conflict requires the means to follow post-conflict developments closely and systematically.[4] Yet the Security Council has only a very weak capacity to interact with other major stakeholders in the consolidation of peace (ECOSOC, the specialized agencies and the Bretton Woods institutions), or with regional and sub-regional organizations engaged in post-conflict processes.

The division of institutional responsibilities makes the development of a comprehensive approach in the consolidation of peace extremely difficult. While the Security Council is primarily in charge of maintaining international peace and security and ECOSOC is first and foremost concerned with development issues, it is the IFIs that have the greatest (financial) clout in multilateral development. The inter-relationship of peace and development agendas has led to renewed efforts to strengthen the capacity of the United Nations to develop a comprehensive approach in the consolidation of peace. Equally problematic has been achieving crosscutting policy goals in interconnected areas such as conflict management and peace-building. At the level of the UN Headquarters, in order to escape those structural deficiencies, four executive committees seek to reduce overlapping competences and improve coordination between departments, funds, and programmes (see Table 4.1). The committees cooperate and coordinate on an ad hoc and informal basis to avoid contradictions in the activities of the various agencies and programmes involved.[5] A key initiative in this regard was the establishment of the UNDG/ECHA Joint Working Group on Transition Issues, formed in November 2002.[6] The Working Group addresses crosscutting problems related to the transformation of conflicts in order to secure a continuum from relief to development and to avoid funding gaps.[7] This is of particular importance, as one can observe a consistent pattern that donors contribute more funds for emergency relief than for post-conflict

[4] The experience of the 1990s, which saw a reversion to armed conflict in Rwanda, Sierra Leone, Somalia, Sri Lanka, and twice in Angola, strongly suggests the need for greater attention to the implementation of negotiated peace agreements.

[5] See Jacques Fomerand, *Mirror, tool, or linchpin for change? The United Nations and Development* (ACUNS, International Relations Studies and the United Nations Occasional Papers, No. 2/2003), p. 32. For example, the Executive Committee on Humanitarian Affairs (ECHA) and the UN Development Group (UNDG) recently established a joint working group for Afghanistan to coordinate relief and recovery programmes in the country.

[6] This occurred in response to ECOSOC Resolution E/2002/32.

[7] See UN Doc. A/58/352, 5 September 2003, para 25. In 2003, the World Bank, in cooperation with DPKO, UNDP, UNICEF, and others, launched a US$ 500 million demobilization and reintegration programme for the Great Lakes region, with two national programmes in Rwanda and Angola, as well as specific projects in Angola and the DRC.

97

Table 4.1. Executive committees of the United Nations

Peace and security

DPA—Department of Political Affairs (Chair)
DDA—Department for Disarmament Affairs
DPKO—Department of Peacekeeping Operations
DPI—Department of Public Information
OCHA—Office for the Coordination of Humanitarian Affairs
OHCHR—Office of the High Commissioner for Human Rights
OLA—Office of Legal Affairs
OSRSG/CAC—Office of the Special Representative of the Secretary-General for
    Children & Armed Conflict
UNDP—United Nations Development Programme
UNHCR—United Nations High Commissioner for Refugees
UNICEF—United Nations Children's Fund
United Nations Security Coordinator
World Bank

Development Group

UNDP—United Nations Development Programme (Chair)
DESA—Department of Economic and Social Affairs
DPI—Department of Public Information
FAO—Food and Agriculture Organization
IFAD—International Fund for Agricultural Development
ILO—International Labour Organization
OHCHR—Office of the High Commissioner for Human Rights
OHRLLS—Office of the High Representative for the Least Developed Countries,
    Landlocked Developing Countries and Small Island Developing States
Office of the Under-Secretary-General/Special Advisor on Africa
OSRSG/CAC—Office of the Special Representative of the Secretary-General for
    Children & Armed Conflict

Regional Commissions

UNAIDS—Joint United Nations Programme on HIV/AIDS
UNCTAD—United Nations Conference on Trade and Development
UNDCP—United Nations Drug Control Programme
UNEP—United Nations Environment Programme

Economic and social

DESA—Department of Economic and Social Affairs (Chair)
DPI—Department of Public Information
INSTRAW—International Research and Training Institute for the
    Advancement of Women
ODCCP—Office of Drug Control and Crime Prevention
OHCHR—Office of the High Commissioner for Human Rights
OHRLLS—Office of the High Representative for the Least Developed
    Countries, Landlocked Developing Countries and Small Island Developing
    States

Regional Commissions

UNDP—United Nations Development Programme
UN-HABITAT—United Nations Human Settlements Programme
UNITAR—United Nations Institute for Training and Research
UNRISD—United Nations Research Institute for Social Development
UNU—United Nations University

Humanitarian Affairs

OCHA—Office for the Coordination of Humanitarian Affairs (Chair)
DPA—Department of Political Affairs
DPKO—Department of Peacekeeping Operations
DPI—Department of Public Information
FAO—Food and Agriculture Organization of the United Nations
OHCHR—Office of the High Commissioner for Human Rights
OSRSG/CAC—Office of the Special Representative of the Secretary-General
    for Children & Armed Conflict
UNCTAD—United Nations Conference on Trade and Development
UNDP—United Nations Development Programme
UNEP—United Nations Environment Programme
UNHCR—United Nations High Commissioner for Refugees
UNICEF—United Nations Children's Fund
UNRWA—United Nations Relief and Work Agency for Palestine Refugees in
    Near East
WFP—World Food Programme
WHO—World Health Organization

UNESCO—United Nations Educational, Scientific and Cultural Organization
UNFPA—United Nations Population Fund
UN-HABITAT—United Nations Human Settlements Programme
UNICEF—United Nations Children's Fund
UNIDO—United Nations Industrial Organization
UNIFEM—United Nations Fund for Women
UNOPS—United Nations Office for Project Services
WFP—World Food Programme
WHO—World Health Organization

Observers
OCHA—Office for the Coordination of Humanitarian Affairs, Spokesman for the UN Secretary-General (UNSG); Director of the Office of the Deputy UNSG; UNFIP—United Nations Fund for International Partnerships; World Bank.

recovery situations. Reducing the dependency on voluntary contributions for assistance is considered essential in this regard.[8]

The lack of coordination in the UN system has been just one of the challenges for countries emerging from conflict. A second has been the deep reluctance at the level of UN member states to become involved in conflicts on the African continent, particularly after the failures of UN engagement in Somalia and Rwanda. In order to overcome such reticence and to mobilize international support, the UN Secretary-General advocated the establishment of informal ad hoc arrangements—that is, groups of friends, core groups, and contact groups—as a means of catalysing regional and sub-regional peace-building efforts such as disarmament, demobilization of forces, and reintegration of former combatants.[9] Inside the Secretariat, the role of those ad hoc arrangements is considered to be primarily positive, as long as they complement UN activities. Furthermore, the formation of these groups helps to identify countries with a pre-existing level of commitment to becoming more closely engaged in a conflict. Coordinating and bundling activities vis-à-vis crisis settings and parties to conflict informal groups have also helped to coordinate activities and parties in the areas of peace-building efforts, reducing the risk of duplication, overlapping, or competing agendas.

Informal groupings have encountered considerable opposition from UN members. By contrast, the ad hoc advisory groups have an explicit mandate from ECOSOC, which specifies their rights and responsibilities and holds them accountable. This significantly enhances the degree of procedural legitimacy, while permitting them to benefit from a high degree of informality and a less bureaucratic structure.

The specific proposal for an ECOSOC ad hoc advisory group on countries emerging from conflict originated in discussions of the UN General

---

[8] See Background Note of UNDG/ECHA Joint Working Group on Transition Issues for Joint Meeting of the Executive Boards, January 2005 (on file with author).

[9] Recent examples of those informal arrangements include the contact groups on Sierra Leone (1998) and Liberia (2002) or the groups of friends of Guinea-Bissau (1999) and the Great Lakes region (2003). The Contact Group on Sierra Leone comprises Belgium, Canada, China, Egypt, France, Germany, Italy, Japan, the Netherlands, New Zealand, Nigeria, Norway, Sierra Leone, Sweden, the United Kingdom, the United States, the Commonwealth Secretariat, the Economic Community of West African States (ECOWAS), the European Commission, the United Nations, and the World Bank; the Contact Group on Liberia is composed of France, Morocco, Nigeria, Senegal, the United Kingdom, and the United States; ECOWAS (coordinator), African Union, European Union; and various UN representatives; the Friends of Guinea-Bissau include Brazil, Canada, France, Germany, Guinea, Italy, the Netherlands, Nigeria, Portugal, Senegal, Sweden, Togo, and the United States; the Friends of the Great Lakes is co-chaired by Canada and the Netherlands and comprises various representatives of the United Nations and of specialized agencies, the African Union, the European Union, the international financial institutions, and 28 other countries.

Assembly's Open-ended Ad Hoc Working Group on the Causes of Conflict and the Promotion of Durable Peace and Sustainable Development in Africa.[10] It built on ECOSOC's earlier establishment of a similar device designed to assist in identifying the needs and drafting a long-term programme of support for Haiti.[11] The case for applying the framework to Africa was strong. The Security Council's involvement in sub-Saharan Africa has significantly increased since 1998. As of September 2006, a total of 18 peace operations are currently directed and supported by the Department of Peacekeeping Operations, nine of which are on the African continent.[12] The UN Secretary-General has therefore stressed the 'need...for greater coordination of priorities, programmes and related financial and technical support for broad-based recovery and reconstruction and to prevent the re-emergence of conflicts'.[13]

The case of Burundi illustrates shortcomings the ad hoc groups were created to address. Table 4.2 points to the lack of joint planning as well as to weak linkages between the various donor reconstruction programmes.[14]

ECOSOC endorsed the idea of an ad hoc advisory group, and indeed of such groups in general, in April 2002 and proposed a mandate, which was formally adopted three months later.[15] The mandate of the ad hoc groups was

> to examine the humanitarian and economic needs of the country concerned: they would review relevant programmes of support and prepare recommendations for a long-term programme of support, based on its development priorities, through the integration of relief, rehabilitation, reconstruction and development into a comprehensive approach to peace and stability. The ad hoc groups would provide

---

[10] See UN Doc. A/55/45, para 48. This proposal was endorsed by GA resolution 55/217, 21 December 2000.

[11] The Ad Hoc Advisory Group on Haiti was established by ECOSOC Resolutions 1999/4 of 7 May 1999 and 1999/11 of 27 July 1999. It comprised five ambassadors of ECOSOC and representatives of the government of Haiti. However, the group had been active for merely three months, since some donors thought that the political situation in the country prevented a large-scale engagement. This changed, however, with the departure of Aristide in February 2004, which led to the reactivation of the Ad Hoc Group the same year; see ECOSOC Resolution 2004/322, 11 November 2004. Now it is composed of the Permanent Representatives to the United Nations of Benin, Brazil, Canada, Chile, Haiti, Spain, and Trinidad and Tobago. The President of ECOSOC and the Special Representative of the UN Secretary-General in Haiti are also invited to participate.

[12] See United Nations Peacekeeping Operations, Background Note, 30 September 2006, available at http://www.un.org/Depts/dpko/dpko/bnote.htm.

[13] UN Doc. E/2002/12, 2 April 2002, para 2.

[14] See International Crisis Group, *A Framework for Responsible Aid to Burundi* (ICG Africa Report No. 57, 21 February 2003).

[15] See UN-Docs E/2002/12, 2 April 2002 and E/2002/L.12, 15 July 2002.

Table 4.2. Institutional shortcomings in the transition from war to peace—the case of Burundi (as of February 2003)[16]

Donors
> ➢ Lack of strategy
> ➢ No effective coordination meetings
> ➢ No coordination unit and secretariat
> ➢ No unified approach toward government, UN, or NGOs
> ➢ Insufficient staff capacity

Governments
> ➢ Lack of a comprehensive transitional strategy
> ➢ No effective coordination meetings or mechanisms
> ➢ A weak inter-ministerial unit
> ➢ Insufficient information on the population's needs and the existing programmes being implemented
> ➢ Insufficient staff capacity
> ➢ Insufficient financial resources

The UN and NGOs
> ➢ No joint and comprehensive strategy: poor linkages between various strategies and plans
> ➢ No joint planning: sector-driven approach rather than focus on the transition process as a whole
> ➢ No linkages with the inter-ministerial unit
> ➢ Poor linkages with donor reconstruction programmes

advice on how to ensure that the assistance of the international community in supporting the country concerned is adequate, coherent, well-coordinated and effective and promotes synergy.[17]

Six features of the groups are worth highlighting.

First, ECOSOC ad hoc advisory groups may provide a 'voice for the weak' by offering an informal platform that can be used for the exchange of knowledge and for agenda-setting. Post-conflict countries that are below the radar of international attention and do not have a large network of development partners need an advocate.

Second, the ad hoc groups have a versatile structure, which is flexible and non-bureaucratic. It can be adapted as changing circumstances require.

Third, ad hoc groups facilitate sustained attention to a conflict and help to avoid (funding) gaps, which typically develop. They do not coordinate the policies of the various actors, the agencies of the United Nations system or the international financial institutions, but they act as a facilitator and convener.

---

[16] Information adapted from International Crisis Group, *A Framework for Responsible Aid to Burundi* (ICG Africa Report No. 57, 21 February 2003).
[17] ECOSOC Resolution E/2002/1, 15 July 2002, para 3.

Fourth, ECOSOC ad hoc advisory groups explicitly recognize the responsibility and the leadership role of the country emerging from conflict. Participation of government representatives in the ad hoc group facilitates an ongoing dialogue, which is important for devising a long-term strategy. The process of peace consolidation is owned by the national authorities, which is paramount for the successful implementation of any peace agreement.

Fifth, the ad hoc advisory groups help to secure a continuous flow of information between the field and Headquarters levels (especially the UN and IFIs). This is of key importance for an effective and comprehensive peace-building strategy. The current framework of formal institutions does not adequately supply such information.

Sixth, advisory groups are expected to work through and to make maximum use of existing structures, linking and bundling parallel activities of formal and informal mechanisms of the UN system, bilateral and multilateral donor groups, regional and sub-regional organizations as well as informal groupings such as groups of friends and contact groups.

4.3. The Workings of Ad Hoc Advisory Groups[18]

This section assesses the role and performance of ad hoc advisory groups in fulfilling their mandate. At the request of the respective governments of the countries concerned, ECOSOC has established two advisory groups on African countries emerging from conflict thus far, on Guinea-Bissau (2002) and on Burundi (2003).[19] In both cases, the further modalities for establishing the groups had been set out by the President of ECOSOC in consultation with member states. Table 4.3 shows the composition of the groups.

4.3.1. Meeting Structure and Institutional Backing

The Ad Hoc Advisory Group on Guinea-Bissau and on Burundi met at the ambassadorial level at the UN Headquarters, with the permanent representatives of Guinea-Bissau and Burundi participating in their respective meetings. Both advisory groups invited the Chair of the Security Council

[18] For a chronology of key activities of the ECOSOC ad hoc advisory groups for countries emerging from conflict, see Appendix 4.1.
[19] See ECOSOC Decision 2002/304, 25 October 2002, and ECOSOC Resolution 2003/16, 21 July 2003.

Table 4.3. Composition of the ad hoc advisory groups

Guinea-Bissau[20]	Burundi[21]
South Africa (Chairman)	South Africa (Chairman)
Brazil	Belgium
Guinea-Bissau	Burundi
The Netherlands	Ethiopia
Portugal	France
	Japan

Ad Hoc Working Group on Conflict Prevention and Resolution in Africa and the President of ECOSOC to participate in their work. In the case of Guinea-Bissau, the Chair of the Group of Friends (convened by the Secretary-General) also attended the meetings.

Both the Ad Hoc Advisory Groups on Guinea-Bissau and on Burundi held regular meetings, which decreased in frequency following the year of their establishment.[22] The frequency of gatherings had been contingent on the political situation on the ground. In addition to the meetings at the ambassadorial level, parallel to the General Assembly's annual general debate, there were high-level meetings with the Heads of State or Government of Guinea-Bissau and Burundi. The Advisory Group on Guinea-Bissau liaised closely with the UNDP Resident Coordinator, the UN country team, the Representative of the UN Secretary-General, the Assistant Secretary-General in the Department of Political Affairs, officials at the international financial institutions, permanent representatives of neighbouring countries and the Group of Friends of Guinea-Bissau and the Community of Portuguese-Speaking Countries (CPLP). After its establishment in 2003, the Ad Hoc Advisory Group on Burundi held a range of consultations with major UN and international interlocutors.

The institutional set-up and the meeting structure of the group helped to secure ownership of the process for the national authorities, principally through participation of the countries emerging from conflict in the workings of the group. This also allowed for a better and constant flow of information and exchange of knowledge between the field and Headquarters levels.

[20] The Chairman of the Group of Friends of Guinea-Bissau (The Gambia), the Chairman of the Ad Hoc Working Group of the Security Council on Conflict Prevention and Resolution in Africa (Angola), and the President of ECOSOC participate in the workings of the advisory group.

[21] The Chairman of the Ad Hoc Working Group of the Security Council on Conflict Prevention and Resolution in Africa (Angola) and the President of ECOSOC participate in the workings of the advisory group.

[22] See UN Doc. E/2006/64, 8 May 2006, para 9.

Although the advisory groups received substantial inter-agency support, they encountered serious difficulties in funding their activities, which limited their effectiveness.[23] While the UN's Department of Economic and Social Affairs (DESA) and the Department of Political Affairs (DPA) provided significant secretarial support and covered some of the operating costs, including travel to Guinea-Bissau and Burundi, securing appropriate resources occurred on an ad hoc basis and remained a constant challenge.

4.3.2. Working to Support Governments

The most important function of the ad hoc advisory groups has been their role as advocates for countries that are not at the forefront of foreign assistance, bringing the issues that had been previously neglected to the attention of policymakers. This is particularly relevant to 'forgotten conflicts' where international engagement tends to be low. In this specific sense, ad hoc groups provide a 'voice for the weak'.[24] Advisory groups may play a key role in 'mobilizing donor support while encouraging the national authorities to establish a conducive environment for increased assistance'.[25]

The Ad Hoc Advisory Group on Guinea-Bissau's original mandate was to prepare recommendations for a long-term programme of support. However, the needs assessment mission in November 2002 concluded instead that 'addressing the short-term needs of Guinea-Bissau would have an impact on the long-term development plans for that country'.[26]

The coexisting Group of Friends of Guinea-Bissau, established in 1999, had been thus far 'little more than a discussion group'.[27] Moreover, substantial differences between the chair of the Friends, Gambia, and the

---

[23] For example, the lack of resources limited the manoeuvring room available to engage with regional and sub-regional organizations.

[24] In August 2005, the Secretary-General concluded that the activities of these groupings 'have led to demand for the creation of similar mechanisms for other African countries emerging from conflict' (UN Doc. A/60/182, 1 August 2005, para 42). However, this perceived demand seemed short-lived, as member states rejected recent efforts by the UN Secretariat to establish an ad hoc advisory group on Somalia. Therefore there are currently no further plans to employ advisory groups in other conflict settings, as the recently established Peacebuilding Commission is expected to take over their functions. However, it is doubtful whether the institutional design and the rules of procedures of the Commission will allow for these tasks to be accomplished.

[25] UN Doc. E/2004/86, 25 June 2004, p. 1.

[26] UN Doc. E/2003/8, 10 January 2003, p. 1.

[27] Teresa Whitfield, 'Groups of Friends', in David Malone (ed.), *The UN Security Council: From the Cold War to the 21st Century* (Boulder: London, 2004), p. 314.

government of Guinea-Bissau rendered this grouping essentially ineffective, and therefore working through the ECOSOC ad hoc advisory group constituted a much more promising alternative, not least because the South African chair had more political leverage at his disposal than the representative from the much smaller Gambia.

The group advocated a partnership approach between the national authorities and the international community: while the government would actively promote policy goals such as the implementation of the rule of law and political stability, international donors would provide the funding for emergency support and technical assistance in a wide range of fields. This partnership approach was particularly visible in the establishment of the Economic Emergency Management Fund (EEMF), an idea that had been developed within and recommended by the ad hoc advisory group.[28]

Based on IMF estimates, the group called for contributions by the donor community in the range of US$ 12–15 million, which would be the minimum required to maintain the functioning of state services until the next inflow of funds.[29] The EEMF channelled financial contributions from the donor community and allocated funds to the most pressing issues such as the maintenance of social services and public administration in order 'to contain potentially volatile social tensions during the transition process'.[30] The potential for social unrest has been very high given that 60 per cent of the country's workforce is unemployed and 88 per cent of the population lives on less than US$ 1 per day. By definition, the EEMF did not seek to address long-term needs of the country but sought to provide transitional relief, contributing to the maintenance of stability during the transition process. Table 4.4 shows the financial contributions by UN member states to the EEMF. A similar mechanism was established to support the planning and implementation of security sector reform in the country.[31]

However, the mobilization of international support was only modestly successful in the context of the Presidential elections in June–July 2005, when the advisory group, in cooperation with the chair of the Group of Friends of Guinea-Bissau and the President of ECOSOC, urged UN

---

[28] See UN Doc. E/2003/8, para 44.
[29] The revenues were expected to come primarily from cashew nut exports and fishing licences; see UN Doc E/2003/8, para 44.
[30] UN Doc. E/2004/86, 25 June 2004, para 18.
[31] See UN Doc. S/RES/1580, 22 December 2004.

Table 4.4. EEMF financing (as of May 2005)

Donor	Amount received (in US$)
The Netherlands	2,137,767.22
Sweden	938,644.23
Portugal through the Community of Portuguese-Speaking Countries (CPLP)	1,801,585.08
France	1,270,398.77
Brazil through the CPLP	49,258.12
Italy	663,129.97
Total	6,860,783.39

Source: UN Doc. E/2005/70, 2 June 2005.

member states to provide funding for the electoral budget of €4.9 million in order to stabilize the situation on the ground. Table 4.5 illustrates the (lack of) contributions by international donors. By December 2005, the transition process in Guinea-Bissau and the return to constitutional order had been completed, with the focus of international assistance shifting to critical areas such as security sector reform.[32] Yet, the lack of progress in the overall socio-economic situation still remains a matter of concern and a source of instability.[33] Despite the establishment of the Peacebuilding Commission, ECOSOC, at its 2006 substantive session, decided to extend the mandate of the Ad Hoc Advisory Group on Guinea-Bissau until 2007 to continue monitoring closely the country's economic and social development.[34]

The situation in Burundi differed significantly from that in Guinea-Bissau, as state institutions had continued to function, even after a decade of conflict. The provision of emergency assistance did not constitute a primary concern. This should not, however, obscure the fact that the country had been in urgent need of international assistance: classified

[32] For the assessment of the Secretary-General's report on developments in Guinea-Bissau and on activities of the United Nations Peacebuilding Support Office see UN Doc S/2005/752, 2 December 2005. The report underlines the instrumental role of the advisory group in bringing the transition process to a successful conclusion.

[33] For example, by mid-April 2006, salaries in the public services had been paid only up to the end of January that year. See UN Doc. E/2008/8, 18 April 2006, para 9. As the report of the advisory group stresses, Guinea-Bissau is in a state of 'structural emergency'. Ibid., para 32.

[34] See ECOSOC Resolution 2006/11, 26 July 2006. The decision seems to reflect the understanding that the Ad Hoc Advisory Group is, for the time being, the best available instrument to monitor the situation on the ground. At the same time, it illustrates the challenge the new Peacebuilding Commission is confronted with: the extent to which the formalization of informal ad hoc processes produces better results.

Table 4.5. Financing of the presidential election in June/July 2005[a]

Donor	Amount received
European Commission	€1.3 million
The Netherlands	€200,000
Algeria (via ECOWAS)	US$ 500,000
Portugal	€350,000
China	US$ 100,000
Central Bank of West African States	€229,000
West African Development Bank	€229,000
West African Monetary Union	€762,000
UN Development Programme	US$ 400,000

[a]In addition, there have been in-kind contributions from Brazil (computer equipment and technical assistance) and Portugal (electoral material).

Source: UN Doc. E/2005/70, 2 June 2005.

as a least developed country, roughly 90 per cent of the population lives on less than US$ 2 per day and more than half on less than US$ 1 per day. Yet, the Ad Hoc Advisory Group on Burundi acted much more as an interlocutor and as an advocate vis-à-vis the donor community.

From 19 to 26 November 2003, the group assessed the situation on the ground and met with government authorities, representatives of UN agencies and programmes, members of the diplomatic community and other development partners. The advisory group participated in the Forum of Development Partners of Burundi held in Brussels in January 2004 where the chairman called for strong budgetary support in order to provide the Transitional Government with greater room to manoeuvre. In addition, the advisory group organized meetings with the Minister for External Relations and International Cooperation, inviting countries, including neighbouring states and major donors, with an interest in supporting Burundi.[35] The group discussed recovery plans prepared by the Burundian government that required support from international donors.[36]

The work of the group focused on four targets: (1) maintaining momentum in consolidating the peace process; (2) promoting stability; (3) engaging in poverty alleviation and sustainable development; and (4) reinforcing international partnerships. In July 2006, ECOSOC decided to terminate the mandate of the Ad Hoc Advisory Group on Burundi, taking into account the decision of the Peacebuilding Commission to

[35] Those meetings took place in Bujumbura in November 2005 and January 2006.

[36] Following those consultations, the group assisted Burundi in preparing for the donor conference held in Bujumbura in September 2006. See UN Doc. E/2006/64, 8 May 2006, para 11.

address the situation in the country.[37] The decision essentially followed a recommendation by the advisory group that had expressed concerns that '[w]hile the existence of an ad hoc body has been suitable to follow the transition process in Burundi, consideration of international cooperation would be better dealt with by a permanent body like the Peacebuilding Commission'.[38] Yet, the success of the Commission faces a key test as to whether it will be in a better position to support the consolidation of peace in Burundi following the deterioration of its political climate after the new government came to power in September 2005.[39] The need to monitor the situation on the ground very closely has become particularly urgent following the departure of UN troops on 31 December 2006.

In conclusion, the workings of both advisory groups underline the challenges in attempting to bridge the traditional division between 'security' or 'political' issues on the one hand and 'economic' and 'development' issues on the other.[40] The setting of the conflicts suggests there is a strong need for an overarching political framework under which development partners can engage in long-term projects to consolidate peace on the ground. Quasi-networks like the ad hoc advisory groups may help to establish such a framework by fulfilling the following functions: (1) they mobilize international support for countries emerging from conflict, (2) they foster international partnerships, and (3) they further the integration of relief, rehabilitation, reconstruction, and development.

4.3.3. *Formal and Informal Institutional Linkages*

Looking at the formal and informal linkages of the ad hoc advisory groups, three aspects should be highlighted. First, the groups helped to foster cooperation between ECOSOC and the Security Council. When the group was established, both Burundi and Guinea-Bissau were on the Security Council's agenda. The engagement of the two UN bodies in the discussion process helped to develop solutions which addressed the problem in a comprehensive way, examining both the socio-economic and politico-security dimensions of the conflicts. In addition, the composition of the groups facilitated collaboration, as the Chairman of the

---

[37] See ECOSOC Resolution 2006/12, 26 July 2006. At its inaugural meeting on 23 June 2006, the Peacebuilding Commission decided to select Sierra Leone and Burundi as the first two countries receiving help from the new advisory body.

[38] UN Doc. E/2006/53, 20 April 2006, para 28.

[39] See International Crisis Group, *Burundi: Democracy and Peace at Risk* (Africa Report No. 120, 30 November 2006).

[40] UN Doc. E/2004/86, 25 June 2004, para 25.

Ad Hoc Working Group of the Security Council on Conflict Prevention and Resolution in Africa and the President of ECOSOC participated in the meetings. In 2003 and 2004, ECOSOC and the Security Council undertook joint missions to Guinea-Bissau to assess the situation on the ground. Interaction between the two principal organs was further strengthened by Brazil's membership on the Security Council in 2004–05, which served as an important bridge and helped to make the case of Guinea-Bissau heard in the Council's chambers.

A second linkage the AHAGs were able to forge was among agencies within the UN system, such as DESA and DPA, the Office of the Special Adviser on Africa, UNDP (both at Headquarters and field levels) and the UN political offices on the ground (the UN Peace-building Support Office in Guinea-Bissau (UNOGBIS) and the UN operation in Burundi (ONUB)). In the case of Burundi, the group also liaised with the Office for the Coordination of Humanitarian Affairs (OCHA). The advisory groups held regular and wide-ranging consultations with other stakeholders such as officials at the IMF and the World Bank, and specialized agencies of the UN system such as the Food and Agriculture Organization (FAO), the World Food Programme (WFP), and the International Fund for Agricultural Development (IFAD).

Finally, the AHAGs succeeded in fostering closer collaboration between the UN system and the international financial institutions vis-à-vis the two post-conflict countries. This has been a significant achievement. In the case of Guinea-Bissau, the IMF established a monitoring and reporting system for the UNDP-managed Emergency Economic Management Fund. The advisory group also helped the national authorities to achieve a more flexible application of the IMF's conditionality criteria.[41] In Burundi, the advisory group closely monitored the post-conflict emergency assistance, encouraged the national authorities to draft a poverty reduction strategy paper, while simultaneously urging donors to contribute to the World Bank's multi-year debt trust fund.[42]

Figure 4.1 provides a simplified model of the multiple formal and informal institutional linkages of the advisory groups at Headquarters level. It illustrates the rather horizontal architecture and decentralized

---

[41] For example, on 28 January 2003, the group organized a meeting with government officials of Guinea-Bissau (i.e. the Ministers of Foreign Affairs as well as Economy and Finance), donors, and the Bretton Woods institutions focused on establishing a partnership approach between the government and the donor community; see UN Doc. E/2005/70, 2 June 2005, para 9.

[42] Both the IMF and the World Bank have considered the collaboration with the ad hoc advisory groups rather positive; see UN Doc. E/2004/86, 25 June 2004, paras 31–34.

nature of the UN system that requires coordination by persuasion rather than authoritative control.[43] While the ad hoc advisory groups engaged with a wide range of divisions within the UN's security and development agencies in order to close institutional gaps, the figure also highlights very clearly how those activities are embedded among other organizations, departments, agencies, and programmes inside and outside the UN system. Strikingly, there are parallel structures, which connect the various units operating in the peace and development fields.[44] Networks can therefore only be successful in the security and development realms if they are able to avoid competing with and complement existing efforts.

4.3.4. Shortcomings in the Implementation of Mandates

The lack of financial resources limited the operational capabilities of the advisory groups and restrained their manoeuvring room. There were also other shortcomings in the implementation of their mandates that went beyond the question of resources.

Although the ad hoc advisory groups actively promoted the integration of relief, rehabilitation, reconstruction, and development efforts through the establishment of various formal and informal linkages, their contribution in this field could have been enhanced by addressing more specific, practical issues related to the transition from humanitarian assistance to development support. Those issues include, *inter alia*, the demobilization, disarmament, rehabilitation, and reintegration (DDRR) of armed forces. At the Headquarters level, there is the potential for enhanced interaction with existing mechanisms such as the UNDG/ECHA Working Group on Transition Issues in order to improve coordination.

At the regional level, many intra-state conflicts on the African continent carry the risk of spilling over from one country to another, and thus regional dimensions must be taken into account when addressing conflicts at the country level. Without consideration of the regional driving forces, conflict management is bound to remain piecemeal. It is here that networks such as groups of friends and quasi-networks such as advisory groups should engage in closer cooperation and task-sharing.[45]

---

[43] See Inis Claude, *Swords into Plowshares: The Problems and Progress of International Organizations*, 4th edn. (New York: McGraw-Hill, 1984), p. 68.

[44] These are represented by the dotted lines in the diagram.

[45] However, this requires a broader comparative assessment of the added value of groups of friends and contact groups in the building of peace.

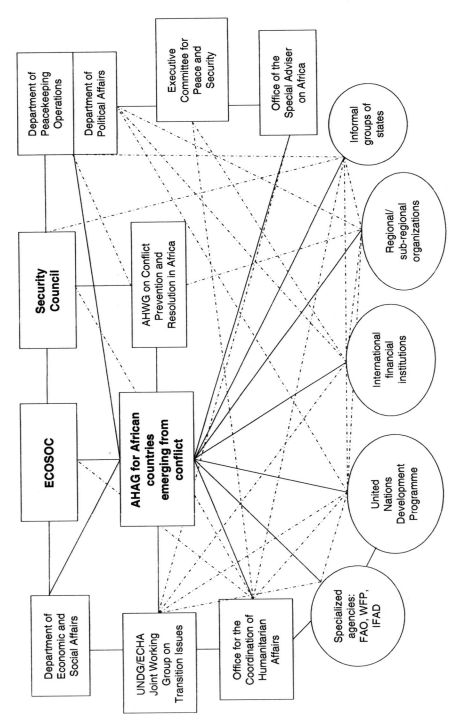

Figure 4.1. Simplified model of formal and informal institutional linkages at headquarters level

In addition, although the advisory groups on Burundi and Guinea-Bissau each saw a clear need to collaborate closely with regional and sub-regional institutions such as the African Union, the African Development Bank, the Central Bank of West African States, and ECOWAS, those exchanges did not occur systematically 'owing to time and travel limitations'.[46]

In mobilizing donors, the impact of the AHAGs was modest. While in principle the EEMF is an innovative and efficient mechanism to meet the emergency needs of the government of Guinea-Bissau, the instrument has never been fully funded. In 2004, the EEMF received only a quarter of the funds that would have been required to cover key administrative functions of the government.[47] Also, financial contributions by international donors to fund the 2005 Presidential elections have been extremely modest.

In fact, in both Guinea-Bissau and Burundi, the discrepancies between donor pledges and actual disbursements were a constant matter of concern and point to a commitment gap on the donor side. While some of the reluctance can be explained by low absorption capacities of post-conflict countries and the high level of uncertainty vis-à-vis the transition from war to peace, the issue of 'good donorship' needs to be addressed. Although the leverage of the advisory groups to change this pattern is quite modest, nevertheless, the naming (and shaming) of 'bad donors' may help.

4.4. Conclusions

Although the ad hoc advisory groups differ significantly from the characteristics of networks as defined by Podolny and Page, the workings of these semi-formal ad hoc arrangements display various network-like features, as this assessment has illustrated. The institutional framework of the groups allows for improved partnerships and better cooperation between the countries emerging from conflict and key players, but without the criteria of hard conditionality. The non-bureaucratic structure and ad hoc nature of the arrangements ensure a high degree of flexibility. The returns of quasi-networks are particularly high for those countries whose situation has remained below the radar of international attention. Both Guinea-Bissau and Burundi had nothing to lose by working through the ad hoc

---

[46] UN Doc. E/2004/86, 25 June 2004, para 39.
[47] See UN Doc. E/2005/70, 2 June 2005, para 30.

advisory groups. They gained a voice in and ownership of the process of steering the countries' transition from war to peace.

Alongside the creation of informal groups, the Secretary-General of the UN has urged member states 'to take a hard look at the existing "architecture" of international institutions and to ask themselves whether it is adequate for the tasks we have before us'.[48] This statement reflects the belief that managerial and network-based changes cannot operate to their greatest potential if they are not matched with adequate formal mechanisms of coordination at the intergovernmental level. Upgrading the role of ECOSOC has been of particular concern, first as a strategic forum to coordinate activities of the UN system with those of the IFIs and the WTO, and second to close the operational gaps in the transformation of conflicts. The enhanced cooperation of ECOSOC and the UN Security Council is considered very important in the implementation of multi-dimensional and long-term approaches to conflict prevention.[49] In addition, closer coordination between the two bodies would facilitate greater attention to and generate a larger focus on the needs of countries emerging from conflict by mobilizing high-level political support. Those considerations informed the recent decision by UN member states to establish a Peacebuilding Commission.[50]

The main purpose of the Peacebuilding Commission is to fill an institutional gap in the United Nations system by establishing 'a dedicated institutional mechanism to address the special need of countries emerging from conflict towards recovery, reintegration and reconstruction and to assist them in laying the foundation for sustainable development' (see Table 4.6).[51] The Commission is a conscious effort to build on some of the successes of the ad hoc advisory groups. As the UN Secretary-General's explanatory note of April 2005 illustrates:

[48] See the UN Secretary-General's report on the implementation of the UN Millennium Declaration, UN Doc. A/58/323, 2 September 2003, para 91.

[49] The Security Council has stressed the importance of greater interaction with ECOSOC in order to enhance the transformation of conflicts. It also emphasized that economic rehabilitation and reconstruction constitute important elements in the long-term development of post-conflict countries and the consolidation of peace; see UN Doc. S/PRST/2002/2, 31 January 2002.

[50] On the Secretary-General's proposal to establish a Peacebuilding Commission, see *In Larger Freedom: Towards Development, Security and Human Rights for All*, UN Doc. A/59/2005, 21 March 2005, paras 114–119. On the decision by the 2005 World Summit to establish the Commission, see UN Doc. A/60/L.1, 20 September 2005, paras 97–105.

[51] UN Doc. A/60/L.1, 20 September 2005, para 97, for an overview of the provisions of the Peacebuilding Commission, as adopted by the 2005 World Summit.

Table 4.6. 2005 world summit outcome—the Peacebuilding Commission[a]

Peace-building

98. The main purpose of the Peacebuilding Commission is to bring together all relevant actors to marshal resources and to advise on and propose integrated strategies for post-conflict peace-building and recovery. The Commission should focus attention on the reconstruction and institution-building efforts necessary for recovery from conflict and support the development of integrated strategies in order to lay the foundation for sustainable development. In addition, it should provide recommendations and information to improve the coordination of all relevant actors within and outside the United Nations, develop best practices, help to ensure predictable financing for early recovery activities and extend the period of attention by the international community to post-conflict recovery. The Commission should act in all matters on the basis of consensus of its members.

100. The Peacebuilding Commission should meet in various configurations. Country-specific meetings of the Commission, upon invitation of the Organizational Committee referred to in paragraph 101 below, should include as members, in addition to members of the Organizational Committee, representatives from
(a) The country under consideration;
(b) Countries in the region engaged in the post-conflict process and other countries that are involved in relief efforts and/or political dialogue, as well as relevant regional and subregional organizations;
(c) The major financial, troop, and civilian police contributors involved in the recovery effort;
(d) The senior United Nations representative in the field and other relevant United Nations representatives;
(e) Such regional and international financial institutions as may be relevant.

101. The Peacebuilding Commission should have a standing Organizational Committee, responsible for developing its procedures and organizational matters, comprising
(a) Members of the Security Council, including permanent members;
(b) Members of the Economic and Social Council, elected from regional groups, giving due consideration to those countries that have experienced post-conflict recovery;
(c) Top providers of assessed contributions to the United Nations budgets and voluntary contributions to the United Nations funds, programmes, and agencies, including the standing Peacebuilding Fund, that are not among those selected in (a) or (b) above.
(d) Top providers of military personnel and civilian police to United Nations missions that are not among those selected in (a), (b), or (c) above.

102. Representatives from the World Bank, the International Monetary Fund, and other institutional donors should be invited to participate in all meetings of the Peacebuilding Commission in a manner suitable to their governing arrangements, in addition to a representative of the Secretary-General.

103. We request the Secretary-General to establish a multi-year standing Peacebuilding Fund for post-conflict peace-building, funded by voluntary contributions and taking due account of existing instruments. The objectives of the Peacebuilding Fund will include ensuring the immediate release of resources needed to launch peace-building activities and the availability of appropriate financing for recovery.

104. We also request the Secretary-General to establish, within the Secretariat and from within existing resources, a small peace-building support office staffed by qualified experts to assist and support the Peacebuilding Commission. The office should draw on the best expertise available.

105. The Peacebuilding Commission should begin its work no later than 31 December 2005.

[a]UN Doc. A/60/L.1, 20 September 2005, paras 97–105.

The ad hoc post-conflict groups under the Economic and Social Council, formed over the past few years, constituted helpful efforts to perform this function of providing sustained attention. It is important that we learn from these, which could inform the workings of the Peacebuilding Commission and ECOSOC. I do believe however that a standing body that draws at different stages on the authority of the Security Council and ECOSOC will be able to provide a more powerful and consistent system of support.[52]

It becomes clear from this statement that the ad hoc advisory groups have taken on the role of agents or catalysts of formal change.[53] However, it poses for us the question of whether the formalization of informal, ad hoc processes is likely to produce better policy outcomes? Seasoned UN scholars like Jacques Fomerand have argued that the complexity of the UN system strictly limits its capacity for major reform:

[I]t should be recognized that change in complex organizational settings like the United Nations is bound to remain incremental, as would be the case in any similar, organizationally complex setting. This process, in which incremental innovations trigger (in fact compel) further incremental changes, offers perhaps a more encouraging view of the capacity of the United Nations to reform itself.[54]

While the establishment of the Peacebuilding Commission is clearly an important step towards filling an institutional gap in addressing the needs of countries emerging from conflict, it also highlights the uses of networks of quasi-networks.[55] First, the Peacebuilding Commission is primarily an intergovernmental advisory body, with all the disadvantages of this sort of agency, rather than a proactive monitoring instrument that can comprehensively assist in the transition from war to peace. Second, the quantity and quality of members of the Commission is determined by the needs of a wide range of stakeholders with potentially competing agendas and divergent interests. The fact that the Peacebuilding Commission acts on the basis of consensus gives each member an effective veto. AHAGs have a smaller composition and more flexible and less cumbersome procedures. Another comparative advantage of the ad hoc advisory mechanisms is the

---

[52] Explanatory Note of the Secretary-General: Peacebuilding Commission, 17 April 2005 (on file with author).

[53] It might be worthwhile to consider whether one can apply this lesson to other organizational settings such as the international financial institutions.

[54] Fomerand, *Mirror, Tool, or Linchpin for Change*, p. 30.

[55] The operational procedures are in the process of being established. The 2005 World Summit decided that the Peacebuilding Commission should begin its work no later than 31 December 2005. See UN Doc. A/60/L.1, 20 September 2005, para 105. For the relevant provisions, see Table 4.1.

clear identification of the chair as the group's leader. It is rather uncertain whether the standing Organizational Committee of the Peacebuilding Commission will be able to work effectively without a clearly defined hierarchy. Finally, simply adding minor institutional fixes such as the Peacebuilding Commission cannot fix the problems fundamental to the structural design of the UN system:

> Functionally speaking, the United Nations was set up as a kind of loose confederation of international agencies... This principle of decentralization modified by persuasive coordination, but not authoritative control from the center, was neither precisely defined nor exclusively applied in the Charter.[56]

The design of the Commission does not fundamentally alter this diffusion of responsibilities and authorities. An intelligent and careful use of (quasi-)networks like groups of friends or advisory groups will remain important for identifying and consolidating countries to become engaged in peace-building activities. AHAGs will also remain important for the development of more effective channels for regular interaction, strategic coordination among agencies and governments, and, most crucially, the exercise of advocacy and leadership.

Appendix 4.1: Chronology of Advisory Groups on Guinea-Bissau and Burundi[57]

Guinea-Bissau, 2002–06

2002

On 25 October 2002, ECOSOC established the Ad Hoc Advisory Group on Guinea-Bissau (ECOSOC Decision 2002/304).

Following a series of consultations with national stakeholders and development partners of Guinea-Bissau in New York and Washington, the group visited the country from 9 to 16 November 2002. Aside from meeting with a wide range of actors on the ground, the advisory group participated in consultations between the government of Guinea-Bissau and representatives of the UN system as well as the donor community. The meeting addressed problems arising from the suspension of the IMF's Poverty Reduction and Growth Facility and the related decrease in donor assistance.

---

[56] Claude, *Swords into Plowshares*, p. 68.

[57] This chronology is adapted from UN Docs E/2004/86, 25 June 2004; E/2005/70, 2 June 2005; E/2005/82, 24 June 2005; E/2006/8, 18 April 2006; E/2006/53, 20 April 2006; and E/2006/64, 8 May 2006.

2003

The Ad Hoc Advisory Group presented its first report to the Council on 10 January 2003 (E/2003/8). The report recommended a partnership approach between the authorities of Guinea-Bissau and the international community, under which the authorities would work on the promotion of the rule of law and political stability, while international development partners would provide emergency financial support and technical assistance in various fields. The Group recommended the establishment of an Emergency Economic Management Fund, to be managed by the United Nations Development Programme (UNDP), to channel international assistance. The report suggested that international financial institutions should consider de-linking peace-building activities from macroeconomic programmes and explore other ways of addressing urgent needs. It also made recommendations for the long-term development of the country.

On 28 January 2003, the Group organized a meeting between the Minister for Foreign Affairs and the Minister of Economy and Finance with donors and the Bretton Woods Institutions, which focused on the establishment of the 'partnership approach' between the Government and the donors. This approach was endorsed by the Economic and Social Council (ECOSOC resolution 2003/1 of 30 January 2003) and subsequently advocated by the Group.

From 26 to 28 June 2003, the Group undertook a mission to Guinea-Bissau jointly with the Security Council. The objectives of the Advisory Group were to promote dialogue with the authorities of Guinea-Bissau, to appeal to the Government to take measures to prepare for the forthcoming elections, to promote better understanding between the authorities and donors, and to address the humanitarian situation in the country. A second joint mission took place in June 2004.

Through the Advisory Group, the working relationships between the Economic and Social Council and the Security Council have improved and intensified. On 4 August and 19 December 2003, the President of the Security Council issued press statements that commended the Group for its role in the follow-up on the situation in Guinea-Bissau. On 18 November 2003, the President of ECOSOC and the Chairman of the Ad Hoc Group were invited to address the Security Council at a private meeting on the situation in Guinea-Bissau and to present the work carried out by those bodies on the development support to the country.

In September 2003, President Kumba Yala resigned from office and a broad political agreement was signed. Immediately after these events, the Ad Hoc Advisory Group issued a statement in which it called on donors to consider extending emergency assistance to Guinea-Bissau to enable it to return to democratic rule and address the deteriorating socio-economic situation.

On 17 November 2003, the Group hosted an informal dialogue between Guinea-Bissau's transitional president, the Minister for Foreign Affairs, United Nations entities, the Bretton Woods Institutions and major donors to discuss ways of providing emergency support to the transitional government.

2004

The report of the Ad Hoc Advisory Group to ECOSOC (E/2004/10, 6 February 2004) describes the recent developments which had/have taken place and describes the nature of international donor support to Guinea-Bissau. The report includes information on the UNDP-managed Emergency Economic Management Fund, the establishment of which was recommended in the Group's initial report. This Fund now channels important financial assistance from donors. The report also stresses that the Emergency Economic Management Plan and the budget for 2004 elaborated by the government with support by the BWIs, the ADB and UNDP have been elaborated with explicit reference to the partnership approach proposed by the Group.

On 6 April 2004, the Group issued a statement in which it congratulated the people of Guinea-Bissau on the successful legislative elections held on 28 March and called for broad donor support to Guinea-Bissau such as contributions to the Emergency Economic Management Fund (EEMF) managed by UNDP in order to meet the population's basic needs.

Responding to a major crisis in October 2004 when factions of the army mutinied over salary arrears, the Advisory Group issued a statement that called on international donors to continue the support for Guinea-Bissau despite the uprising, especially with emerging budgetary support and the restructuring of the armed forces.

2005

In April 2005, on the advice of the Advisory Group, the President of ECOSOC urged member states to provide support for the Presidential elections in June/July and for the EEMF.

On 20 September 2005, at the margins of the 2005 World Summit, the Ad Hoc Advisory Group, in collaboration with the Group of Friends, held a meeting with a delegation from Guinea-Bissau and led by Prime Minister Carlos Gomes Junior to discuss the situation on the ground and how to best mobilize international support.

On 7 December 2005, the Ad Hoc Advisory Group sent a letter of appeal to international donors calling for additional contributions to the EEMF in order to cover salaries and other expenses in the public services.

2006

On 26 July 2006, ECOSOC extended the mandate of the Ad Hoc Advisory Group on Guinea-Bissau until the Council's substantive session in 2007 (ECOSOC Resolution 2006/11).

Burundi, 2003–06

2003

On 21 July 2003, ECOSOC established the Ad Hoc Advisory Group on Burundi (ECOSOC Resolution 2003/16).

Following its establishment, the Group held a series of briefing sessions and meetings in New York with major United Nations and international agencies, including the Bretton Woods institutions, to discuss development support to Burundi. The Group also met H. E. Mr. Domitien Ndayizeye, the President of Burundi, in September 2003.

The Group undertook a mission to Burundi from 19 to 26 November 2003, during which the Group met the government authorities, major socio-economic actors, United Nations entities active on the ground, the diplomatic community, and other development partners.

The President of ECOSOC was invited to address the Security Council at a meeting on the situation in Burundi held on 4 December 2003. The Security Council welcomed the work of the Group in a presidential statement of 22 December 2003 (S/PRST/2003/30).

2004

The Group was represented at the Forum of Development Partners of Burundi, held in Brussels on 13 and 14 January 2004. Participants at the Forum pledged US$ 1.032 billion of assistance to Burundi.

On 11 February 2004, the Advisory Group on Burundi presented its report to the Council (see E/2004/11). In this report, the Group underlines the various and interlinked challenges that the country is confronted with, in order to embark on the road from relief to development. It encourages the efforts made by Burundi to cope with these challenges and stresses the fact that in view of the considerable humanitarian, economic, and social needs of the country, a strong partnership with the international community is required for these efforts to yield results. The Group makes recommendations for consideration by the Council on the following themes: (1) maintaining the momentum and consolidating the peace process, (2) promoting stability, (3) engaging in poverty alleviation and sustainable development, and (4) reinforcing international partnerships.

On 3 May 2004, the Council adopted draft resolution E/2004/L.6, in which it noted with appreciation the Group's report and welcomed its recommendations.

The Chairman of the Group presented an oral report to ECOSOC on 21 July, in which he urged donors to disburse the promised funds pledged during the Forum of Development Partners, held in Brussels in January 2004.

In September 2004, the Group met with the President of Burundi at the margins of the General Debate of the 59th session of the UN General Assembly. Discussions focused on problems related to the disbursement of aid as well as on the possibility of a follow-up mission to Burundi by the Advisory Group.

On 10 December 2004, the Advisory Group met with the UNDG/ECHA Working Group on Transition Issues. Members of the Working Group presented their main findings related to Burundi.

2005

On 4 February 2005, the Chairman of the Group presented an oral report to ECOSOC, emphasizing that despite some progress in finding international assistance, more support was needed from development partners in order to consolidate the peace process and to support the transition from relief to development.

On 24 June 2005, in its report to ECOSOC, the Ad Hoc Advisory Group called for an increase in international assistance in response to short- and medium-term needs in the transition from relief to development.

On 29 November 2005 and 26 January 2006, the Group held meetings with the Burundian Minister of External Relations and discussed the government's development plans.

On 13 December 2005, the Burundian government officially requested that the Ad Hoc Advisory Group assist in the preparation of a conference with donors for development, which was ultimately held in September 2006.

2006

On 26 July 2006, ECOSOC terminated the mandate of the Ad Hoc Advisory Group on Burundi, taking into account the decision of the Peacebuilding Commission to address the post-conflict needs of the country (ECOSOC Resolution 2006/12).

5

The Commission for Africa: A View Through the Prism of Networks

Myles Wickstead

5.1. Introduction

In 2004, British Prime Minister Tony Blair brought together 17 people to form a Commission for Africa. Their task was to define the challenges facing Africa, and provide clear recommendations on how to support the changes needed to reduce poverty. The initiative had echoes of the Brandt Commission, an international panel brought together by World Bank President Robert McNamara in 1977 to break through the international political impasse in North–South negotiations for global development and to formulate basic proposals on which global agreement would be 'both essential and possible'.

The Commission for Africa had no formal authority to make decisions. Like the earlier Brandt Commission, individuals participated in their personal capacity and independently rather than as official representatives. It was thought that the Commission could influence thinking and policy by sharing ideas, furthering knowledge, and disseminating a new set of proposals through the wide networks of the members of the Commission. The Commission would be, in effect, a network of networks, whose members would learn from one another, generate a consensus among themselves, and use their official positions to press for action.

5.2. The Emergence of the Commission for Africa

In 2005, it was the turn of the UK to be President of both the G8 and the EU. Prime Minister Tony Blair saw this as an opportunity to put Africa at the top of the international agenda. Africa had, in his view, been unduly neglected by the rest of the world, an opinion he had articulated at the Millennium Summit in 2000 when he described Africa as 'a scar on the conscience of the world'. This was initially a moral agenda, without a clear plan for implementation; with no clear audience in mind (should recommendations be addressed to African leaders or to the international community as a whole?), and without specific targets or outcomes.

A comprehensive institutional framework already existed for managing relations with Africa. This included the International Monetary Fund (IMF), the World Bank, the African Development Bank, the Commonwealth, the Francophonie, and the G7/G8 for coordinating rich countries' policies. Blair was fully supportive of Canadian and French efforts to give priority to Africa at the Kananaskis and Evian G7 Summits in 2002 and 2003, but was disappointed that the commitments made on those occasions were rarely implemented. For Blair, the G7/G8's failure to come through on its promises to Africa revealed a serious problem with status quo development institutions: they reflected an unequal world order in which the rich and powerful made the decisions which affected not just themselves, but everyone else in an increasingly globalized world. Some of the existing institutions—notably the IMF and World Bank—were perceived by some to be part of the problem rather than part of the solution, and too dominated by the interests of the major economic powers. Others (like the Commonwealth) were less formal, but perceived as insufficiently universal or effective.

The major international institutions were mostly set up a half-century ago to govern the world which emerged after the Second World War. Their shortcomings for governing the vastly altered international system of the late-twentieth century had become evident long before the beginning of the new millennium. For the poorest countries an important step towards redress had been made in the adoption of the Millennium Development Goals (MDGs) at the UN Millennium Summit in New York in 2000. Building on a precursor—the International Development Targets—the MDGs highlighted increasingly obvious inequalities within and across countries. However, while the MDGs were very relevant to the debate about Africa, they were not merely about African development. Using them as the primary means of focusing on the challenges facing the continent ran the risk of becoming mired in complex and politically sensitive issues of UN reform and seats on the Security Council. For all the reasons above, none of the other existing institutions seemed adequate to address Africa's particular problems. Each institution had a legacy and a certain inertia which made adaptation to new challenges difficult.

For policymakers concerned with African development, the new millennium signalled a need to look beyond the existing institutions based on formal, inter-governmental political and economic relations towards new arrangements which might better reflect a relationship between Africa and the rest of the international community based more on partnership.

The political context was ripe for a new approach when Sir Bob Geldof, a British rock-star, turned advocate for Africa, met Prime Minister Blair in late 2003 and proposed that Blair establish a Commission for Africa. Geldof had made his name in advocacy for Africa through his efforts in 1984–95 with Band Aid and Live Aid to raise money to alleviate famine in Ethiopia and elsewhere. Prior to meeting with Blair in 2003, Geldof had visited Ethiopia, where continuing drought and uncertain weather patterns had created conditions which left open the possibility of a famine on the scale of those seen by the country in 1984. In his view, a 'Marshall Plan' for Africa was required if Africa was ever going to be able to stand on its own feet. It was time to take another look at Africa, and address the key challenges that it faced, in the same way that the Brandt Commission had looked at the world more generally 25 years earlier.[1, 2]

The decision to create the Commission was not taken instantly. Decisions had to be made as to whether more progress could be made by using existing, formal mechanisms and establishing a process which would explicitly not be about establishing a new, permanent mechanism, but about exerting political pressure on existing mechanisms to deliver real change. A Commission would almost certainly be less biddable and

[1] The Brandt Commission was convened in 1977 under the chairmanship of the former German Chancellor Willy Brandt after then World Bank President Robert McNamara proposed establishing a commission of experienced, respected politicians and economists who would not be official representatives of governments and who should work independently to formulate 'basic proposals on which global agreement is both essential and possible' to break through the international political impasse in North–South negotiations for global development.

[2] 'North–South: A program for survival', *Report of the Independent Commission on International Development Issues under the Chairmanship of Willy Brandt* (1980). 'Common Crisis. North–South: Cooperation for World Recovery', The Brandt Commission (1983).

subject to control than other potential mechanisms—indeed, its independence would be a key test of its legitimacy. Was the British Government, and specifically the Prime Minister, ready to run the risks inherent in establishing such a body, which could have significant political and financial implications? After some weeks of consideration, the decision to establish the Commission was taken, and it was launched formally at the end of February 2004.

5.2.1. *Establishing the Commission*

In the early stages, few elements of the Commission were clear. There were no Terms of Reference, and its modus operandi remained undecided, as did its composition, although there was already a recognition that it needed to be broadly representative both of Africa and the international community. The experience of the Brandt Commission offered some useful pointers—it, too, had functioned primarily as a network, but largely because its members (all of whom had been significant actors on the world stage at its inception) no longer held the same degree of control. One way in which the Commission for Africa could make a real difference would be to have as its members people who were not only able to function together effectively as a network but were also key players in the institutions in which crucial decisions were taken. Those institutions needed to be political as well as economic (one criticism of the composition of the Brandt Commission was that it had been too dominated by economists). Commissioners would be invited to participate in a personal capacity rather than as official representatives of their countries or organizations. At the same time, however, many of them would be in positions of power either within Africa or the international system. The Commission would be, in effect, a network of networks, whose members would potentially be in a position to press for action within existing inter-governmental bodies.

Creating the right network was difficult. The Commission had to have wide-ranging influence, but it also had to be of a manageable size. If it was to be seen as broadly representative, it needed not just national politicians but representatives of civil society and international organizations. It had to have a reasonable gender balance. It was important to engage the G8 and the EU, but it also had to be representative of the regions of Africa and to involve African institutions. Whatever the final shape of the Commission, there were inevitably going to be tensions between comprehensiveness and selectivity, between plugging into certain networks and leaving others out. It was clear from the beginning that this would need very careful handling.

From the outset it was thought that a reasonable size would be approximately 15 people (in the event, there were 17 Commissioners). Three of those places were effectively pre-empted by the Prime Minister (Tony Blair), the Chancellor (Gordon Brown) and the International Development Secretary (Hilary Benn). It would fall to them to chair key meetings under the G8 and EU Presidencies at which crucial decisions affecting Africa would be taken, so they necessarily had to be part of the process. A fourth slot was taken by Bob Geldof. So this meant only a dozen or so places remained to meet the goals described above—a formidable task. When the creation of the Commission was announced on 26 February 2004 its composition was still unclear: a number of individuals had already been approached to join the Commission, some had responded positively, some negatively, and some not at all. Others were under consideration.

It was already clear that it would not be possible to invite individuals from all of the G8 countries to join the Commission. And while those individuals who were involved in domestic politics would explicitly not be representatives of their governments, the Commission needed attention from national governments. It was clear that there must be a French Commissioner or this would be seen as just an anglophone, Commonwealth initiative, and the French had pushed forward the Africa agenda under their G8 Presidency in 2003. There also had to be a Canadian Commissioner, since Canada had been responsible for putting Africa on the agenda and inviting African leaders to the G8 Summit at Kananaskis in 2002, and combined a British and French heritage. Finally, the USA, which held the G8 Chair in 2004 and whose (at least tacit) support was essential, could not be excluded.

Several G8 members had to be left out. Russia and Italy accepted philosophically the fact that they would not be represented, while both Germany and Japan protested strongly at their omission. The German Africa Personal Representative, Uschi Eid (whose own commitment to Africa has never been in question) felt undermined—both personally and institutionally—by the establishment and composition of the Commission. As Khadija Bah notes in this volume, a visit by Commission officials to the NEPAD Secretariat in late 2004 was followed within days by a visiting German senior official warning that the Commission did not necessarily reflect the views of G8 Governments, and that whatever recommendations it might make would not necessarily be endorsed by the G8 leaders.

Japan—at least at first—felt even more strongly. It was not just that the Japanese felt left out; it was that a decision to include China had been taken at an early stage. Any process which aspired to being globally comprehensive could scarcely ignore a country which contained 20 per cent of the world's population and was likely to become the biggest economy in the world within a generation. Furthermore, China was already developing a significant economic and political relationship with an increasing number of African countries. However, seen from Japan, China was its rival as the dominant power in eastern Asia and the Commission was composed at the time when there were particular tensions between them. The Japanese also asserted—correctly—that they had an exceptionally well-qualified individual in Mrs Ogata, formerly Head of UNHCR and at that point the Head of Japan's Development Ministry. Following Japanese pressure, the decision was taken to invite her, but ironically she declined to accept the position because she had too many other commitments.

The complexities applied similarly to Africa. The new African Union (AU) had as its building blocks the regional economic communities and the five regions of Africa. Numbers meant that it was difficult to incorporate representatives from all of those regions; and in any case, there were not always individuals who came quickly to mind. Ultimately, the Commission included Commissioners from three of the five regions. There were no representatives (but equally no demands to be represented) from central Africa; but North Africa—while recognizing that the Commission was primarily concerned with sub-Saharan Africa—felt that they should be represented, and Egypt and Algeria (both important because of their membership on the NEPAD Steering Committee) made their case forcefully.

Selecting members for the Commission also required considering the various regional and international institutions. Alpha Konare, the recently appointed Head of the African Union Commission Secretariat and ex-President of Mali, was an obvious candidate for the Commission; articulate, passionate, and francophone. He had made it clear to the Head of the Commission Secretariat (then the British Ambassador in Addis Ababa) on a number of occasions that he recognized Tony Blair's commitment to Africa and he expected him to use his Presidencies in 2005 to do something extraordinary for Africa. Having taken legal advice, however, he concluded that he could not himself be a member of the Commission because of possible conflict of interest—though he would use his position and influence to help.

This support was welcome, but created problems of its own. In particular (and this would have been true whether or not Konare was a member of the Commission), there were complications over the relationship between the African Union and the New Partnership for Africa's Development (NEPAD). This has been covered admirably elsewhere in this book by Khadija Bah, who notes that NEPAD was essentially a network of a number of key African leaders, created with honourable intentions, but without consultation with African civil society and many other African leaders. Konare was clear that NEPAD had to be 'a programme of the African Union' even though NEPAD pre-dated it. While this was publicly acknowledged by the NEPAD leaders, it was not clear how far they wanted NEPAD to come under Konare's control rather than their own. These tensions raised potential complications for the Commission.

By the time of its first meeting in May 2004, the composition of the Commission was more or less complete, lacking only a Chinese representative (the Government of China had been invited to propose an individual of the right calibre and experience, which resulted in mid-2004 in the appointment of Ji Peiding to the Commission). At the May discussion, the Commissioners agreed on a number of important issues, most importantly the Commission's objectives. These were as follows:

- To generate new ideas and action for a strong and prosperous Africa, using the 2005 British Presidencies of the G8 and European Union as a platform;

- To support the best of existing work on Africa, in particular the New Partnership for Africa's Development (NEPAD) and the African Union, and to help ensure this work achieved its goals;

- To help deliver implementation of existing international commitments towards Africa;

- To offer a fresh and positive perspective for Africa and its diverse culture in the twenty-first century, which challenges unfair perceptions and helps deliver changes; and

- To understand and help fulfil African aspirations for the future by listening to Africans.

5.2.2. The Work of the Commission

Effectively achieving the goals of the Commission required working in several different ways. The Commission would need to be agenda-setting, influencing other institutions and the coordination of their policies. But equally it would need to be consensus-building and to produce and disseminate ideas.

Early on, the Secretariat of the Commission had been given the task of defining and building a consensus. Initially staffed by about 16 people, the Secretariat was supposed to identify, develop, and use networks to develop the consensus. This was a mammoth task. Furthermore, it soon became clear that, rather than just building on existing work on Africa as had been originally intended, some serious new thinking (and commensurate new resources) would be required. Although there was agreement on some issues, in early 2004 there was no consensus on key issues such as the importance of agricultural research, tertiary education, and infrastructure. For that reason, Sir Nicholas Stern was appointed as Director for Policy and Research, with the primary responsibility of producing the Commission's final report, while the Head of the Secretariat was charged with managing the consultation and networking process. In practice, these roles became intertwined through necessity, and most of the senior members of the Secretariat had dual responsibilities for writing and consultation.

The Commissioners had between them an extraordinary collection of networks linking them to existing formal political and economic structures. Though there was no member who was currently working in the IMF and World Bank, Michel Camdessus was a former Managing Director of the IMF; Gordon Brown was then Chair of the International Monetary and Financial Committee, which oversees the organization; and Trevor Manuel, the South African Finance Minister, was Chair of the Development Committee, which performs a similar function for the World Bank. Ralph Goodale, Hilary Benn, and Linah Mohohlo were all Governors of the Bretton Woods institutions, K. Y. Amoako was a former Executive Director at the World Bank, Nicholas Stern had previously been the Chief Economist at the World Bank, and the Head of the Secretariat had been the UK Executive Director at the Bank and Fund. So having a basis for discussion and dialogue was straightforward, and was crucial in delivering the debt package (more on this below). Similarly, the Commission had close connections with the United Nations, as two Commissioners were senior UN officials and had the tacit support of Secretary-General

Kofi Annan who, like World Bank President Jim Wolfensohn, saw the Commission as a potential ally in focusing efforts on the MDGs and Africa.

Missing from the heart of the Commission for Africa was a direct link to the leaders of NEPAD, and to francophone and North Africa. The support of the AU and NEPAD, without which the Commission would have fallen at the first hurdle, has already been mentioned. That said, while Commissioners President Mkapa and Prime Minister Meles had good relations with the NEPAD Steering Committee (Presidents Mbeki of South Africa; Obasanjo of Nigeria; Wade of Senegal; Bouteflika of Algeria; and Mubarak of Egypt) there was always a risk that those leaders would see the Commission as undermining their own pre-eminence. In particular, the Commission was viewed with a good deal of scepticism by francophone and North Africa in the early stages, which created significant difficulties, though ultimately the NEPAD Steering Committee rallied behind the initiative and their Governments welcomed Commission-related events in their countries. Individuals like Ismael Serageldin, who might reasonably have anticipated a place on the Commission, played an enormously helpful role in the consultation process.

Scepticism about the Commission was shared by many within (and beyond) Africa. For some, it invoked a sense of weariness, a sense that similar initiatives had been tried and had failed time and time again. For others, the mistrust was more concrete—the 'Blair Commission' was simply an effort by the British Prime Minister to restore his international reputation after Iraq, or it represented yet another attempt to impose an external agenda on Africa. It was, they argued, not only unnecessary but also potentially harmful. Africa now had its own mechanisms and strategies—the AU, NEPAD, and the Africa Peer Review Mechanism (APRM)—and the Commission was otiose. As Khadija Bah has described in Chapter 6 of this book, the NEPAD Secretariat certainly felt very threatened in the early stages by what might transpire.

An uncomfortable overlap existed between the Commission and the Africa Personal Representatives (APRs), a group of senior officials who had been appointed at the Kananaskis G8 Leaders Summit to monitor performance on the G8 commitments and regularly to report back to the G8. While two of the APRs, Michel Camdessus and Hilary Benn, were also members of the Commission, there was a good deal of resistance to the Commission by other APRs, who feared the Commission would create a new network of influence and axis of cooperation which would undermine and disempower their own network.

A further overlap existed with the Millennium Review Summit in New York, which reviewed progress made towards the Millennium Development Goals (MDGs) that had been set following the Millennium Summit in 2000. The overarching goal was to halve the proportion of people in the world living in absolute poverty by 2015, among a number of other desired outcomes which focused largely around improving education and health indicators. It was already evident by the time the Commission was established that, while a number of countries (particularly China and India, which accounted for one third of the world's population) were making very good progress towards achieving these goals, the whole continent of Africa was being left a long way behind. It was equally evident that the key elements of the Commission and Millennium Review Summit had to be broadly aligned if they were not going to undermine one another.

Finally, two other initiatives overlapped with the Commission. A Millennium Task Force had been established in New York under the leadership of Professor Jeffrey Sachs to analyse progress (or the lack of it) towards the achievement of the MDGs and to make recommendations for the Millennium Review Summit.[3] An increasingly powerful and vociferous coalition of international NGOs had come together under the campaign to 'Make Poverty History', determined to press for international action, focusing in particular on the need to address the issues of aid volume, debt, and trade policy. Nowhere was that lobby more active than in the UK.

5.3. The Work and Influence of the Commission for Africa

The work of the Commission emerged through two sets of intertwined networks: one national (within the United Kingdom) and one international. The Commission was chaired by the British Prime Minister, two other UK Cabinet Ministers were also members, and the Secretariat was nested within the UK Government. But the goal of the Commission was to build international as well as national support for the Africa agenda, not just within government but among NGOs, civil society, academics, and the private sector.

The Commissioners recognized from the outset that their participation in the process was crucial. They decided to hold a series of ten regional

---

[3] Jeffrey Sachs, 'Investing in Development: A Practical Plan to Achieve the Development Goals', www.unmillenniumproject.or/ (2005).

consultations in Africa, two in each region (one would be general and the other would focus in particular on the private sector). This provided at least some counter-weight to the perception that the Commission was an elite grouping with little accountability. In addition, the Nelson Mandela Foundation was contracted to carry out a series of regional seminars.

The Secretariat was very soon given a key role. Following the first meeting in London in May, the Secretariat was mandated to draw up a consultation document—a very preliminary outline of some of the issues which might provide the main themes of the final Report—which would form the basis of an outreach strategy. The strategy would need to be comprehensive and in particular target those who questioned the need for a new Commission or those who felt omitted from it.

Outreach and collaboration were crucial from the start. Opportunities were seized; where meetings were already planned by others and where networks were already operating, the Commission was to piggyback on those efforts. For example, at the time of the second meeting of the Commission in Addis Ababa in October 2004, there was also a meeting of several hundred African women for a 'Beijing plus 10' conference. This provided an excellent opportunity for the Commissioners to discuss with them issues such as the gender dimension of governance and conflict prevention. The World Economic Forum meeting in January 2005, hosted by Trevor Manuel in South Africa, provided the perfect opportunity to get the support of African Finance Ministers for the Commission Report.

How did these elements of the Commission's work come together and with what tensions and implications for the network effects the Commission was hoping to leverage?

5.3.1. *The Secretariat and the UK Base of the Commission*

The Secretariat was charged with putting together a consensus which built from and drew support from governments across the world as well as NGOs, civil society, academics, and the private sector.

A serious challenge for the Secretariat was how to make use of its position nested within the UK Government but without becoming driven by 'Whitehall priorities' or compromising its independence. While the Secretariat included a number of non-civil servants, some of them foreign nationals (two of them based in Africa), it comprised primarily British civil servants on secondment from a number of Whitehall

Departments—from the DFID (from whose resources the Secretariat was funded) but also from the Foreign and Commonwealth Office, the Treasury, Education, Environment, and elsewhere.

On the positive side, the Secretariat was able to use ready-made cross-governmental networks to draw on expertise from across Whitehall both in developing contacts and in constructing the Report. The Secretariat also benefited from the support of the Prime Minister—and the very strong signals from the Prime Minister's office that this was something to which the Prime Minister attached particular importance (as evidenced by regular Whitehall coordination meetings). That support and attention pushed government departments to perform.

On the challenging side, the Secretariat sat amidst several different government departments. Every department wanted to shape the agenda to suit its own priorities. As mentioned above, the Secretariat had to make use of the expertise available, but try not to be driven by particular Whitehall priorities or compromise its independence. Help in the task of negotiating across the government came from the Africa All-Party Parliamentary Group, a cross-party Parliamentary Committee. It was particularly helpful in creating awareness and consensus in support of the Commission's work within the British Parliament. But it also took evidence from government departments on the issue of the coherence of UK policies towards Africa. It used its own networks to influence parliamentarians in other countries, particularly within the EU.

The link to Parliament, through the Africa All-Party Parliamentary Group and the International Development Select Committee, was important in helping to build support within the UK—across all parties—to reach the international target of 0.7 per cent of GNI for development assistance. This political consensus would have been inconceivable five (or even two) years earlier, and represented a huge step forward in the significance of development issues generally and African issues in particular within the UK. While that political consensus was not an explicit objective when the Commission was established, it is likely to be one of the Commission's lasting legacies.

Broader outreach within the UK was also vital to the work of the Commission. Both before and after the publication of the Commission Report (March 2005) and the G8 Summit (July 2005), strong links and a programme of activities had been put together. Organizations like the British Council, the BBC, and the British Museum played significant roles in building public support, primarily through mobilizing their networks. The British Museum, for example, played a leading role in developing the concept of 'Africa '05', a year-long festival to celebrate the diverse cultures of Africa, becoming a lead partner with the South Bank Centre and the Arts Council. The creation of an 'Africa Garden' at the British Museum by the BBC 'Ground Force' team attracted over 5 million viewers. A number of exhibitions on the theme of 'Made in Africa' were held in or supported by the Museum. New relationships with African museums and institutions were established. This could not have fitted better with the emphasis in the Commission Report on the importance of understanding Africa's heritage, traditions, and cultures, and provided the basis for a continuing interest in Africa.

5.3.2. *Relations with Other International Actors and Institutions*

The challenge at the international level was to show that adequate and serious consultations had been undertaken both within and beyond Africa so as to imbue the Report with legitimacy. Within Africa, this meant engaging with the AU, with the NEPAD leaders and the NEPAD Secretariat, and with those parts of Africa that felt, or might feel, ostracized from the process (particularly the North and the francophone). This was not merely about engaging with politicians, but with civil society and the private sector as well. Beyond Africa, the same principles applied.

Within Africa, President Mkapa and Prime Minister Meles in particular used their influence to persuade the key NEPAD Heads of Government that the Commission, far from being a threat to NEPAD, was designed primarily to encourage the international community to put its weight and resources behind the positive changes that were increasingly evident in Africa. Cooperation between the Commission Secretariat and the NEPAD Secretariat increased as mutual trust developed. By the autumn of 2004, the Head of the NEPAD Secretariat shared a platform in New York with the Head of the Commission Secretariat and the relationship was cemented through a visit by several members of the Commission Secretariat to their NEPAD colleagues. Gradually, the key NEPAD leaders began to give their support—first Obasanjo and Mbeki, then Wade, and finally Bouteflika and Mubarak. After its initial scepticism, NEPAD became a key supporter.

The relationship with the G8 was important, though not always easy. Commissioners used every opportunity to promote the Commission's work. The Secretariat visited every G8 capital for meetings with all the different arms of government at senior levels, and were invariably given a good hearing. This did not mean that G8 Governments and representatives necessarily liked the momentum which was beginning to build behind the Commission's work, but their prior scepticism was replaced by a sense that the Commission might succeed, and that therefore they should be informed and engage.

Relations with key EU member states were also vital, especially the countries holding the EU Presidency before and after the UK's term. These were not always easy. Relations with the European Commission were important but made complicated by the changeover of the Commission in November 2004. That said, relations with the EU proved fruitful. The European Development Commissioner Louis Michel was very supportive of the Commission initiative, and the European Commission's 2005 Africa Strategy was entirely consistent with the Commission Report. The decision taken under the Luxembourg Presidency in May 2005 that the traditional EU member states would reach the 0.7 per cent target for flows of official development assistance (ODA) by 2015, with the new member states committed to 0.33 per cent within the same timetable, helped to create a very positive environment for the G8 Summit several weeks later, and has further caused the development of a new network of governments, NGOs, and academics in Eastern Europe with an interest in Africa, again at least in part as a legacy of the Commission.

The UN system was generally very supportive throughout the process, and helped to give publicity to the Commission at existing events, such as the 2004 UN General Assembly meetings. The IMF and World Bank were also very constructive, and it proved relatively straightforward—particularly with two Commissioners holding the reins of the IMFC and the Development Committee—to use regular meetings of networks associated with the institutions to take forward the work of the Commission.

5.3.3. *The Report and its Implementation*

By the end of 2004, the first phase of the consultation process had come to an end. It would have been difficult in the time available to cast the net for consultations any wider. The challenge now was to concentrate on writing the final Report, as the third (and final) meeting of the Commission was to take place in London at the end of February 2005, but to do so in such a way that people recognized that their views and ideas had been taken into account. This was vital for cementing the credibility of the consultation process and the legitimacy of the Commission.

When the Report was finally launched on 11 March 2005,[4] it was received warmly both within and outside of Africa. It was generally perceived to be comprehensive and well written, to give a credible account of the positive changes happening within Africa, and to identify the changes that were required for the continent. On this basis, it was thought to make a convincing case for a substantial increase in international support. The Report noted that the G8 and others could not pick and choose from this particular menu—it was a package and had to be treated as such. Of course, there were financial implications, which were not universally welcomed, but the intellectual coherence of the Report tilted the debate away from those against doing more to support Africa, and in favour of a powerful and increasingly significant coalition of new networks. Within the UK, the Report became official policy when the Prime Minister declared his support for the Report in its entirety at the launch on 11 March 2005 and supported the specific objective of making it G8 policy. This marked an important shift but a serious challenge for the Commission.

Would the recommendations of the Commission be implemented? While the Commissioners and the Secretariat continued to press the case for their recommendations, holding a series of events in Africa in the second quarter of the year to explain how the ideas of the different networks had been incorporated into the Report, the primary responsibility to deliver—once the Report had been launched with strong UK endorsement—rested with the British Government.

Serious problems arose in the G8. The Report became the basis for discussion of Africa by the Sherpas, sous-Sherpas, and other G8 networks and more formal mechanisms responsible for preparing for the Summit. This move exacerbated tensions with the Africa Personal Representatives (APRs), who thought their own document should form the basis for discussion at the Summit. In the same way that the Sherpas and sous-Sherpas had felt their network threatened by the creation of the APR network in 2002, so the APRs in 2004 and 2005 felt their network threatened by the Commission. They succeeded in reducing the Commission to a single reference in the G8 Communiqué, but the Commission Report remained the basis for the logic, sequence, conclusions,

---

[4] 'Our Common Interest: Report of the Commission for Africa'. 2005 (www.commissionforafrica.org). 'Our Common Interest: the Commission for Africa, An Argument'. 2005.

and recommendations of the Communiqué. All the efforts with the AU and NEPAD leaders paid off; the AU Summit held just days before the G8 Summit welcomed the Commission Report, committed its members to fulfil Africa's side of the bargain, agreed to keep the position under constant review, and urged the G8 to deliver on its side of the partnership.

Although implementation remained problematic, the Report bolstered the case of civil society and other groups campaigning for more support for Africa. One campaign in particular was fortified: the 'Make Poverty History' (MPH) campaign. While the Commission Report contained some 90 Recommendations, and the MPH focused only on 3 (aid, trade, and debt), there was no inconsistency between the two, and the NGOs were generally very supportive of the Commission Report. Their efforts gathered momentum as the G8 Summit got nearer, and Bob Geldof in particular was instrumental in developing popular support both by working closely with the NGOs and organizing the 'Live 8' Concerts.

Finally, the Report catalysed further advocacy and consensus-building among private sector groups. This was a less public but equally significant element of the Commission's work. The Chancellor, Gordon Brown, had established a number of private sector working groups early on in the Commission's existence, and Commissioner William Kalema in particular had vigorously championed the role of the private sector throughout. A 'private sector Summit' was held in the week before the G8 Summit to develop support for its Recommendations (e.g. on the creation of an Investment Climate Facility), and launched 'Business Action for Africa' (a continuing initiative, and an important network in its own right).

5.4. Conclusions

Did it all work? There is one very clear indicator that the Commission was successful: the extent to which the G8, to whom most of the Recommendations are addressed, endorsed the Commission Report in the Gleneagles Communiqué. There are two other important indicators—the extent to which those agreed recommendations are implemented in practice (though in many cases it will not be possible to attribute this with any certainty to the Commission), and the degree to which Africa remains on the international agenda as a consequence of the Commission's work.

As noted above, the Gleneagles G8 Communiqué on Africa followed the logic and sequencing of the Commission Report, recognizing the importance of taking a holistic approach rather than cherry-picking. Most of the Commission Recommendations were accepted in their entirety; some lost some of their specificity (such as estimates of what it would cost to implement particular recommendations); and some were bypassed altogether. On the three 'campaigning' issues, the language on aid (and in particular, the endorsement of a doubling of aid to Africa between 2005 and 2010) and debt was very positive, though much less so on the trade agenda.

The Commission succeeded in building a consensus around which governments were prepared to make commitments. However, although the G8 accepted the commitments recommended by the Commission, their implementation is another story. In the immediate aftermath of the Commission, it was unclear whether all G8 countries were increasing their development assistance in line with the agreed increases—though support by some or all of the G8 countries for initiatives like the replenishment of the Global Fund, the International Finance Facility for Immunization, and the Infrastructure Consortium for Africa was promising.

On debt, the outcome has been very positive. Commissioners Gordon Brown and Trevor Manuel were at the forefront of those arguing successfully at the IMF/World Bank meetings in September 2005 for full international support for the debt package proposed by the Commission, a good example of how effectively a network can feed into more formal decision-making processes. Trade remains a major disappointment. There has been real progress on some other issues (developments which may or may not have occurred without the influence of the Commission) including the ratification of the UN Convention against Corruption, the commencement of negotiations on an Arms Trade Treaty, and the launch of the Investment Climate Facility.

Networks are characterized by their informality, by the determination of their members to use their contacts to make progress in a particular area, and by their ability to 'get on' in pursuit of a common interest, characteristics which provide the potential for 'a more flexible, flat and non-hierarchical means of exchange and interaction which promises to be more innovative, responsive and dynamic'.[5] One of the truly remarkable

[5] Mohan Henry and Yanacopulos, 'Networks as transnational agents of development', *Third World Quarterly*, 25: 5 (2004), pp. 839–55.

elements of the Commission for Africa was how well its members inter-acted with each other, as evidenced by the meeting in Addis Ababa in October 2004, which saw significant discussion on critical development issues such as the effective role of the state. Unlike more formal structures, where personality becomes virtually irrelevant, it is hard to conceive of a network functioning effectively if its members do not gel. Perhaps more by luck than good judgement, the Commissioners developed a strong sense of camaraderie and mutual respect, which meant that they were even more willing to press for the implementation of Commission Recommendations and conclusions in the more formal mechanisms and structures of which they were also part.

There has undoubtedly been a shift in the profile of Africa as a result of the Commission's work, which has in turn given rise to changes in both formal and informal mechanisms for follow-up. The German Pres-idency became committed to developing a statement at the G8 Summit in mid-2007 about the progress made towards meeting the G8 commit-ments in Africa and (as agreed at the St. Petersburg Summit under the Russian Presidency in 2006) identifying priorities for future work. This would be based in part on the work of the Secretariat to the Africa Partners' Forum, established to monitor progress by Africa, the G8, and other donors against their commitments, which made its first Report in October 2006.

Of course, new networks will develop to remind the G8, EU, and African Governments of their commitments. Some will be very informal groupings of NGOs and civil society groups. Some will be more formal, with a small secretariat—for example, the 'Africa Monitor' established in 2006 by the Archbishop of Cape Town to hold African leaders to account. Perhaps the most significant of all will be the Africa Progress Panel (APP), an independent monitoring mechanism to be chaired by for-mer UN Secretary-General Kofi Annan and initially comprised of around eight members, most of whom were closely involved with the work of the Commission and two of whom (Michel Camdessus and Bob Geldof) were actually Commissioners. Such a mechanism was recommended in the Commission Report, but not picked up in the Gleneagles Commu-niqué, not because the G8 leaders thought it would not be effective, but because they feared it would be. The APP is likely to have much in common with the Commission, not least because it will likely oper-ate as a network of networks. It will, like the Commission, lack the capacity to implement or enforce decisions, but is likely to have the credibility and authority—as the Commission did—to create, exert, and sustain the moral pressure required to ensure continuing progress in Africa.

A commentary by Sir Nicholas Bayne

As Myles Wickstead shows, British Prime Minister Tony Blair set up the Commission for Africa in 2004 to underpin the African component of the G8 summit which he was due to chair at Gleneagles the following year. The summit had already done a lot of work on Africa, from 2001 onwards, and had launched an 'Africa Action Plan' intended to underwrite the New Programme for Africa's Development (NEPAD). But after a hopeful start, the initial impetus was running out of steam. Promised commitments in aid, trade, and debt relief were slow to materialize or were not being met at all. The Americans had largely left Africa off the agenda for the 2004 summit. The G8 and African components were following parallel but separate tracks, as the G8 did not want to undermine African 'ownership' of NEPAD. Both in Africa and G8 countries, the approach was being criticized by civil society groups, as being imposed from the top down.

Tony Blair brought Africa back onto the G8 agenda for 2005 and developed a strategy intended to correct the weaknesses that had emerged. Jointly with his Finance Minister, Gordon Brown, he promoted measures for 100 per cent debt relief for poor debtor countries and for accelerated aid spending through a new International Finance Facility. The Commission for Africa was an essential part of this strategy. Its aim was to bring together Africans and non-Africans, government and non-government participants, in an informal setting outside the circuits of state institutions, to generate persuasive new thinking about Africa's prospects and potential. This process was intended to lead to clear recommendations on the measures that needed to be taken, that would stimulate the G8 to greater collective effort than they had taken before.

During its life of just over one year, from its launch in February 2004 to the issue of its report in March 2005, the Commission was very successful. This emerges from Myles Wickstead's paper, from the Commission's own report and from other contemporary references. In particular,

- A strong collegiate spirit developed within the Commission, with good bonding between all the members.

- The Commission successfully overcame initial resistance in Africa and won the confidence and cooperation of the key institutions, like NEPAD and the African Union. It was accepted as representative, despite the low presence of Francophones and North Africans.
- It produced, on time, an extremely well-written report. This argued its case eloquently, in clear, concise, and jargon-free language.

The content of the report reinforced and expanded the underlying approach to African development that had been gaining ground since the launch of NEPAD in 2001 and the G8 Africa Action Plan at the Kananaskis summit of 2002. The key elements of the report were the following:

- Africans should define their own approach to their development and take responsibility for it.
- Better political governance in Africa is a pre-condition for progress.
- There were precise and clearly costed recommendations in fields such as education (going beyond primary education), health care, agriculture, infrastructure, trade, and business development. Some of these, like infrastructure and trade, reflected African aims hitherto neglected by the G8.
- The detailed recommendations justified the Commission's call for aid to Africa to double in three to five years, making available an extra $25 billion per year, while heavily indebted poor African countries should have 100 per cent of their debts forgiven.
- The report finally called for a monitoring mechanism to track the progress made, led by two senior figures, one African and one from the donor community.

These recommendations were presented as a package, not to be taken piece by piece. The report earned the full endorsement of the African Union summit in July 2005, just before the G8 met at Gleneagles.

But while the African impact of the Commission worked well, its impact on the G8 fell short of what was intended. Blair wanted the G8 leaders explicitly to endorse the Commission for Africa's report and to make its recommendations the foundation for the Gleneagles summit's conclusions. Though Myles Wickstead claims this in his paper, a comparison of the Commission's report and the G8 Africa document from Gleneagles suggests only partial success. In particular,

- There is only one grudging reference to the Commission's report in the summit's Africa document.
- Many of the specific recommendations were picked up, so that the G8 Africa document may be said to follow the logic and sequence of the Commission report, as Wickstead suggests. But, as he admits, some parts of the package are missing, many are heavily qualified and all have lost the precise costings that gave such strength to the report.
- There was strong resistance to any follow-up mechanism to the Commission for Africa. However, the G8 did agree to strengthen the Africa Partners Forum and give it some staff (based in the OECD), as it had not proved very effective up till then as a monitoring instrument.

The headline targets, on trade liberalization, debt relief, and aid volume, were accepted by the G8 at Gleneagles. The trade commitment came to nothing; the debt relief proposals, which pre-dated the Commission for Africa, were successfully implemented in the IMF and World Bank. The doubling of aid to Africa, with a 2010 deadline, was widely welcomed after Gleneagles, notably by civil society campaigners. But the $25 billion figure had become detached from the detailed calculations that justified it. Though the G8 repeated its pledge at the next two summits, St. Petersburg in 2006 and Heiligendamm in 2007, actual aid spending by most G8 members (though not the UK) was falling well behind the target. Severe doubts were emerging that it would be met.

The short conclusion is that the Commission did well among the Africans, but much less well among the G8. To explain this, it is necessary to look more closely at how the two halves of the Commission operated and how they contributed to its effectiveness as a network.

Myles Wickstead has aptly characterized the Commission for Africa as a 'network of networks' where each member was able to tap into the other networks to which he or she belonged, both to enrich the Commission's own work and to facilitate wider acceptance of the Commission's findings. This outreach process did apply not only to other networks but also to formal institutions, both international, like the IMF and World Bank, and African, like NEPAD, the AU, and the UN Economic Commission for Africa.

Wickstead's paper shows that the nine African members of the Commission used their standing in other networks and institutions to good effect. All made a specific contribution and there were no passengers. For example, though none of the four founders of NEPAD were on the Commission, the African leaders that were (Meles Zenawi and Benjamin

143

Mkapi) made sure that they were engaged. The four non-government African members worked hard with business and civil society networks. In the IMF and World Bank, Trevor Manuel (chair of the Development Committee) made a powerful team with Gordon Brown (chair of the International Monetary and Finance Committee), while two more of the Africans were part of the UN system. The cumulative effect of this successful networking was that the Africans had a sense of ownership of the Commission.

Networking by the eight non-African members appears less effective. Gordon Brown's pivotal position in the IMF has already been noted and made an essential contribution on debt relief. Even so, he was unable to win wide support for his International Finance Facility. Bob Geldof's high profile in the NGO community ensured a favourable response from civil society, but there was no one from business. Michel Camdessus ensured strong backing from Chirac—Blair's closest ally throughout—and helped to gain acceptance among Francophone Africans. But the American, Canadian, and Chinese members exerted little influence even within their national networks. The British and French members were part of the EU network, but there was no one who could represent the European Union as such; the UK only took over the Presidency after the Commission had reported.

The most conspicuous failure, as already argued, was to engage the G8 governments collectively in the enterprise. The G8 often behaves like a network, when its members combine to gain acceptance of their initiatives in wider institutions like the IMF or WTO. But it is nonetheless an institution, which makes formal commitments on the basis of voluntary cooperation among its members. It has well-defined methods of decision-making, both at summit and lower levels. In particular, because the G8 is so small, all members expect to speak for themselves and to be involved in its decisions. There were therefore high risks in setting up a network explicitly intended to influence the G8 in which not all G8 participants were present.

On this basis, the composition of the eight non-African members of the Commission looks less coherent than the nine Africans and did not avoid these risks. The UK took three places (Blair, Brown, and Hilary Benn) as well as providing most of the Secretariat. Geldof, though Irish by nationality, was also considered to be in the British camp. One of the four remaining seats was given to China: a far-sighted move, as events have shown, but unwelcome to the rest of the G8 at the time. This left only three places for other G8 members, so that over half were absent—Japan,

Germany, Italy, the European Commission, and Russia (who would chair the 2006 summit). The Canadians supplied a member, but still disliked the Commission because it departed from the G8 machinery they had created in 2002.

As a result, the other G8 members (except for France) came to regard the Commission as a British manoeuvre to circumvent the standard G8 preparatory process. They rejected the Commission because they saw it as being owned by the British, not by the G8 as a whole. With hindsight, this rejection might have been avoided if the British had contented themselves with two places, not three, and left China off the list. That would have freed up two places, which could have been filled by Japan and by the European Commission, whom Germany and Italy could have accepted as a European voice. In this way, only Russia would have been wholly unrepresented.

These problems over participation and ownership, however, concealed a deeper problem over the G8's approach to Africa. From the outset, the G8 has recognized the collective achievement of the Africans in creating NEPAD and the African Union, and declared its wish to support those bodies. But the G8 has been reluctant to develop collective policies towards Africa of its own. Each G8 participant wants to retain the freedom to develop distinctive aid and development policies, in forms that will win support from domestic constituencies. The USA is most conspicuous in doing this, but no G8 member is immune from this trend. G8 work on Africa still largely consists of the juxtaposition of the existing policies of its members. When the G8 leaders meet, they are able to agree joint statements which identify shared areas of activity and set common targets for the future. But these often crumble away when it comes to implementation.

The Commission for Africa was intended to bring the G8 closer to a genuine collective approach to Africa. It failed to do so because, in the event, the G8 members did not feel sufficiently involved in its work. It is in fact doubtful whether an informal network could have succeeded in changing their national approaches to development policy, even with a more balanced composition and greater sense of ownership. Change of this kind might have been stimulated by the Commission, by creating a coherent rationale for collective policymaking, but it would need stronger institutional machinery to make it happen.

Blair and his team had rightly perceived that the G8 Africa Personal Representatives (APRs) created in 2001–02 did not have sufficient authority, as its members carried unequal weight in their national systems. Improving collective performance would require more formal disciplines than the APRs could provide. But the Commission did not make recommendations on this; its informal nature and wide composition left it ill-placed to do so. The decision that emerged from Gleneagles—to strengthen the Africa Partners Forum—has not yet solved the problem, to judge from the results from the 2007 Heiligendamm summit. So, in some respects, the Commission for Africa was attempting a task beyond the capacity of an informal network.

In conclusion, the Commission for Africa has not had the success in determining policy that the quality of its report deserves. It certainly influenced the outcome of the 2005 Gleneagles summit: the African content of the summit would have been much weaker without the Commission's work. But it has not produced the decisive move towards a more collective G8 approach to Africa that Blair hoped and intended. Two years on, by the Heiligendamm summit of 2007, the G8's performance on Africa is being regarded with growing scepticism.

6

Africa's G4 Network

Khadija Bah

6.1. Introduction

This chapter examines the functioning of African political networks, two in particular—the New Partnership for Africa's Development (NEPAD) and the African Peer Review Mechanism (APRM). Within each, there are several formal, institutionalized networks. These include the NEPAD Heads of State and Government Implementing Committee (HSGIC), the APR Forum, the NEPAD Steering Committee, the APR Panel of Eminent Persons, and various national networks in member states.

This chapter will demonstrate that behind these formal networks is an informal, non-institutionalized network of the Heads of State of four of Africa's most influential states, a group I call 'Africa's G4'. The group is comprised of Presidents Thabo Mbeki of South Africa, Olusengu Obasanjo of Nigeria, Abdelaziz Bouteflika of Algeria, and Abdoulaye Wade of Senegal. This group was the force behind the evolution, adoption, and implementation of NEPAD and its APRM. This chapter explores the extent to which Africa's G4, working through NEPAD and the APRM, has been able to change African politics and influence the industrial-ized North not only to recommit to the continent's development but to do so on the basis of a new equal partnership based on mutual accountability.

This chapter is divided into three parts. In the first I examine the various processes and negotiations leading to the evolution and adoption of the NEPAD Plan by the Organization of African Unity (OAU) and the key decisions in the development of the APRM review areas and indicators. It will analyse why the G4 chose to create NEPAD and the APRM rather than continuing to use existing institutions. The second part of this chapter will examine the G4's capability to exert influence on regional politics through NEPAD and the APRM and to inspire a new commitment from the industrialized nations to the continent. The last section looks at the strengths and limitations of Africa's G4 as a network and draws conclusions.

6.2. The Emergence of NEPAD and the APRM

The goal behind the creation of NEPAD was to induce a paradigm shift in Africa's regional politics and relationship with the international community by making explicit the link between development and stability.[1] In its strategic document, NEPAD is described as:

a pledge by African leaders, based on a common vision and a firm and shared conviction, that they have a pressing duty to eradicate poverty and to place their countries, both individually and collectively, on a path of sustainable growth and development and, at the same time, to participate actively in the world economy and body politic. [It] is anchored on the determination of Africans to extricate themselves and the continent from the malaise of underdevelopment and exclusion in a globalising world.[2]

NEPAD is perceived to be striving to make democracy, accountability, and good governance core values of African politics while seeking a new, more equal partnership with the industrialized nations.[3] Thus, the NEPAD strategy can be seen as a dual compact on the one hand between African leaders and African constituencies to improve good governance and human rights and on the other between African leadership and developed nations. In exchange for accountability among African leaders, the industrialized world would commit to Africa's development with enhanced Overseas Development Assistance (ODA), debt relief, favourable

---

[1] Chris Landsberg, 'NEPAD: What is it? What is missing?', *NALEDI* (South Africa, 2003).

[2] NEPAD Secretariat, *The New Partnership for Africa's Development* (Johannesburg, South Africa, 2001), 1.

[3] Among others Kempe Ronald Hope Sr., 'Towards Good Governance and Sustainable Development: The African Peer Review Mechanism', *Governance: An International Journal of Policy, Administration, and Institutions*, 18: 2 (2005), 283–311; Alex de Waal and Jajudeen Abdul Raheem, 'What is the Value of NEPAD?', *Africa Analysis*, 44 (20 February 2004); Landsberg (2003); and Jimi O. Adesina, 'NEPAD and the Challenge of Africa's Development: towards the political economy of a discourse', unpublished paper, Rhodes University (South Africa, 2002).

trading terms, and direct foreign investments.[4] NEPAD is an institution-alized commitment of African states to enhance democratic processes in the continent in order to attract foreign aid.

In spite of its positive agenda, NEPAD was not without controversy. To its architects and proponents, NEPAD embodies an African renaissance aimed at addressing the continent's development challenges, such as poverty and poor governance. Some have even called NEPAD the African 'Marshall Plan'. By contrast, NEPAD's detractors see it as a 'top down' neo-liberal project aimed at promoting a Western economic agenda on the continent. This view of NEPAD is particularly strong among African civil society organizations (CSOs). Others have even characterized NEPAD in Marxian terms as a 'class project'.[5]

NEPAD's most ground-breaking feature is the African Peer Review Mech-anism (the APRM), which was formally adopted by the NEPAD Heads of State and Government Implementing Committee (HSGIC) of the OAU in March 2002, and later endorsed by the African Union (AU) in July 2002 at the Durban Summit. The mechanism requires member states to enhance political, economic, corporate, and socio-economic governance. It repre-sents the efforts of African leaders to honour their side of the new part-nership pact with the African constituency and the industrialized world.

The APRM is a mutually agreed, self-monitoring instrument created by the participating member states. Membership in the APRM is open to all member states of the African Union on a voluntary basis. The APRM aims to promote among its member states the adoption of the NEPAD guiding principles of political stability, high economic growth and sustainable development. States can accede by signing a Memorandum of Understanding (MOU), thereby agreeing to be reviewed by peers on a periodic basis to ensure adherence to the NEPAD political, economic, and corporate governance codes and standards contained in the *Declaration on Democracy, Political, Economic and Corporate Governance*, a document approved by the AU Summit in July 2002 (NEPAD Secretariat 2003). As of this writing 23 African countries have signed the APRM MOU.

6.2.1. *The Birth of NEPAD: Three Leaders, Three Plans*

The idea behind the creation of NEPAD began with South African President Thabo Mbeki's idea of an African renaissance to counter

[4] Ibid.

[5] See, for example, Adesina (2002) for an overview of NEPAD as a neo-liberal class project.

Afro-pessimism in the outside world. Mbeki believed that if the continent's economic and political energies were unfettered, it could achieve accelerated development.[6] It was to this end that Mbeki initiated his 'new agenda for Africa' calling for more democratically accountable African states and a new commitment by the industrialized nations to address the continent's vast development challenges.[7] Mbeki was aware that an African agenda based on a South African plan and leadership, no matter how compelling, was likely to fail. To succeed, he needed to garner the support of key African states, namely Algeria, then chair of the OAU; and Nigeria, chair of the G77 at the time.[8]

While Mbeki was promoting his 'new Agenda for Africa', the OAU Heads of State were concerned about the continent's ever-increasing debt and were seeking a rapid solution to the fiscal crisis. To this end, a specific mandate was given to Presidents Abdelaziz Bouteflika and Thabo Mbeki in the *Sirte Declaration* of the 4th Extraordinary Session of the Assembly of Heads of State and Government in September 1999. The mandate was for them to work in consultation with the OAU Contact Group on Africa's External Debt, 'to engage with African creditors on our behalf on the issue of Africa's external indebtedness, with a view to securing the total cancellation of Africa's debt, as a matter of urgency'.[9]

The mandate did not include President Obasanjo of Nigeria. However, at the 35th Ordinary Session of the OAU Heads of State in Algiers in 1999 alongside a 'commitment to exclude those who came to power by *coup d'état* from attending OAU sessions', the Heads of State discussed President Obasanjo's proposal on peace and security issues, known as the Conference on Security, Stability, Development and Cooperation in Africa (CSSDCA) initiative, which was adopted formally a year later at the 36th OAU Assembly of Heads of State and Government Session in Lomé in 2000.[10]

The CSSDCA was a Nigerian initiative developed in 1991 by then Major General Obasanjo before he was elected President of Nigeria. The goal was to gradually build consensus around a set of benchmarks, standards, and timetables for a continental peer review mechanism that deals with interstate security, democracy, human rights, good governance, economic, and development issues.[11] The CSSDCA was also intended to address

---

[6] Among others, de Waal and Raheem (2004); Landsberg (2003); and Adesina (2002).

[7] Landsberg (2003); Adesina (2002); Jakkie Cilliers, 'NEPAD Peer Review Mechanism', *Institute for Security Studies*, 64 (November 2002).

[8] Adesina (2002).   [9] OAU in Adesina (2002, 6).   [10] Adesina (2002, 5).

regional integration and collaboration, which was to be coordinated by the Regional Economic Communities. The CSSDCA membership was to be inclusive, open to all OAU/AU member states. Its benchmarks were specific and time-bound, making it difficult for avoidance or ambiguity. The CSSDCA framework also called for country reports and visits by a panel of eminent, reputable Africans to be conducted in two-year cycles.

In July 2002, the AU was officially launched and its first Assembly of the Heads of State was convened in Durban. Following the launch, leaders adopted a memorandum of understanding, setting out a framework and process for the CSSDCA peer review process. The framework included a set of core values and commitments, and 50 specific key performance indicators on democracy, human rights, security, economic issues, and development. In endorsing the CSSDCA, the Heads of State and Government 'reaffirmed the centrality of the CSSDCA Process... as a monitoring and evaluation mechanism for the African Union'.[12] The CSSDCA Unit within the AU Commission was instructed to elaborate a comprehensive work programme and time schedule for '... overseeing the monitoring process, with diagnostic tools and measurement criteria for assessing performance, as well as deficiencies and capacity restraints that impede them'.[13]

There are overlapping areas between the CSSDCA peer review framework and the APRM, a notably proposed panel of eminent Africans, country visits, and country reports. The key differences between the two frameworks are (a) the membership—the CSSDCA is inclusive of all 53 AU member states, while the APRM is voluntary, exclusive, and discriminatory and (b) the CSSDCA benchmarks are specific and time-bound, making avoidance or ambiguity difficult, whereas those of the APRM are a series of best practices culled from international institutions such as the UNECA and the OECD. Many of the APRM benchmarks would require considerable national resources to implement.

Endorsement of the CSSDCA by the AU meant that this initiative was already in the process of being implemented. It was not implemented because this would have meant that Africa's G4 would have had to work within the OAU/AU structures, something they did not want to do. However, components of the CSSDCA were integrated into the APRM, largely to appease Nigeria.

---

[11] Cilliers (2002).   [12] AU in Cilliers (2002, 64).   [13] Ibid.

The convergence between Mbeki's 'new agenda for Africa', the mandate to Presidents Bouteflika and Mbeki to deal with Africa's debt crisis, and President Obasanjo's CSSDCA seems to have led to the three presidents operating as a troika, using their collective influence to push Africa's development agenda. The timing and convergence of these various initiatives also contributed to the view that NEPAD was authorized by the OAU Assembly of Heads of State.

NEPAD proper only began to take root following the High Level Summit in Okinawa between a number of G8 leaders and developing countries (including Algeria, Nigeria, South Africa, and Thailand) on 20 July 2000, a day before the official opening of the Okinawa G8 Summit. A report on the summit by the Japanese Ministry of Foreign Affairs notes that the Summit represented the first time a dialogue of this magnitude had taken place between the G8 and developing countries. It was also noted that 'the developing countries expressed the desire that they would like to continue this meeting at the G8 Summit in Italy next year'.[14] The concern of Mbeki, his colleagues, Presidents Bouteflika and Obasanjo, and the Thai Prime Minister was debt relief for developing countries in general, but African countries in particular. However, the dialogue extended beyond debt relief to include foreign direct investment (FDI) and official development assistance (ODA) on the argument that debt relief alone will not be sufficient to help developing countries achieve growth.[15]

After the Tokyo meeting, the G8 called for African leaders to direct a workable plan on the basis of a new compact, which might meet the demands of the three African Presidents. The G8 response was illustrative of the growing demand for 'reciprocity' by the developed nations, as mentioned in the Cotonou Agreement and the World Trade Organization (WTO).[16] President Mbeki was then given a mandate by Presidents Bouteflika and Obasanjo to develop the Plan demanded by the G8. The subsequent Plan developed by Mbeki was the Millennium African Renaissance Programme, or MAP. It was developed by a drafting team in Pretoria guided by two interlinking projects: the African Renaissance Project of Mbeki,[17] and the South African Growth and Employment and Redistribution (GEAR)[18] macroeconomic framework.[19]

---

[14] MoFA, 1.

[15] Ministry of Foreign Affairs, *Kyushu-Okinawa Summit Meeting 2000* (*Dialogue meeting with Developing Countries*) on www.infojapan.org.

[16] Adesina (2002).

[17] Signed into law in November 2000 by Mbeki, as the African Renaissance and International Cooperation Fund Act No. 51.

[18] Adopted in 1996.   [19] Adesina (2002).

The Millennium African Renaissance Programme (MAP) was first unveiled at the World Economic Forum (WEF) six months after the Tokyo Summit. In his briefing about the MAP, President Mbeki stated that the Programme would initially be a club of 'African leaders [who] would form a compact committing them to the programme, and a Forum of Leaders who would make decisions about sub-programmes and initiatives and review progress on its implementation'. While participation was open to all African countries, there was an opt-in clause: those intent on participating would have to be prepared and ready to commit to the underlying principles guiding the initiatives.

The MAP was not an initiative of the OAU or its Assembly of Heads of State and Government. The processes used in the development and unveiling of the Plan did not follow the normal channels of OAU procedures. On his return to Pretoria following Davos, President Mbeki gave a briefing on the events leading to the development and unveiling of the MAP.[20] The account suggests that President Mbeki took an active lobbying agenda in the preceding year (2000) among the political leadership of the developed world—the north discussing and seeking commitments to 'the idea of a new concerted effort to address, among others, the challenge of African poverty and underdevelopment'.[21] The process was therefore in large part a personal initiative of Mbeki, without and before 'coming to any agreement with other African leaders and African civil society'.[22]

The presentation of the MAP at the World Economic Forum as a firm commitment by all African leaders caused tension among some African leaders. Some have argued that as a result, President Wade of Senegal left Davos and developed his Omega Plan to counter the MAP. However, this view is questionable. At Davos, it was reported that President Wade welcomed the MAP 'while issuing his own strong appeal for international support for Africa's infrastructure and educational systems'.[23] President Wade had presented a plan for Africa with a primary focus on infrastructure at a Yaoundé Summit on 17–19 January 2001,[24] before the 2001 WEF Summit and the unveiling of the MAP on 28 January. President Wade also presented his Omega Plan in Algiers in May 2001. It soon became clear that to succeed, the two competing initiatives would each need the support of the same continental and international stakeholders.

---

[20] Adesina (2002).   [21] Mbeki in Adesina (2002, 7).
[22] Nabudere in Adesina (2002, 7).
[23] World Economic Forum, 2001. *A Plan for Africa*. www.weforum.org, 1.
[24] Wade, President Abdoulaye. *The OMEGA Plan* (2001, 4) www.nepad.org.ng.

To garner international support for his Omega Plan, President Wade convened an international conference of experts in Dakar in June 2001. Following the conference, Wade and his supporters envisioned presenting it at the 2001 OAU Summit in Lusaka a month later. However, President Mbeki and the proponents of the MAP had a similar plan to present their alternative formulation at the same Summit. Fear of a potential francophone/anglophone rift over the plans prompted the proponents of the MAP to force President Mbeki to consult with President Wade for a merger of the two plans.[25] Without some sort of a compromise, the environment was ripe for a possible splintering of camps along francophone/anglophone lines.

Diplomatic efforts ahead of and during the 2001 OAU Summit led to the integration of the two plans as the New African Initiative (NAI). In spite of the continued tension within the OAU and among the Heads of State on the framework and its mode of implementation, the NAI was formally adopted as the NEPAD Plan by the 37th Summit of Heads of State and Government of the OAU, in July 2001 in Lusaka, Zambia.[26] Seen primarily as a pro-Western, neo-liberal economic framework that does not precisely reflect Africa's development priorities, many wondered whether the Heads of State read the NEPAD document prior to signing it,[27] particularly given the pre-existence of OAU declarations like the Lagos Plan of Action and the CSSDCA.[28]

In a keynote address at the African Forum in Nairobi in April 2002, Adebayo Adedeji expressed anguish over the lack of political will and courage by African leaders to implement their own agenda, notably the Lagos Plan of Action.[29] Adedeji's lament was also questioning the creation of NEPAD in the face of similar existing OAU-authorized plans. For the purposes of this chapter, it sharpens the question: whose initiative was NEPAD?

6.2.2. The Drivers Behind the Initiative: Africa's G4

The origins of NEPAD are as controversial as the initiative itself. NEPAD is a composite of several initiatives that converged to form the framework. The general consensus today is that NEPAD was mandated by the Organization of African Unity (OAU). While there are aspects of the

---

[25] Adesina (2002).   [26] Adesina (2002); Cilliers (2002).   [27] Adesina (2002).
[28] The NEPAD Plan differs from these two earlier OAU declarations, both of which preceded NEPAD by several years.
[29] Adedeji in Adesina (2002).

Plan that were undeniably authorized by the OAU,[30] as we have seen, NEPAD in its current form did not emerge from the OAU. NEPAD is a 'leadership-driven initiative'[31] pursued primarily by four of Africa's most powerful leaders—presidents Thabo Mbeki of South Africa, Olusengu Obasanjo of Nigeria, Abdelaziz Bouteflika of Algeria, and Abdoulaye Wade of Senegal. These four leaders (and to some extent the HSGIC) have set and controlled NEPAD's agenda. They also represent and speak on behalf of the continent with little or no consultation with its other stakeholders.

The group initially began as a troika of Mbeki, Obasanjo, and Bouteflika. At the time of the troika's evolution, Mbeki was chair of the Non-Aligned Movement (NAM) and was also developing and promoting his vision of an African Renaissance, Obasanjo was chair of the G77, and Bouteflika was chair of the OAU. The collaboration among the troika began with a mandate issued by the OAU Heads of State to Presidents Mbeki and Bouteflika to address Africa's external indebtedness, which in 2000 stood at US$ 206.1 billion.[32]

Along with Obasanjo, the chair of the G77, the troika came to represent the continent at the first ever summit between African leaders and G8 leaders in Tokyo a day before the Okinawa G8 Summit in July 2000. President Abdoulaye Wade of Senegal joined the group following the integration of his Omega Plan with the Millennium African Renaissance Programme (MAP) to form the New African Initiative (NAI) as part of reconciliation to avoid a francophone-anglophone divide over the plans.

Africa's G4 has become, for all intents and purposes, the voice of the continent in international affairs involving Africa. More often than not, the G4 is likely to be the group of African leaders invited to represent the continent at international gatherings. For example, the meeting in Tokyo prior to the Okinawa Summit opened the door for the participation of African leaders in subsequent G8 Summits. The leaders are also invited in smaller sub-groupings (i.e. simply Mbeki and Obasanjo) or individually to represent Africa in various international processes.

Internally, among the G4 there are frequent exchanges among the four leaders, their personal representatives, and their offices. That said,

---

[30] The OAU mandate was limited to Africa's external indebtedness.

[31] Simon Maxwell and Karin Christiansen, 'Negotiation as simultaneous equation: Building a new partnership with Africa', *International Affairs*, 78(3), 477–91. Published online 16 December 2002.

[32] Adesina in Adesina (2002, 6).

there is tension and discord, with President Wade somewhat as an outsider. His constant and numerous pronouncements against NEPAD and his colleagues have brought to light the discord and infighting both within the G4 and the wider African leadership, causing a fracture along linguistic lines. However, it was (and still is) crucial to its proponents that NEPAD be seen and acknowledged as an OAU mandate. One such example is the 2002 statement by Aziz Pahad, Deputy Foreign Minister of South Africa, that Presidents Bouteflika, Mbeki, and Obasanjo were authorized by the OAU Heads of State 'to develop the plan' during meetings of the African Economic Community in Algiers.[33] In fact, President Mbeki attended the meeting in Algiers and delivered a statement on the challenges of globalization and his concern about putting in place the right mechanisms and procedures to evaluate progress at the national, bilateral, and regional levels towards the objectives of the Abuja Treaty. However, Mbeki's statement provoked uneasiness among the other Heads of State, who perceived it as magisterial in tone.

In essence, NEPAD was a top-down, G4-driven initiative, with little or no consultation with the wider OAU leadership and African society. The need to promote NEPAD as mandated by the OAU, Adesina argues, lies in its sponsors' (Africa's G4) need to legitimize the initiative. Equally, Africa's Western partners, who had demanded a plan for a post-Washington-consensus era of ownership, transparency, and accountability, needed to portray the framework as an African initiative, developed by the African leadership,[34] and 'owned' and endorsed by the African people.

6.2.3. The Relationship of NEPAD to Other Institutions and Initiatives

Why was it necessary to create NEPAD given the existence of the Lagos Plan of Action and the CSSDCA? To answer this, we must examine NEPAD's relationship to two key regional organizations: the Organization of African Unity (the OAU) and the United Nations Commission for Africa (UNECA).

The Organization of African Unity was established on 25 May 1963.[35] Its charter was signed by the Heads of State and Government of the 32

---

[33] Padad in Adesina (2002, 5).

[34] Implies the 53 OAU Heads of State and Government.

[35] I am focusing on the OAU and not the African Union (AU) because at the construction of NEPAD, it was the OAU and not the AU that was in existence. NEPAD pre-dates the AU.

independent African states. The stated objectives of the OAU were to rid the continent of the remaining vestiges of colonization and apartheid; to promote unity and solidarity among the independent African states; to coordinate and intensify cooperation for development; to safeguard the sovereignty and territorial integrity of member states; and to promote international cooperation within the framework of the United Nations.[36]

Unlike NEPAD, membership of the OAU was opened to all 'independent sovereign African States and neighbouring Islands'. Member states pledged to harmonize their policies and cooperate in politics and diplomacy, economics, education, health, science and technology, and defence and security. The OAU was seen as the continent's most effective peacekeeper; the UN General Assembly even paid tribute to the organization for its contribution to the maintenance of international peace and security.

By most accounts, the OAU was an effective organization in its first two decades but began to decline in effectiveness, which led to its dissolution in its fourth decade. Many factors contributed to the decline and eventual disbanding of the OAU, but the single most significant is the end of apartheid in South Africa, which put the country in direct competition with the OAU for dominance in the political affairs of the continent.

Though confronted by its own internal challenges, post-apartheid South Africa was much better placed to take the lead in the political affairs of the continent with its exemplary leadership, its relatively strong institutions, and its developed infrastructure. With Mbeki's vision for an African Renaissance increasingly taking root, the disbanding or restructuring of the OAU was all but inevitable. The OAU had become increasingly ineffective in addressing the continent's escalating challenges. The decline of the organization was further exacerbated by a combination of internal problems including ineffective leadership, poor governance, and corruption. The organization therefore could not have been entrusted with a framework like NEPAD aimed at the rebirth of the continent.

The United Nations Economic Commission for Africa was established in 1958 under the administrative direction of United Nations (UN) Headquarters. It is the regional arm of the UN in Africa mandated to support the economic and social development of the 53 member states, foster

---

[36] AU website, www.a-u.org.

regional integration, and promote international cooperation for the continent's development. The ECA reports to the UN Economic and Social Council (ECOSOC).

The fundamental principle of African ownership and leadership, which underlies the NEPAD vision, made it politically unacceptable for the ECA, as a non-African institution, to carry out the mandate of NEPAD and its APRM. In addition, the Commission was plagued by its own internal problems, including resource constraints.

In summary, the widespread distrust in Africa's leadership[37] and in the existing institutions to address the continent's ever increasing development challenges led to the creation of NEPAD and the APRM outside these existing structures. Bayne argues that 'Africa's problems are rooted in the continent's lack of strong political institutions and protracted conflicts', which 'has influenced the construction of NEPAD and the Africa Action Plan'.[38]

The distrust in the continent's leadership and existing institutions had extended beyond the region to the outside world. To Africa's industrialized partners, Mbeki and his allies were a breath of fresh air—a new breed of African leaders ready and willing to develop 'radical interventions' to put the continent on a path of sustainable development based on the principles of democracy and human rights.

In the same way, Mbeki and his supporters, aware of the high stakes, were not prepared to entrust their renaissance vision for the continent to the same discredited 'old guard regimes' without a formal commitment to the guiding principles underlining the vision. Likewise, Africa's defunct existing institutions could not be trusted to carry out the mandate of the NEPAD vision with the required efficiency and urgency. Indeed, the attraction of NEPAD was that it was developed outside of the existing OAU structures.

6.3. The Workings of Africa's G4 Network

NEPAD and its peer review mechanism faced two key challenges. The first was how to change the African political culture so as to enhance democracy, accountability, and good governance in the region—all

---

[37] Meaning the 'old guard regime' with its chronic corruption and overt abuse of human rights.

[38] Sir Nicholas Bayne, *Staying Together: The G8 Summit Confronts the 21st Century*, UK (2005), 9.

pre-requisite for political stability and socio-economic development. The second was forging a genuine partnership between African leaders and the G8 industrialized nations—two very unequal partners. What sort of influence could Africa's G4 exert on the G8 to get them not only to take Africa seriously but also to re-engage with the continent on the basis of an equal partnership with mutual accountability and responsibility? This question is pertinent as the NEPAD pact seeks to redefine and alter power relations aimed to enhance partnerships between African leaders and the wider African society, and between the world's poorest region and the rich and powerful industrialized North.

6.3.1. *Internal Networking and Politics within Africa*[39]

A key goal of NEPAD was to build partnerships within the African continent. However, the exclusive focus on external partnerships with the G8 all but overshadowed this aspect of NEPAD, which has contributed to the view of NEPAD as a top-down neo-liberal initiative to serve the agenda of the West. This view is particularly prevalent among Africa's civil society organizations. NEPAD's external focus and top-down approach are a consequence of the processes that led to its evolution.

As we have seen, NEPAD was a product of three different initiatives, which included Mbeki's African Renaissance Project, Obasanjo's CSSDCA, and Wade's Omega Plan. Each was primarily developed and propagated by the initiating leader with little or no consultation with either their fellow leaders or with African constituencies, with the exception perhaps of the CSSDCA. In spite of some areas of overlap, each of these initiatives had a different agenda. Whereas Obasanjo's CSSDCA was more inward looking, Wade's Omega Plan and Mbeki's MAP were outward looking; the priority was to win the buy-in and support of the industrialized North and their financial institutions. Had NEPAD emerged from an OAU mandate to all 53 leaders of its member states to develop a continental framework to address Africa's development needs, the environment would have been engendered for wider consultations with the citizenry, at the local, national, and continental levels. The end product would likely have been a more bottom-up and truly African process. As it was, the differing

---

[39] Except where indicated, this section borrows heavily from Cilliers (2002).

agendas of the initiatives which informed the NEPAD Plan fractured the leadership.

The tension and the political struggle, which started over the MAP and the Omega Plan, did not dissipate with the integration of the two plans into NEPAD: it carried over to the APRM negotiations. The battle was between South Africa and Nigeria, over the indicators, review areas, ownership, and the location of the APRM. South Africa initially wanted to model the APRM entirely after the UNECA Governance Project, with UNECA coordinating the process. There was even a proposal to house the APRM at UNECA, notwithstanding the fact that Mbeki had earlier objected to a UNECA-based proposal because the institution was outside the framework of the OAU Assembly of Heads of State and Government.[40] Nigeria's Obasanjo was against UNECA, using Mbeki's argument that UNECA is not an African institution.[41] Obasanjo argued that the responsibility should be rightfully that of the AU.

An implementation workshop held by the NEPAD Secretariat in Addis Ababa in August 2002 nonetheless turned to UNECA and the Africa Development Bank (ADB) to develop the indicators and benchmarks for the APRM. Did South Africa's role as one of the chief architects of NEPAD, its dominance in the affairs of the NEPAD Secretariat (including its staff) and in continental politics influence the decision? It is a plausible argument. The decision later influenced another key decision: the harmonization of the NEPAD APRM and the CSSDCA—two peer review mechanisms in competition with each other.[42]

In the early negotiations on NEPAD, it was understood that the issue of political governance—democracy, human rights, and good governance—should be the domain of the OAU/AU, and not that of the NEPAD APRM. To this effect, the OAU was already developing a peer review mechanism, the CSSDCA initiated by Obasanjo discussed above.

Nigeria saw the creation of the NEPAD APRM as a parallel process, in direct competition with the CSSDCA. The differing positions between Nigeria and South Africa generated a great deal of tension and threatened the timely implementation of the APRM. The situation was further complicated by the expectations of Africa's development partners, who saw political review as a crucial aspect of the new partnership pact

---

[40] Cilliers (2002).
[41] Ibid.   [42] Ibid.

between the G8 countries and African leaders towards a common commitment to democracy and political governance.

To move the agenda forward, a compromise was made to harmonize the two peer review mechanisms in a manner that would appease Nigeria and South Africa, while also taking into consideration donor sensitivities. A few days before the 5th NEPAD HSGIC meeting in Abuja in 2002, South African Deputy Foreign Minister, Aziz Pahad, announced that the APRM would be limited to economic and corporate governance, with UNECA handling economic governance issues and the ADB the corporate issues.[43] The AU would be responsible for the political review[44] through its structures, some yet to be developed.

The reaction among Africa's development partners, as well as the African media and civil society, was strong opposition. The restructuring of the OAU into the AU has not dispelled the old distrust of the organization as inadequate and ineffective in handling the governance woes of the continent. Donors, African media, and CSOs alike had expected democracy and political governance to be an important review area of the APRM. However, in the words of Pahad, the final compromise, while not what the donors had hoped for, was 'inevitable and politically necessary'.[45]

Following the Abuja Summit, one can only assume that there must have been a great deal of lobbying behind the scenes and pressure on the proponents of NEPAD to make democracy and political governance a review area of the APRM. Democracy and political governance is presently one of the four[46] review areas of the APRM. Without democracy and political governance as a central part of the NEPAD APRM, Africa's new partnership with the industrialized North would have been compromised.

NEPAD and its APRM are based on the principles of democracy, human rights, and good governance. Yet the architects of NEPAD, Africa's G4, have not themselves followed these principles. The top-down approach and lack of consultations in the development of NEPAD and its APRM went against the principle of African ownership. It is difficult to own a process on which one was not consulted.

This was an unfortunate missed opportunity to have conveyed the crucial message that NEPAD is the new way to do business in Africa.

---

[43] Banking and financial standards.   [44] Democracy and governance issues.
[45] Cilliers (2002, 64).
[46] The review areas are (i) democracy and political governance; (ii) economic governance and management; (iii) corporate governance; and (iv) socio-economic development.

By consulting and effectively engaging the wider African leadership and population, Africa's G4 would have set an important example by their own actions, thereby rebuilding trust in African leadership and institutions. As it was, the limited popular participation and ownership in the development of NEPAD not only undermined the ownership principle but also conveyed the message that where democracy and good governance are concerned, it is business as usual—reaffirming the generally held view that African leaders cannot be trusted.

One should not assume, however, that broad consultations by Africa's G4 would have resulted in a general acceptance of NEPAD and the APRM. Regardless of the consultation process, NEPAD would still have had its critics and sceptics. However, a meeting of the minds in advance is not a necessary condition for successful partnership. Hence the critics and cynics of NEPAD do not necessarily have to agree initially with its proponents. All the same, making the sceptics part of the process from the start would have encouraged ownership, promoted learning, and left the door open for later engagement.

The above arguments may seem to imply that the efforts of Africa's G4 to transform the African political landscape through NEPAD and the APRM have been negligible. While this may be largely the case, a view of NEPAD and its APRM as a work in progress paints a slightly different picture. In this regard, it is best to look at the processes that have been unleashed from various developments (including NEPAD and the APRM), which are currently taking shape across the African continent.

There is a growing awareness of, and demand for, democratic processes, human rights, and political governance across the continent. Even the tension among the architects of NEPAD should be seen as a call for more democratic approaches in decisions pertaining to the continent. For example, Wade's initial rejection of the MAP programme as not representing the collective voice of Africa is an exercise of his democratic right to question and provide an alternative view. The same is also true of Obasanjo's opposition to the role of UNECA, and his support (albeit also driven by self-interest) for the CSSDCA and the legitimacy of the AU in the process. These incidents should also be seen as African leaders holding each other accountable by questioning their respective decisions and presenting alternative views.

Moreover, there are the growing voices in Africa's civil society organizations, the African media, and the African diaspora that are increasingly calling for more transparency and accountability from African leaders.

When and where necessary, the separate and collective voices of these groups have campaigned effectively against the decisions and actions of African leaders deemed problematic and/or not to be in the interests of the continent. For example, in Uganda, there is a network of parliamentarians demanding to veto external loans deemed not to be in the interests of the country and its people. In Sierra Leone in 2004, the country was brought to a standstill by a massive national strike organized by the Sierra Leone National Union[47] to force the government to provide them with a copy of the country's draft Poverty Reduction Strategy Paper, in whose preparation the Union was not invited to participate.

Africa's G4 may have been negligent in respecting the democratic and political rights of the continent's citizenry. Despite this, the winds of change blowing across the continent are whispering songs of democratic processes into the ears of Africans urging them to exercise their political and human rights to demand more accountability from their leaders including Africa's G4.

6.3.2. The Impact of NEPAD on the G8

A second way to measure the impact of Africa's G4 on Africa's partnership with the G8 is to assess the progress on the implementation of the G8 Africa Action Plan. The G8 Africa Action Plan (AAP) is the G8's response to the NEPAD partnership compact between African leaders and their bilateral and multilateral partners.[48] It was developed by the G8 at its Summit in Genoa, Italy in 2001 upon the presentation of the New African Initiative (NAI).

The Plan gives explicit support to the NEPAD strategy[49] and welcomes the commitment of African leaders to focus on good governance and human rights as the necessary pre-conditions for the development of the continent.[50] The Plan further identifies economic growth and economic governance as the 'engine for poverty reduction'.[51] In short, the Plan spells out the terms of Africa's new compact with its bilateral and multilateral partners. The AAP groups G8 commitments in eight areas—two political (peace and security, and governance), and six socio-economic

---

[47] The umbrella organization of all trade unions.   [48] Hope (2005); Landsberg (2003).

[49] The G8 Plan support of the NEPAD strategy was also endorsed by the international community through UN Resolution 57/7 of 2002, resulting in the formation of the Africa Partnership Forum (NEPAD Secretariat, 2005).

[50] Hope (2005); NEPAD Secretariat, *Proposals for Accelerating the Implementation of Nepad in Partnership with the G8 and the International Community* (Johannesburg, South Africa, 2005).

(trade and investments, debt relief, knowledge, health, agriculture, and water resources).

AFRICA'S 'MARSHALL PLAN'?

The Africa Action Plan is so central in the NEPAD pact with the G8 countries that many have called it Africa's 'Marshall Plan'. However, this analogy is misplaced. A crucial difference between the NEPAD and the Marshall Plan is the power relations between donor(s) and beneficiaries. No one would argue that following the end of the Second World War, the USA was in a much stronger position of influence than Western Europe, which had been weakened by the devastating impact of the war. However, the power relations between the USA and Western Europe were relatively more balanced compared to those between Africa and the G8 countries. Africa's relationship with its Western 'partners' has historically been asymmetrical, with Africa at a disadvantage. In a non-binding pact, power relations are crucial. They determine whether or not the parties in a compact honour their commitments, and how effectively they honour them.

The nature of development assistance provided by the Marshall Plan and that promised by the G8 AAP is another crucial difference between the two plans. The Marshall Plan was an agreement between 16 Western European countries and one donor, the USA. The Marshall Plan funds were not only guaranteed but also offered collectively as grants and sustained over several years. The predictability of the Marshall Plan funds was crucial to its success. In fact, it was the ineffectiveness of the 'piecemeal' loans provided by the USA (and Canada) to war-torn Europe from 1945 to 1947 that prompted the development of the Marshall Plan.[52] In the case of the G8 AAP, there are potentially 53 countries with diverse needs and priorities asking for aid from 8 Western countries with differing agendas, priorities, and programmes. The financing promised in the G8 AAP is by no means guaranteed; it is highly complex and uncoordinated.

The AAP also does not address some of NEPAD's key priorities. For example, the Plan does not support NEPAD's proposal for infrastructure and a more liberal debt relief. The AAP's response to trade access is also weaker than what the NEPAD Plan calls for. Bayne writes that the USA was prepared to suffer some economic disadvantage to ensure Europe's economic revival and the achievement of the Marshall Plan's political objectives. The G8 countries, on the other hand, appear not to be willing

---

[51] G8 Summit in Hope (2005).   [52] Bayne (2005, 3).

to make such sacrifices for African countries, as illustrated by the foot-dragging of some of its member states in removing agricultural subsidies.

The African leaders had hoped the G8 would see NEPAD as a serious demonstration of their commitment to enhance democracy, human rights, and good governance in the continent, and respond likewise with a concrete commitment on the part of the industrialized nations to help relieve the continent of its debt, enhance its flow of ODA, increase its market access and help build its capacity.[53]

The inequality of the partnership between the G8 and NEPAD countries became evident early on upon the presentation and adoption of the G8 Africa Plan of Action at the Kananaskis Summit in 2002 by Africa's G4. The G4 had gone to Kananaskis hoping that the development of the AAP and the implementation of the APRM would indicate a commitment on their part, and that the G8 would react accordingly with a commitment to the principle of mutual responsibility and accountability.[54] The outcome was largely disappointing for Africa's G4. What they got were announcements by the USA, Canada, and Britain of increased aid and trade access for Africa. However, these were uncoordinated and complex national initiatives.[55] The G8 countries were particularly non-committal on debt relief, market access, infrastructure development, and ODA reforms. The issue of mutual accountability through peer review mechanisms—which would have concretized the partnership and ensured that both parties would live up to the commitments made under the NEPAD pact and the G8 AAP—was never even discussed.[56]

Nonetheless, following Kananaskis in 2002, the G8 countries reaffirmed their commitment to the G8 AAP on several occasions.[57] At the G8 Summit in Evian in 2003, the first report on the implementation of the Plan was presented, and again there was an agreement to 'strengthen the partnership between Africa and the developed world'.[58]

In spite of the above reaffirmations to support the NEPAD process and the G8 AAP, a big gulf remains between 'promise and delivery'.[59] The year 2005 was seen as the pivotal year for meeting the MDGs, particularly in

[53] Hope (2005); Landsberg (2003).   [54] Landsberg (2003).
[55] Bayne (2005).   [56] Landsberg (2003).
[57] For example, in February 2003 following the G7 finance ministers and central bank governors, a press release stated, 'consistent with the G-8 Africa Action Plan, we are ready to provide substantial support to African countries that implement [the] New Partnership for Africa's Development (NEPAD) principles and are committed to improving governance and demonstrate solid policy performance'. Also, in a working paper on aid effectiveness issued by the same finance ministers and central bank governors, the support to NEPAD was again re-stated: 'with respect to Africa, we renew our support to the NEPAD process'. Government of Canada, 2003 in Hope (2005, 301).

Africa, and therefore many assessments were conducted during that year on the progress made thus far on the implementation of the G8 AAP—which was thought to be critical, if Africa is to meet the MDGs and achieve sustainable development. The general consensus from sources ranging from the UN Millennium Project to the Commission for Africa is that some progress has been made, mostly on the part of African leaders. But the continent has yet to access the bulk of the resources promised in the G8 AAP by the G8 countries to finance the MDGs.[60]

COOPERATION WITH THE CFA

The collaboration between NEPAD and the Commission for Africa (CFA) is illustrative of an effective partnership based on mutual accountability. Although the relationship started on shaky ground, the CFA invested the necessary effort to effectively engage NEPAD in a genuine partnership of mutual accountability for the outcome. Moreover, the CFA also conducted five sub-regional consultative workshops with a cross-section of key African stakeholders. The cooperation with NEPAD and the continental consultations resulted in a CFA report that better reflected Africa's development realities and priorities. As a result, the report was welcomed and endorsed widely across the continent and in the diaspora. Furthermore, the recommendations made by the CFA Report reflect the NEPAD priorities better than the G8 AAP. While, like the G8 AAP, the recommendations call for good governance, development of capacity, investment in human capital, and peace and security, unlike the G8 AAP, the CFA Report also recommends support for infrastructure as 'a priority in the future', the total removal of agricultural subsidies and trade barriers, and 100 per cent of debt cancellation for African countries that need it.

The close relationship of the collaboration—NEPAD working directly, and one on one with the CFA—also contributed to the positive outcome of the process. There were numerous exchanges between the two Secretariats including telephone calls, email messages, and visits. Interestingly, the internal politics and differing agendas of the G8 countries necessitated a visit by a senior official of the German Government a day or two following a visit by senior CFA officials to the NEPAD Secretariat. The purpose of the visit by the German official was to warn the Secretariat that the UK does not have the authority to speak or act on behalf of the G8 countries; therefore there is no guarantee that the

[58] NEPAD Secretariat (2005).   [59] Landsberg (2003).   [60] NEPAD Secretariat (2005).

recommendations of the CFA will be endorsed by the G8 at the 2005 Summit.

OBSTACLES TO AAP IMPLEMENTATION

According to the NEPAD Secretariat, one of the key obstacles to the implementation of the G8 AAP 'has been the lack of concrete development strategies and action plans, sufficiently quantified and detailed'.[61] The Secretariat added that the development of the 'AU/NEPAD sectoral strategies and the Report of the Commission for Africa have bridged this gap'.[62]

From a purely economic standpoint, the G8 countries stand to gain or lose very little whether or not they honour the NEPAD compact and the G8 AAP. However, the political aim of preventing those African countries who meet the grade from falling into anarchy and becoming havens for terrorists' recruitment and activities has led to a selective implementation of the Plan. The only two components of the G8 AAP where significant progress has been made (relative to funding and support) are good governance and peace and security.[63] In this respect, Africa is seen as more of a threat to international security than a serious development or trading partner.

The slow progress in the delivery of the resources promised in the G8 AAP illustrates a limitation on the part of Africa's G4 to enforce the compact with their rich and powerful G8 partners. To put it bluntly, African leaders simply lack the leverage necessary to hold their industrialized partners accountable and make them deliver on their commitments. Moreover, the G4's largely weak position leaves them with few options to counter the lack of delivery by their northern partners with punitive measures, while the G8 has the option of suspending development aid as a punitive weapon. In this regard, the NEPAD strategy could be seen as more a unilateral 'pledge' to the G8 countries than a contract with them. For example, the NEPAD pact calls for mutual accountability and while the African leaders want a mutual monitoring mechanism, the G8 countries have simply chosen to ignore the issue while demanding that African leaders be more accountable.

For NEPAD to have been a genuine partnership, what was needed was 'symmetrical accountability' which would have required the conditions

---

[61] NEPAD Secretariat, 1.   [62] Ibid. 1.

[63] Henning Melber, 'South Africa and NEPAD: "Talking local, acting global" and/or "talking global, acting local"', *Looking at South Africa Ten Years on International Conference*, University of London, 10–12 September 2004.

applying to Africa's industrialized partners to be clearly spelled out—for example, the size and composition of aid flows, the pace and sequencing of trade liberalization and the flow of debt relief.[64] This form of symmetrical accountability should have been an integral part of the NEPAD compact and the G8 AAP given the unequal power relations upon which the compact is based. The value-added likely would have been the timely implementation of the G8 Africa Action Plan.

The slow delivery on the G8 commitments in the Africa Action Plan does not signify a complete failure on the part of Africa's G4; if anything, the mere existence of the Action Plan should be seen as an accomplishment. But even more importantly, Africa's G4 accomplished a significant task in putting and keeping Africa on the agenda of the G8 countries since 2000. Following the 11 September terrorist attacks against the USA and the resulting war on terrorism, Africa and its needs were on the verge of being relegated into the abyss of the developed world's priorities. Thanks in large part to President Mbeki's vision of an African renaissance and NEPAD, the isolation and marginalization which would have been Africa's fate in a post-9/11 world was averted with remarkable urgency, and the continent went from the margins of global affairs to its centre.[65]

6.4. Conclusions

The collective weight of Africa's G4 is sufficient to change the African political landscape and Africa's international affairs. However, the group lacked transparency and accountability in the processes leading to the development of the NEPAD Plan. This engendered an atmosphere of distrust and suspicion, which led to the alienation of the continental force the G4 needs to validate and legitimize it as the representative voice of Africa within the continent and the world at large.

The exclusive focus on the G8 countries cost Africa's G4 the opportunity to rebuild trust between the African leadership and the African

---

[64] Maxwell and Christiansen (2002, 480).

[65] Africa has been on the agenda of every G8 Summit since 2001, culminating in the unprecedented global focus on the continent in 2005. The continent was the key focus of two of the year's most significant reports, the Millennium Project Report and the UK Commission for Africa Report. In addition, Africa was also the priority of the UK concurrent presidencies of the G8 and the European Union, and a major focus of the UN Summit on the half-term review of the Millennium Development Goals.

people. The exclusion of the wider African society from the NEPAD process has also led to a sense of betrayal in the collective mind of the continent.

In addition to building international partnerships, Africa's G4 also needs to focus on building strong partnerships within the continent, with an aim to strengthen public–private collaborations. They can begin by listening to and addressing the increasing voices of dissent in the continent, particularly those from within civil society and the private sector. Africa's G4 should see these dissenting voices as less of a threat and more as part of the success of NEPAD. It is the principles underlying NEPAD which have unleashed these voices, and they can no longer be silent or ignored.[66] Above all, intra-partnerships are critical for mobilizing internal resources, which in the long run are more sustainable than external aid.

Furthermore, Africa's G4 should use its influence to encourage cohesion and enhanced cooperation among Pan-African institutions. A starting point should be the integration of NEPAD into the AU Commission. The sustained tension between NEPAD and the AU over the issue does not engender confidence within the continent and in its northern partners, and has the effect of weakening our position that we are ready to take the lead in our own development. For how can we expect the West to trust African leadership with billions of their aid money (as they are being asked to do), when it appears the same leadership cannot manage their own housekeeping?

NEPAD was a political necessity at the time of its creation. The Plan and its proponents have accomplished the incredible feat of keeping Africa alive in a post-9/11 environment. However, it is time for NEPAD to integrate into the AU Commission to avoid the existence of parallel structures competing for limited resources. Africa's G4 needs to engage the rest of the AU leadership in a continental dialogue to determine an effective role for NEPAD as Africa's socio-economic framework in the twenty-first century, perhaps with a focus on intra-partnerships and regional integration, and strengthening external partnerships with the industrialized nations and south–south collaboration.

Africa's G4 also needs to use its collective influence (with the support of the entire AU membership) to hold the G8 accountable for the delivery of commitments made in the Africa Action Plan. It is time to shift from affirmations to implementation. Africa's G4 needs to lobby effectively

---

[66] Jonathan Katzenellenbogen, 'NEPAD vision a victim of African realpolitik', *Business Day 1st Edition* (Johannesburg, South Africa, 2002).

for mutual accountability and mutual monitoring mechanisms to assess progress on the implementation of the G8 Africa Action Plan. Africa's G4 should also call for the coordination of the G8 Africa Action Plan with recommendations of the report of the Commission for Africa, among others.

7

The Heavily Indebted Poor Countries' Finance Ministers' Network

Matthew Martin

7.1. Introduction

The Heavily Indebted Poor Countries' (HIPCs') Finance Ministers' Network was established in 1999 as a response by Finance Ministers of the HIPCs to the creation of the HIPC Debt Relief Initiative in 1996. It stemmed from the actions of a wider technical capacity-building programme (the HIPC Debt Strategy and Analysis Capacity Building Programme) in which they had come to have a considerable degree of trust since its establishment in 1997. Their growing dissatisfaction with the construction and progress of the original HIPC Initiative led them to request the creation of a forum where they could have frank discussions among themselves (and sometimes with representatives of like-minded donors and the Bretton Woods Institutions, or BWIs) about prospects for debt relief. Over time, the network also became a forum for discussing poverty reduction strategies, new development financing prospects, and their capacity-building needs, and its membership has grown from 16 to 34 countries.

The network has fostered learning among HIPC Finance Ministers and their officials, by allowing them to exchange information and views on the progress of their debt relief, poverty reduction, and new financing. It has also served as a mechanism for HIPC Finance Ministers better to exercise voice in the international system, to access enhanced debt relief and better quality new financing, and to decide autonomously their collective positions on international debt and development financing issues.

The HIPC Finance Ministers' Network did not have any formal organizational authority to arbitrate and resolve disputes, nor any hierarchy for decision-making. Nevertheless, the network has proven remarkably successful in leveraging the influence of the smallest and poorest heavily indebted countries in global institutions and with the wider international community, as well as fostering learning and cooperation among HIPCs.

The rest of this chapter is structured as follows: the first section examines the origins and structure (membership, participation, means of contact, and institutional support) of the HIPC Finance Ministers' Network (FMN); the second section analyses the functioning of the FMN (activism of members, tensions and splits, cooperation and sanctions, and competition with other networks); and the final section examines the impact of the network (its successes and limitations in playing different network functions and the preconditions for its effectiveness) and presents concluding lessons.

7.2. The Emergence of the HIPC Finance Ministers Network

The HIPC FMN emerged in June 1999 as a result of a suggestion from senior HIPC country debt management officials. During the 1980s and 1990s, many of the poorest countries had become 'heavily indebted', especially to multilateral organizations such as the IMF and World Bank, and were clearly not in a position to continue paying these debts. As a result, creditors gradually became more flexible in providing more space for debt relief, culminating in 1996 in the establishment of the 'Heavily Indebted Countries' Debt Relief Initiative', popularly known as the HIPC Initiative. One major innovation of this initiative was that the amount and form of debt relief would be based on the results of a 'tripartite' analysis of whether the debt was affordable ('sustainable'). The analysis would be conducted by the country government, as well as the Bretton Woods Institutions. Previous debt relief initiatives had based relief on the opinions of and political compromises among creditors, informed by some limited analysis by the IMF.[1]

[1] For more details on the HIPC Initiative and the evolution of debt relief initiatives for the poorest countries as well as discussion of debt sustainability issues, see the various publications and papers available on www.hipc-cbp.org.

During 1993–96, various like-minded donors and UN agencies had been working with the poorest countries to assist them in expressing their own views about their needs for debt relief, and had listened to these views by designing innovative systems to provide relief on multilateral debt, beginning with Uganda's 'Multilateral Debt Fund' which has often been described as a country-specific precursor of the HIPC Initiative. Once the HIPC Initiative opened the door to listening more specifically to the views of the HIPC countries, the same donors realized that there was a dramatic lack of capacity within these countries to express their views on their own debt relief needs.

As a result, these donors[2] funded from 1997 a programme (the HIPC Debt Strategy and Analysis Capacity-Building Programme, or CBP) to provide capacity-building support to HIPCs for expressing their debt relief needs and negotiating them with the international community. It achieved this through institutional support to reform structures, laws, and personnel procedures through inter-regional, regional, and national training workshops and through information products such as publications, newsletters, and a website.[3]

HIPC officials suggested in 1998 that the HIPC CBP should extend its mandate to bring Finance Ministers and their senior officials together on a regular basis to advocate greater and more reliable debt relief, and to exchange views with Development Ministers from the funding donors of the programme. Donors agreed to this idea, on the basis that sensitizing HIPC Ministers to the continuing need for capacity-building and demonstrating to them through the process of preparatory briefing for such meetings the capacities which their own staff had already developed with HIPC CBP assistance, would reinforce country commitment to developing and implementing their own debt strategies rather than depending on external technical assistance.

However, it is important to realize that donors and international organizations played no role whatsoever in the genesis of the network (apart from donors agreeing to fund its meetings). Its creation was entirely driven by demand from the HIPC Ministers themselves (and their senior officials), based on their perception of a double institutional gap. The first gap was the absence of a forum where HIPC Ministers could exchange information with their peers on how to respond to ideas Bretton Woods

---

[2] Austria, Denmark, Sweden, Switzerland, and the UK—who were joined in 2002 by Canada and Ireland.

[3] For more details on the work of the HIPC CBP, see www.hipc-cbp.org.

institution about their debt relief needs and to creditor proposals for debt relief in order to strengthen their hand in negotiations. The second gap was the absence of a forum in which they could agree on common positions relating to international advocacy on how the HIPC Initiative should function.

These gaps reflected the fact that other forums for such discussion were either dominated by non-HIPCs (e.g. the Group of 24/Latin American Caucus Meetings of the BWIs), held jointly with donors (e.g. the Commonwealth and Franc Zone meetings), or focused on much wider issues (e.g. African Union, UNECA Ministerial Meetings, and African/Latin American Caucus meetings of the BWIs). There was also a perception that the formal speechmaking and communiqué-negotiating nature of some of these meetings was a barrier to effective information exchange and advocacy. As a result, even though many of these institutions conducted very high-quality analysis of debt relief and HIPC issues, they were not perceived by HIPCs as fully expressing their voice. The gaps also reflected the lack of 'voice' (in terms of voting power or representation) of HIPCs in the Bretton Woods Institutions themselves, which was essentially limited to the two African Executive Directors in each institution, who received only occasional support from Latin American Executive Directors (whose constituencies were much wider, containing many non-HIPC members, making them less able to express a 'HIPC voice'). Finally, the gaps reflected the unbalanced structure of debt relief negotiations, notably in the Paris Club of OECD creditor governments, in which creditors agreed common positions but debtors were treated separately and on a case-by-case basis.[4]

In addition, it is vital to recognize that, although the network facilitated discussion between HIPC Ministers and donors/BWIs, at no stage were donors or BWI representatives allowed to determine the agenda or conclusions of the meetings. At one point in 2005, a donor attempted to influence the agenda of the discussions in advance, but the secretariat, after consultation with the President of the HIPC Network, reiterated to the donor concerned that the agenda and conclusions of the meetings were entirely a matter for the HIPC Finance Ministers. Such independence guaranteed a very high level of ownership by HIPC Governments, which could rely on the network to express their views accurately and without interference from others.

---

[4] For more details on the functioning of the Paris Club, see the publication available on www.hipc-cbp.org.

The first meeting of the network was held in Copenhagen in December 1999. Over time, the HIPC Ministers asked that the network expand the subjects covered in order to allow HIPCs to advocate their positions on a wider range of issues related to debt relief, notably poverty reduction strategies, the Millennium Development Goals, and new development financing. It also provided a forum for exchanging information on best practices in debt management and related capacity-building. Finally, for a few of the meetings and on a pilot basis, it provided a forum for the exchange of views with the Bretton Woods Institutions and civil society.

7.2.1. Membership

The members of the network were initially 18 HIPCs, which had committed themselves to designing their own debt management and debt relief strategies.[5] It expanded over time, reaching 34 countries by 2005.[6]

The membership covered almost all of the countries listed as Heavily Indebted Poor Countries and qualifying for HIPC debt relief, apart from Liberia, Myanmar, and Somalia, which did not have internationally recognized governments. Other HIPC countries, which did not benefit from HIPC debt relief, did not participate (Kenya, Lao PDR, Vietnam, and Yemen). Only one HIPC country receiving HIPC relief (Madagascar) decided not to participate, partly due to political instability.

From 2003, participation at the Ministers' dinners during the IMF and World Bank Annual Meetings was reduced for cost reasons to five Ministers, one representing each of the regions into which Ministers are grouped (Eastern and Southern Africa, Anglophone West Africa, the CFA Franc Zone, and Latin America and the Caribbean). These Ministers were selected through a process of discussion by regional institutions with their member states. The selection was partly linked to those chairing the regional executive-level forums run by such organizations; partly to those chairing other international groupings such as the Africa caucuses of the IMF and World Bank meetings, the Annual Meetings themselves, the G24, and the Commonwealth HIPC Ministers' Forum; and partly to the degree of activism, interest, and experience in the issues shown

---

[5] Benin, Bolivia, Burkina Faso, Cameroon, Ghana, Guinea, Guinea-Bissau, Guyana, Malawi, Mali, Mauritania, Mozambique, Nicaragua, Sao Tome, Senegal, Tanzania, Uganda, and Zambia.

[6] Those listed above plus Angola, Burundi, CAR, Chad, Comoros, DR Congo, Republic of Congo, Cote d'Ivoire, Ethiopia, Gambia, Honduras, Niger, Rwanda, Sierra Leone, Sudan, and Togo.

by individual Ministers. Attention was also paid to ensuring wherever possible a linguistic balance among countries whose official languages are English, French, Portuguese, and Spanish.

Participation in the network was limited to Finance Ministers or their representatives because, in virtually all countries, they had the leading role in debt management and debt strategy formulation and execution. However, occasionally (especially in early meetings, or standing in for Ministers of Finance) Governors of Central Banks and Ministers of Planning or Economy participated, where they also played a leading role in debt management and debt strategy in their countries.

Countries were invited and almost always represented at Minister, Deputy Minister, or Permanent Secretary/Secretary of State level. The fact that they continued to be represented at such high levels over a period of seven years was reflective of their commitment to advocacy on these issues and the perceived usefulness of the group. In the beginning, Ministers often insisted on being accompanied by technical officials who briefed them and prepared their interventions, in part due to lack of detailed knowledge of the technical issues. However, over time, many Ministers experienced a learning process after which they no longer required technical support and were happy to come to meetings alone. On the other hand, in a few countries, especially those which were beyond the post-HIPC completion point (and which made the key concerns of the group less relevant), Ministers increasingly deputed representation to lower level officials such as Director-Generals or Directors. Nevertheless, those officials had been fully briefed by Ministers and were able to take positions on behalf of their country.

The network was chaired by two Finance Ministers on a rotating basis, with each co-chairperson generally lasting 18 months in order to provide continuity. However, when new chairpersons were not forthcoming, some chairs remained in office for 24–30 months. The chairmanship rotated across different regions to ensure balanced representation, but the choice of individual Ministers was based on his or her individual willingness, interest, and knowledge, rather than on any formal election process.

External participants in network meetings have varied. Initially, the main annual meetings in the first half of the year were held in donor capitals and therefore attracted very high-level participation by donors (Ministers). During 1999–2001, donor-country Ministers also co-signed the letters covering the declarations made at these meetings to encourage the Bretton Woods Institutions and G8 to respond. However, once the network became recognized as the key forum for expressing HIPC views, donors withdrew from this role. In addition, from 2003, the location of the main meetings was shifted to the HIPCs themselves, reducing considerably the level of donor participation.

7.2.2. Means of Contact

Ministers adopted a two-phase strategy in contacts for networking and advocacy during each calendar year. During the first semester they held a major one- to two- day meeting which produce a declaration, the aim of which was to feed into G8 discussions on debt issues, especially the G8-Africa discussions (linking into other such networks has proved crucial to the network's success). In the second semester, they focused their activities on promoting HIPC views in the discussions at the Annual Meetings of the IMF and the World Bank and holding a dinner to update their communiqué and produce a press release.[7]

Regardless of the level of detail of the declarations, two factors were vital in ensuring the impact of the declarations. First, they struck a good balance between criticism and praise, avoiding either moaning or excessively congratulating the international community, and provided constructive criticism and constantly suggested new ideas for moving forward. Second, they were very precisely and technically worded, rather than making vague declarations or suggesting unclear ideas. This often contrasted with the carefully negotiated, sanitized language of many other official communiqués. It reflected in turn the working style of the Ministerial Meetings—where Ministers were urged to be precise and as technical as possible, and to make positive suggestions for improvement.

At various stages, the Ministers also invited the participation of BWI officials, on the suggestion of senior BWI officials. However, their presence reduced the frankness of the dialogue by HIPC Ministers and turned the discussion into more of a defensive debate. As a result, the network switched more recently to a system of organizing separate meetings between top officials of the BWIs (Deputy Managing Director or Director in the IMF; Managing Director or Vice-President in the World Bank) and the chairs of the network to discuss the Ministerial Declaration. These

---

[7] There were only two important exceptions to this: in 2001 the BWI Annual Meetings were cancelled due to the events of 9/11, and the overall meeting was replaced by a smaller Ministerial Meeting for the Eastern and Southern African region, in Maputo. In 2004, due to funding shortages at the end of phase 3 of the HIPC CBP, no major ministerial meeting was held in the first semester.

meetings were found to produce a much more focused and productive discussion. The chairs then reported back to other Ministers on these discussions at the subsequent meetings.

In addition, Ministers have taken the views of their HIPC colleagues into their other discussions at the IMF/World Bank Annual Meetings. Such transmission has been particularly effective in helping African Ministers to agree their caucus positions at the African Group and express African positions in the IMFC and Development Committee meetings. It has been less effective for LAC Ministers, whose caucus discussions and Committee speeches tend to focus more on issues of interest to larger members, except when HIPCs have been leading members of the constituencies.

Another problem with the network has been that, in spite of efforts from both sides at close coordination, Executive Directors' offices in the BWIs have been so overwhelmed by other work pressure's that it has not been possible to involve them in all meetings. Nevertheless, network chairs have taken the opportunity to visit them and to share the results of the declarations with them to inform their work on the BWI Boards.

Ministers have also disseminated their declarations/communiqués to a wide range of international stakeholders. These include Finance and Development Ministers of the G8, as well as like-minded funding donors, the heads of the Bretton Woods Institutions, heads of UN institutions (including the Secretary-General's office, UNCTAD, UNDP, and UNDESA), the European Union, the Commonwealth Secretariat, and the G24. Dissemination did not produce much of an immediate direct response from the recipients beyond letters of acknowledgement from heads of institutions (apart from some personal letters from the BWI and EU heads in 2000). However, it has generally led to the citing of HIPC declarations in publications by the Comsec, G24, UN and BWIs, including major consideration of their views in the IMF review of the PRGF and PRSP (which invited a HIPC representative to speak on behalf of the network to a conference in Washington), the World Bank OED review of the HIPC Initiative (which held a consultation meeting with HIPCs in London back-to-back with the meeting of March 2002), and a UNDP Policy Paper on debt for the UN system.

Where necessary, the chairs pursued individual lobbying steps on key issues. At the particular stage in 1999–2000 when the Enhanced HIPC Initiative was being formulated, Ministers engaged in more concerted lobbying. They assigned each of six Ministers a role in lobbying a key G8 donor (Senegal–France; Bolivia–USA; Guyana–Canada; Rwanda–UK;

Malawi–Japan; Ethiopia–Italy; Zambia–Germany), and allowed Senegal to coordinate the presentation of their views to the G8 Summit, which was being held in France. This process was highly effective in relation to France and the UK. Ministers did the same thing in 2003 when the G8 began to discuss a new debt relief initiative.

Another key aspect of dissemination has been the discussion of Ministers' views with the press and with wider civil society. Each year since 2000 (apart from 2001 when the Annual Meetings of the IMF and World Bank were cancelled), the Ministers have held a press conference at the IMF–World Bank Annual Meetings.[8] Due to intensive prior work with the press and civil society by CBP partner organizations, this press conference became an event which was highly valued by both press and civil society. It attracted around 60–70 participants (two to three times as many participants as similar press conferences held by the G24 and the African Finance Ministers). These press conferences produced an average of three to four specific articles a year plus news agency reports from AFP, AP, Reuters, and Bloomberg. They also resulted in further interviews with individual Ministers, allowing them to advocate issues relevant to their own countries. According to G8 sources, the timing of such articles (as well as the communiqué)—around 24 hours before the IMFC meetings—has been very important in influencing the G8 discussions.

Perhaps the most effective impact of the network has been via civil society contacts. These were initially established at the press conferences but have been followed up in many ways: CSOs established direct links with individual countries for research and advocacy purposes, invited Ministers to speak at major CSO advocacy events and parliamentary hearings, and published articles by Ministers in CSO publications. All of the major CSOs and coalitions conducting advocacy on debt issues (ActionAid, Christian Aid, Eurodad, Jubilee 2000, Jubilee USA, Oxfam, Save the Children, and Swiss Coalition) have drawn extensively on the views of HIPC Ministers to justify their positions with input from developing-country sources. Given that they have themselves played a key role in debt relief advocacy, their reliance on this source has been crucial to getting HIPC messages across. NGOs have taken up key issues based in part on HIPC Ministers' views, including debt service/revenue ratios, the inclusion of domestic debt in debt-sustainability analysis, and

---

[8] Attendance by Ministers at the press conferences was generally by the chairs of the network. However, quite often, during the BWI Annual Meetings, it was impossible for chairs of the network to attend press conferences due to other meetings requested by the BWIs. As a result, during the dinner, other Ministers were asked to step in.

fending off lawsuits against HIPCs. Oxfam, as part of its 1,000 Lawyers for Development initiative, cooperated closely with the HIPC CBP in mobilizing top-quality pro bono legal assistance for HIPCs against such lawsuits.

Finally, the network has been effective in disseminating the views of HIPC Ministers through a wide range of publications, including studies commissioned from the secretariat organizations of the network, which have been produced by the UNDESA/FFD, UNCTAD/G24, the UNECA, the Commonwealth Secretariat, FONDAD, the Dutch and Swedish governments, the North–South Institute of Canada, the African Economic Research Consortium, and the UK Commission for Africa. These studies have covered the HIPC Initiative, the G8 debt relief initiatives, debt sustainability, domestic debt analysis, aid quality and effectiveness, the role of the IMF in low-income countries, and improving international financing facilities to combat exogenous shocks.

7.2.3. Institutional Support

Institutional support in the form of a secretariat for meetings was initially supplied by Debt Relief International (DRI), a UK-based non-profit organization which was selected by the HIPC CBP donors as the project manager for the HIPC CBP, in conjunction with officials from the host or chair countries of the meetings. These officials acted as rapporteurs, mobilized their Ministers to send out declarations, and handled most aspects of local logistics, while DRI assisted in international flight logistics, financial management, and translation of communiqués.

Over time, some functions of the Secretariat were decentralized to regional capacity-building organizations, owned by the HIPCs themselves. These organizations have taken responsibility for mobilizing the participation of their Ministers in events and briefing them in advance, organizing and chairing events, translating the communiqués into appropriate languages, and for discussions with journalists in different languages.

The network was funded by the seven donors of the HIPC CBP—Austria, Canada, Denmark, Ireland, Sweden, Switzerland, and the UK, on the basis of successive two- to three-year phases of funding. Having access to secure financing was extremely helpful to the functioning of the network, as it allowed forward planning of events.

7.3. The Workings of the HIPC Finance Ministers' Network

The activism of different members varied from meeting to meeting. In part this depended on who was representing each country: those Ministers with more experience, dynamism, and technical knowledge were the most active. It also depended on their countries' stage in the HIPC process, as well as on the level of sustainability of their external and domestic debt and on any problems they were having with new financing. Typically, the most active were governments about to make major policy decisions on debt relief, having problems with their progress in the HIPC Initiative, or undertaking intensive discussions with the BWIs on their financing policies. The open and non-hierarchical structure of the network was essential to allowing those who were most committed to play the most prominent roles, rather than confining them through the use of regional caucuses and automatic rotation of chairs and spokespersons.

Several countries were crucial to the evolution of the network, largely due to the activism of their individual Finance Ministers or officials. Generally, the most active countries correlated with those who self-selected as chairs of the network. The vast majority of the countries were very active in meetings and used the ministerial declarations in international forums. Nevertheless, particular tribute should be paid to Ministers Gabriela Nunez de Reyes of Honduras, Abdoulaye Bio-Tchane of Benin, Gerald Ssendaula of Uganda, Luisa Diogo of Mozambique, Javier Comboni of Bolivia, Lamine Ali Zeine of Niger, and especially Donald Kaberuka of Rwanda, who co-chaired the network for two years.

However, given that the agendas of meetings and the resulting communiqués were decided on the basis of consensus, the role of active countries was most important in chairing meetings and in transmission of the conclusions. In this regard it was vital to have chairs of the network who were fully conversant with both political and technical issues and were therefore able to handle discussions with the press, donor Ministers, and senior BWI officials. A key factor in the successful transmission of conclusions was that leaders of the network emerged on the basis of their personal interest, rather than through a formal nomination process, which might have produced lower-quality transmission.

Another general difference in the level of activism was between more experienced and new Ministers, with more experience generally correlating with more activism. Also, the activism of Ministers was based on the level of capacity among their senior technical officials, who provided them with briefings before and during the meetings. Most Ministers who were interested in debt and aid issues were rapidly integrated into the network and soon began to contribute fully. Apart from technical briefings, their most important source of learning was being told by FMN chairs and the secretariat that they were expected to intervene on precise technical issues rather than make speeches.

One problem with the network has been that the flexibility in terms of participation by countries as chairs and press spokespersons has meant that at times the level of participation was severely disrupted by the last-minute absence of key countries due to urgent other meetings (this reached a peak in 2004 when only one Minister attended the press conference).

Another problem has been security and logistics. Since 2001, the dramatically enhanced security at BWI Annual Meetings has sometimes undermined the participation levels of Ministers, as they had major physical difficulties reaching the locations of dinners or press conferences.

7.3.1. *Tensions and Splits*

There were virtually no tensions and no splits within the network. This reflected the fact that the network was created to exchange information and lobby on a set of issues on which consensus existed among members—that debt relief and new development financing were insufficient, allowing insufficient progress on financing poverty reduction in their countries.

The network's unity also reflected the fact that the agenda and communiqués of Ministers were developed by consensus and allowed the preoccupations of all types of members to be included in the documents, regardless of their stage in the HIPC process. There were clearly different points that members felt more passionately about depending on their own country experiences, their stages in the HIPC process, and their views on new development financing, and so they insisted strongly on the insertion of stronger phrasing on these issues into communiqués. This generated little tension given that there was no cost to other members from these proposals.

There was a remarkable degree of consensus, for example in supporting the UK's proposal for an International Financing Facility, the EU proposals for taxing airline tickets to fund development, and the UK's proposals for additional debt relief by the G8 launched in September 2004.

There were only two issues on which there were divergences:

(1) Debts owed by HIPCs to other HIPCs. This was relatively small compared to total debt owed by HIPCs (less than 5 per cent) but was seen as an embarrassing potential source of tension between poor heavily indebted countries. The creditor HIPCs were sometimes reluctant to have this issue raised in the meetings, but after considerable discussion in one meeting it was agreed that all future communiqués would make the case that HIPCs themselves could not afford to provide relief to other HIPCs and therefore request the donor community for assistance. Unfortunately in most cases donors did not respond to this request (apart from Austria funding cancellation of Uganda's debt to Tanzania, and some inter-HIPC debts being included in IDA commercial debt reduction operations). As a result of this lack of action, some HIPCs almost started suing others (Angola suing Sao Tome, Burundi suing Uganda, Cote d'Ivoire suing Burkina Faso), and meetings of the network as well as other meetings organized by the HIPC CBP played important roles in convincing them to drop such ideas of lawsuits.

(2) The G8 proposals on debt relief agreed at the 2005 G8 Summit. At the time of the dinner at the BWI Annual Meetings the details of the proposals (and whether they would be adopted by the meetings) were still somewhat unclear, and therefore some Ministers were doubtful about endorsing them wholeheartedly. However, by the end of the Ministerial dinner the position was much clearer and Ministers were able to reach a full consensus on issues to raise in the communiqué. This was partly due to a frank discussion between HIPC Ministers, the G8 representatives, and representatives of other like-minded donors on the issues. HIPC Ministers indicated that because the dinner focused on the specific issue of debt, and allowed them to get direct explanations from OECD representatives, they came away from the dinner with a much clearer idea of the strong/weak points of the G8 Initiative than they had received in several days of preparatory meetings organized by other institutions. To this extent the FMN provided a valuable forum for donors to provide information and views—but, as already mentioned above, donors were not at any stage allowed to influence the agenda, dominate the debate (preference was always given in meetings to HIPC speakers) or suggest conclusions.

7.3.2. Cooperation and Sanctions

As already discussed in Section 7.3, cooperation increased over time with more countries becoming involved in the network. On the other hand, some countries tended to downgrade their participation slightly once they had been through the debt relief process.

However, there was never any formal non-cooperation, and therefore no need for sanctions. This may in part have reflected the fact that in particular there was no requirement for any financial contribution by countries and therefore no formal need for sanction for non-payment.

7.3.3. Competition

As already discussed, the HIPC FMN arose from a (correct) perception that no other organization or network was effectively fulfilling the function of allowing all HIPCs to exchange their views on key debt relief issues. The network therefore benefited immensely from the fact that there were no directly competing networks with the same aims and membership. While almost all global developing-country fora have discussed debt issues extensively in recent years, they (e.g. the G24) are dominated by non-HIPCs and therefore do not compete in terms of membership and providing a voice for HIPCs in international discussions. Indeed, one of the factors in the success of the network was that most HIPCs had relatively few other chances to express their voices in international fora.

In 2002, a Commonwealth HIPC Finance Ministers Forum was established. It holds one major annual meeting a year in the first quarter which produces a lengthy communiqué, as well as a brief meeting at the Commonwealth Finance Ministers' Meetings in order to feed into Commonwealth Finance Ministers' declarations just before the IMF and World Bank Annual Meetings. This forum dealt with many similar issues, and provided a valuable function in transmitting HIPC views to G8 members of the Commonwealth—Canada and the UK and via Commonwealth Ministers to the IMF and World Bank. However, it did not really constitute competition in terms of membership because it included only 11 HIPCs (the HIPCs which are members of the Commonwealth) and two G8 members. In addition, it acted in a more formalistic way than the HIPC CBP Ministerial Network, not assisting HIPC Ministers to interact with BWI staff, or holding press conferences at the Annual Meetings, though from 2003 it began to encourage interaction with civil society through the Commonwealth civil society fora.

Nevertheless, it was agreed by all parties in 2004 that Commonwealth HIPC Ministers should not be asked to participate in two major meetings and two smaller meetings on these issues every year. At the initiative of the then chair of the Commonwealth Forum, it was agreed that it would be desirable to merge the two fora in order to reduce demands on HIPC Ministers' time and donor funds. In addition, the HIPC CBP and Commonwealth agreed to involve the Agence Internationale de la Francophonie in funding participation of non-Commonwealth HIPCs. Informal cooperation began with participation of the Commonwealth Secretariat at the Ministerial dinner in October 2004. The first joint Ministerial meeting was then held in Maputo in March 2005. At this time the Commonwealth Secretariat organized a Commonwealth caucus while the HIPC CBP and the AIF organized a non-Commonwealth caucus. These were then finalized in a plenary which brought all views together and a joint press conference. The chair of the Commonwealth Forum, Minister Chang of Mozambique, also participated in the press conference of HIPC Ministers in Washington in September 2005.

7.4. Successes, Limitations, and Prerequisites for Success

This section of the chapter attempts to assess the successes and limitations of the HIPC FMN, first in narrative terms and then by using a more formal structure linked to the potential functions of networks. It then assesses the prerequisites for successes by examining the characteristics of the FMN which led to such prerequisites being met, again through a formal framework analysing the characteristics of networks.

7.4.1. Successes and Limitations

The network has had considerable successes. It has fostered a large amount of learning by HIPC Finance Ministers and their senior officials, both on technical details of how debt relief and new financing are provided, and also through exchanging experiences with one another on best practices in negotiating debt relief, new financing and poverty reduction programmes. The technical quality of discussions among Ministers (and with other actors) improved dramatically over time.

Facilitating learning within the network have been the 'rules of engagement' in meetings, which asked Ministers to avoid formal speeches, thanks, and repetition of points made by earlier speakers, and asked Ministers to focus on very specific additional technical points and issues of concern to their countries. Another important factor has been the existence of parallel capacity-building training measures to enhance the skills of officials who brief Ministers, as well as national sensitization seminars to explain the technical issues to Ministers, and information sharing mechanisms through publications, newsletters, a website, and regular listserves for country debt managers. The existence of such an integrated programme has accelerated the learning immensely.

The existence of the network has allowed HIPCs to decide autonomously (and with credibility given the high numbers of countries participating and their participation at Ministerial level) their collective positions on international debt and new financing issues, without dilution by incorporation into a wide group of countries. It has provided a moderately successful mechanism for HIPC Finance Ministers to increase status, legitimacy, and voice in the international system. Greater legitimacy has been seen notably in influencing the design and implementation of the Enhanced HIPC Initiative (HIPC II), and the design of the long-term debt sustainability analysis framework by the BWIs, though to a much lesser extent in recent G8 debt relief and new financing initiatives. Particular results of this input were the greater focus on ratios relating to budget revenue in the design of HIPC II; the reduction and narrowing of threshold levels for the long-term framework; the equal weight given to ratios relating to revenue and service ratios in the LTDS framework (though not in its application to IDA 14); and the commitment to analyse domestic debt issues and thresholds in more detail (which has yet to materialize). It is of course difficult to isolate this influence from that of many other actors, but the fact that HIPC Ministers' views were cited so widely and that they originated and insisted on certain ideas for long periods—which then came to be taken into account in later initiatives—indicates some considerable impact.

Agenda-setting has also been achieved at times by the HIPC Finance Ministers' Network (though they were not the sole sources for such ideas). A notable example of this was the issue of lawsuits against HIPCs by their creditors, which after much delay is finally bearing fruit in initiatives by Oxfam and the Commonwealth Secretariat.

However, the main influence of the network has been through lobbying G8 members and benefiting from the members' partnerships with key HIPCs, Northern CSOs, multilateral organizations, and the press/publications, because the international system offers few opportunities for small, low-income countries to express their views formally. This lack of interest in the views of small low-income countries has been the main limitation of the network.

On the other hand, the visibility of the FMN, involvement of senior donor officials in its discussions, and the perception that country capacity was growing rapidly, encouraged the Ministers to contribute more funding to activities designed further to build country technical and political capacity via the HIPC CBP (though this effect fell sharply once FMN meetings were moved away from donor capitals).

The network has provided many opportunities for countries to learn from one another about both debt relief and about how to improve the quality of new external financing. There are several examples of this. Benin and Gambia were able to learn from Nicaragua about the need to exclude re-exports from the export denominator of HIPC Initiative debt sustainability ratios, and allowing them to qualify for the Initiative. Many countries were able to learn how to negotiate greater debt relief from non-OECD creditors. HIPCs were strongly dissuaded from suing each other by peer pressure. Countries were able to prepare themselves better for decision and completion points (e.g. in advocating frontloading of debt relief in the early years after decision point, or 'topping up' of debt relief at completion point) and therefore benefit from maximum relief at those points. Countries were able to improve the mobilization of new finance by learning about multi-donor budget support mechanisms, successes by other countries in improving the share of grants, the concessionality of loans, the reduction of conditionalities and the share of budget support in their aid programmes, and then to apply these lessons in producing the same results. Countries were encouraged by their peers to give a higher priority to debt strategy (and wider debt management) capacity-building, to support the creation of new country-owned units for this purpose in the CFA Franc Zone and among the African countries whose official language is Portuguese, to reinforce the mandates of other institutes in this area.

The difficulty—and clear limit to the network's impact—has been influencing donors. In spite of in-country capacity-building assistance, countries have found it very difficult to get donors to change new financing policies and listen at a country level. This has been particularly true where the number of 'like-minded/flexible' donors is very limited, in particular in parts of Francophone Africa.

Table 7.1. Strengths and weaknesses of HIPC FMN

Function	Strengths	Weaknesses
Knowledge production and exchange	• Dissemination of new knowledge and studies conducted by their technicians (or based on their work) to Ministers • Dissemination of Ministers' views back to technicians through workshops • Dissemination of Ministers' positions beyond network (see text—to press, G8, BWIs, etc.) • Very strong information exchange and therefore very precise communiqués	• Insufficient formalization of dissemination structures, therefore relatively little formal feedback from BWIs/G8
Agenda-setting (or expansion?)	• Dissemination of several major points—domestic debt, burden on budget revenue, lawsuits	• Constant battle to get ideas listened to given lack of interest in HIPC voice—required openness in G8 and BWIs, sponsorship by G8
Consensus-building (within or beyond network?)	• Major success in building consensus among HIPCs, with like-minded donors and with NGOs, demonstrated by high level of attendance • Less with G8 and BWIs	
Norm diffusion	• No real norms to adhere to except recognition of need for capacity building and not suing each other, in which achieved considerable success	n/a
Impact on other institutions	• Impact on design of policies by UN, NGOs, G8, BWIs	• Slightly weakened by intermittent nature of formal contact
Policy coordination	• Coordinated policy in lobbying G8 and talking to press	n/a

Table 7.1 below summarizes the successes and limitations of the Finance Ministers' Network supported by the other activities of the HIPC Capacity-Building Programme. It appears to have played a strong role in knowledge production and exchange, to and from both Ministers and their technical staff, as well as beyond the network to other groups and, though it lacked a formal structure which required feedback from the BWIs and G8, it frequently received such feedback and was spontaneously asked for inputs of knowledge by such groups. It also helped to expand and set the agenda for discussions as discussed above, though it was not the sole source of ideas, and it was a constant battle to get its ideas on the table given the frequent lack of interest in HIPC voice. Its biggest success was in building consensus among HIPCs, with moderate success building consensus beyond the FMN, with like-minded donors and NGOs. It was not really intended to work on norms or policy coordination, though it did pass messages to Ministers about the need for capacity-building and cooperation among HIPCs, and facilitate coordinated advocacy by HIPCs. The degree of impact this advocacy had on other institutions is described differently depending on the stakeholder group: HIPC Ministers and NGOs indicate that it had a strong effect, G8 officials and some in the BWIs suggest a moderate effect, and some in the BWIs ascribe only a weak effect.

7.4.2. Characteristics and Pre-Conditions for Effectiveness

What can we learn about the pre-conditions for effectiveness of networks from the experience of the HIPC FMN? The case study suggests several conditions. First, the establishment, agenda, and advocacy conclusions of a network need to be demand-driven, with no pre-determined agenda by the secretariat (which can complicate or divert from the core agenda of members). Second, there needs to be agreement from the start on common interests among members, and in this the HIPC FMN was assisted by the relative homogeneity of HIPCs, which engendered clear commonality of the group interests of HIPCs in improving the effectiveness of debt relief and new development financing. Third, the subject area of the network should not be too broad. It is much easier to produce highly concrete and innovative recommendations in a more specific area, and therefore to enhance the credibility of a network's dialogue with other actors. This was facilitated in the HIPC FMN by a close focus on debt relief and new official financing for the Millennium Development Goals.

Even with this narrow focus, the impact of the network on new financing issues was considerably less than on those related to debt.

The structure of the network has also been important. There should be flexibility in the structure and representation of members in order to allow the network to benefit fully from the different levels of commitment, expertise, and time availability of its different members. In the case of the HIPC FMN, the rotation of the chairmanship when new chairs volunteered, the flexibility to have different representatives as chairs of meetings and participating in press conferences, and to allow different levels of participation by each country, were essential to success in advocacy objectives.

Finally, the demand for the views of the network is an important element to consider, or put differently, the openness of the international community to listen to the network. This requires some pre-conditions from the network itself: in particular that the issues treated in communiqués should be very current and very concretely expressed, focusing on substantive proposals for reform and progress; and that those advocating the network views should either know the technical issues very well themselves, or be thoroughly briefed and prepared for advocacy meetings and press conferences beforehand. In this regard the HIPC FMN has worked relatively well, though the September 2002 meeting was much less successful than the others (see above).

In spite of the relatively successful transmission of advocacy messages, it remains the case that the fundamental dialogue about reform to debt relief initiatives was held more among G8 governments. However, in 1999–2000 during the construction of the Enhanced HIPC Initiative, civil society organizations in the North and the managements of the BWIs were also very prominent. This allowed HIPCs to have voice by liaising more with these different organizations and groupings. This political backdrop subsequently changed again and when the UK government was constructing its debt relief initiative in 2004, the views of HIPCs were taken into account in so far as they had long focused on the liquidity burden of debt service on the budget, and the initiative aimed to reduce this burden. However, in 2004–05, when the G8 was constructing its new debt relief initiatives, the discussions were confined largely to a compromise among the G8 itself, and therefore HIPCs had much less input into the final design of the initiative.

Table 7.2 summarizes the prerequisites for effectiveness. The FMN began as only partially inclusive, relatively effective, and partly transparent.

Table 7.2. The effectiveness of the HIPC FMN

Characteristic/ prerequisite	Characteristics and prerequisites for effectiveness	
	Strengths	Weaknesses/trade-offs
Inclusiveness	• Initially only some HIPCs represented • Later all HIPCs participating in HIPC Initiative represented	• Less possibility to include other stakeholders (donors and BWIs) without risk of reducing HIPC frankness • Not serious problem because they have plenty of other fora, and because HIPCs themselves decided on separate BWI talks
Efficiency	• Generally well focused, quick in producing background documents, communiqués, press conferences • Always rapid but not initially fully effective	• Initial problems with effectiveness of G8 contacts, lack of interest by BWIs, lack of knowledge of FMN by press

Informality	• Informal to right degree: not dependent on formal institutions/constraints
	• But sufficiently formal in own procedures to be credible
		• Varied with dynamism of Presidents of FMN
		• Perhaps some reduction of credibility with BWIs but:
		  o overcome by activism of Ministers
		  o a trade-off worth making for ownership

Transparency	• Principle of complete transparency from start, but not implemented due to resource constraints • Currently all on web, disseminated through listserves, newsletter, letters to stakeholders	None
Accountability	• Is full accountability of communiqué—(consensus) • Is accountability to technical level • Is verbal report back by presidents on meetings with BWIs but not formalized • Held accountable by review and update of previous communiqué	None
Overall average		

Over time it became entirely inclusive and transparent and more effective, and developed informal accountability mechanisms.

7.4.3. Lessons Learned

The HIPC Finance Ministers' Network has had a considerable input into recent international decisions on debt relief and new development financing, as well as important practical effects in the delivery of debt relief and new financing to individual countries. In this regard it has been considerably more effective than some other more formal structures, which have existed for many more years. Key attributes of the network which have contributed to its success include: it has been demand-driven; its members have had clear common interests; the network has had a specific focus; the structure of and membership in the network has been flexible; and a multiplicity of tools and fora have been used to foster learning and advocacy.

However, the network has not achieved as much as might have been hoped. In the early stages of the network this was to some extent due to a low level of experience in such aspects as advocacy and press/NGO relations and the limited mandate of the network as defined by the funding donors, but these problems were fairly rapidly resolved.

More recently, the impact of the network has been limited principally by the limited willingness of the international system to listen to HIPC views. Though cooperation among HIPCs has been strong, the international system is established in such a way as largely to ignore these views unless 'sponsors' for HIPCs exist among the G8, multilateral organizations or Northern CSOs.

Finally, there are several lessons which might be drawn for future improvements to the network. Most important, the network needs to fit even more closely with other channels for advocacy to the G8 and the BWIs. This will mean working even more closely with BWI EDs offices, the Africa Partnership Forum, and the Commonwealth Secretariat/Agence Internationale de la Francophonie. More systematic and regular cooperation with NGO networks needs to be created, going beyond discussions at the BWI Annual Meetings to regular contacts elsewhere. The subject focus of the network needs to be rethought to focus on maintaining debt sustainability after debt relief through high-quality new financing, as well as more attention to institutional and legal reforms by HIPCs themselves in order to promote high-quality debt management. There could be slightly less flexibility for members in the sense of firmer advance commitments to chair meetings, organize lobbying processes, and address the press. And finally, Secretariat support needs to be made more sustainable by fuller decentralization to regional organizations run by HIPCs themselves so that costs to donors are reduced.

Commentary by Gerald Helleiner

Emeritus Professor, University of Toronto

The HIPC Finance Ministers' Network (HIPC FMN) illustrates both the potential strengths and some of the major problems of inter-governmental networking among the relatively weak. There can be little doubt that this essentially demand-driven, focused, and flexibly structured network has been very helpful to many, even most, of its participants. Among its other accomplishments, it has successfully strengthened the voice of previously marginalized and virtually unheard governmental actors on the global financial stage.

Its most important contribution has probably been the information exchange, learning, and capacity building that it has fostered among HIPC Finance Ministers and financial policymakers. While a few of the governments and Finance Ministries of the HIPCs had previously been quite well served by their financial analysts and advisers, most to this day remain uniquely weak among the world's financial decision-makers. It has been no small achievement to develop a direct mutual support system that is largely unfiltered by and independent of aid donors, international institutions, other networks, or private sources of finance, each of which have other agendas to pursue. If Matthew Martin's description of network meetings is to be believed, there has been remarkable success in curbing the delivery of setpiece speeches—usually the particular bane of meetings in which participants are inexperienced or weakly prepared—and in generating productive technical discussion of complex policy issues. In consequence of the existence of this network, the relevant policies both of the HIPCs as a group and of its individual members have undoubtedly been more ably developed, expressed, and implemented. Indeed, at the group level there were no expressions of common HIPC positions prior to the development of the network!

Improved information, learning and capacity building and the more informed policies—domestic as well as international—that are their probable result are certainly all desirable in themselves. Perhaps we should content ourselves with such successes as these and inquire no further. And yet, how can one not also address the degree to which this network and the common policy approaches to which it has contributed have actually impacted upon 'high' international policies and specific donor or creditor practices? What is the ultimate international product of all of this relatively effective networking within the HIPC financial policymaking community? Improved and strengthened 'voice' in the international arena can be of little avail if traditional power relationships and/or inappropriate bureaucratic structures continue to determine outcomes which take little account of it. Martin is, of course, fully aware of this problem. He calls particular attention to the fact that it is difficult to find those who will listen. He recognizes that negotiations among major powers, in which HIPCs were not involved, were what finally determined the precise character of HIPC debt relief. He also notes that success in altering the nature of new financing remains, in some individual HIPC cases, quite limited. The collective strength of all of the HIPCs, speaking now more frequently with one voice, however significant that voice may seem to Northern NGOs, remains too little to make much of an impact upon G8 diplomacy. Nor have the HIPC FMN's statements and declarations been able to do much to bolster African or other friendly Executive Directors' still very limited influence upon IMF and Bank policies. These problems impose tight limits upon what is possible for any such cooperative endeavour to achieve. The HIPC Finance Ministers' Network by itself will, it seems, continue to have quite limited influence upon overall debt relief and financing policies or practices.

But that is not necessarily the end of the matter. There are at least two elements of hope for greater influence for the HIPC Ministers upon global approaches to debt and development finance. The most immediate and practical relates to the potential for improvements in financing modalities at the level of individual HIPCs (and individual donors or groups of donors). Unanimity among donors is not required in order for progress to be achieved toward the kinds of reforms in approaches to development finance that the HIPC network pushes. There is nothing to prevent individual aid donors, or groups of them, from responding sympathetically and productively to the representations of individual HIPC Finance Ministers and Governments. HIPC Finance Ministers, now better informed—through their network—of others' practices and precedents (and donor declarations of intent) are in a much stronger position to argue for and negotiate improved terms and relationships with development financiers than ever before. More attractive modes of aid financing—grants rather than loans, budget support rather than project finance, less stringent and inappropriate conditionality, etc.—and mechanisms that more adequately support local ownership of programmes are possible; and there is plenty of both supportive donor rhetoric and practical precedent for them. There remains a wide gap between expressions of general donor intent and the realities of their country-level practice. Individual HIPCs now more readily can and should negotiate improved financing mechanisms with whichever donors are willing, while hoping for and encouraging donor peer pressure and successful example eventually to bring the laggards along. Collectively agreed positions and better information have already proven valuable to some HIPCs as they press for improved development finance and better programmes. It is likely, then, that it is at the country level rather than at the global level that the HIPC FMN has so far had, and is likely to continue to have, its greatest practical productive impact.

The second hope—perhaps a little speculative—is the continuing possibility of developing (or re-developing) informal HIPC Ministerial network exchanges not only with NGOs, as has to some considerable degree already been done, but also directly with the Finance (and Development) Ministries of like-minded and/or more progressive G8 governments. Although, by Martin's account, some Northern Development Ministries and agencies were very much involved in the creation and early support of the HIPC Finance Ministers' network, there have not been many direct contacts between the HIPC FMN and Northern Finance Ministries. The HIPCs are not represented in the G20 Finance Ministers group; nor are their main traditional Northern sympathizers. Their positions have not so far been very effectively presented within the IMFC, the Development Committee, or the Boards of the IMF or World Bank, either. If the positions on which their network has reached agreement are to be taken seriously, let alone advanced, the HIPC Finance Ministers ultimately require more powerful allies. Realistically, such fresh North-HIPC exchanges (a.k.a. expanded networking) could probably only be sporadic rather than continuous, and in order to be productive they would have to be highly focused upon specific practical issues. The potential for productive 'extended' HIPC FM networking of this kind would depend upon the political circumstances of individual developed countries, and, of course, the willingness of the relevant actors to participate. Its productive potential would obviously vary with donor countries and over time. But it is clear that such temporary and issue-specific alliances have been successful for the HIPCs in the past. They can be again; and the HIPC FMN provides the ready mechanism for their promotion. HIPC Ministers should be alert for new windows of such HIPC/North networking opportunity. So should sympathetic non-governmental actors who could again play a useful facilitating role.

Appendix 7.1: Meetings of HIPC Ministerial Network

Date	Location	Chairs	Press conference participants
December 1999	Copenhagen	Burkina Faso, Honduras	
June 2000	Geneva	Burkina Faso, Honduras, Benin	
October 2000	Prague	Honduras, Benin	Honduras, Benin, Uganda
June 2001	London	Honduras, Zambia	
November 2001 (regional meeting for Eastern and Southern Africa)[a]	Maputo	Uganda, Mozambique	Uganda, Mozambique
March 2002 (not focused on ESA)	London	Rwanda, Chad	
September 2002	Washington	Cameroon, Uganda, Gambia	Niger, Mozambique
April 2003	Kigali	Rwanda, Senegal, Guinea-Bissau	
September 2003	Dubai	Rwanda, Bolivia	Rwanda, Bolivia
October 2004	Washington	Rwanda, Bolivia, Sierra Leone	Rwanda
March 2005 (jointly with Commonwealth and AIF)	Maputo	Mozambique, Sao Tome e Principe	n/a
September 2005	Washington	Niger, Benin, Mozambique	Niger, Benin, Mozambique

[a]BWI Annual Meetings were cancelled due to events of 11 September 2001.

8

Networking of Senior Budget Officials

Alex Matheson with contributions from Mickie Schoch and Dirk-Jan Kraan

8.1. Introduction

This chapter examines a network which has strengthened national policy-makers through exchanges of knowledge and peer support. The main network—the Senior Budget Officials' Working Party (SBO) of the Organization for Economic Cooperation and Development (OECD)—is one of the oldest and arguably one of the most successful of the OECD's many technical networks.[1] This chapter explores how it has worked and also how two groups of developing and transition economies—one in Eastern Europe and the other in sub-Saharan Africa—are creating their own networks of senior budget officials following the OECD SBO model. These networks are, respectively, the Central Eastern and South Eastern Europe Senior Budget Officials Network (CESEE) and the Collaborative African Budget Reform Initiative (CABRI). This chapter is therefore about the promise and the challenges involved in emulating developed-country networks and applying the model to a developing- or transition-economy context.

Unlike some of the other networks in this book, which deal with matters of international finance, the focus of the networks covered here is decidedly domestic. Their business is public financial management, which ranges from technical budgeting issues to wider considerations

---

[1] The OECD was established in 1961. It currently has 30 members: Australia, Austria, Belgium, Canada, Czech Republic, Denmark, Finland, France, Germany, Greece, Hungary, Iceland, Ireland, Italy, Japan, Korea, Luxembourg, Mexico, the Netherlands, New Zealand, Norway, Poland, Portugal, Slovak Republic, Spain, Sweden, Switzerland, Turkey, the United Kingdom, and the USA.

of the political economy of budgeting, public expenditure management, performance, accounting, arm's length agencies, delivery structures, inter-governmental grants, intervention policies, accountability, tax expenditures, reallocation, parliamentary oversight, and public sector reform.

8.1.1. *The Aims of SBO Networks*

Networks of senior budget officials (SBOs) primarily aim to influence national rather than international financial governance. The core proposition is that the way a country's central budgeting and financial management works has an important impact on both governance (i.e. the role of the legislature, fiscal transparency, and government accountability) and management (i.e. aggregate control and technical and allocative efficiency). By producing and exchanging knowledge and norms in key areas, these networks help finance ministries introduce beneficial changes to their national systems, provided that the political will for adopting such measures exists. At the same time, SBO networks can bring about a process of convergence across countries with regard to budgeting, reporting, and accounting language, which can lead to the creation of mechanisms for external and peer scrutiny, and, ultimately, to greater fiscal transparency.

An SBO network can also set formal international standards (the OECD, for instance, has done precisely that in the area of budget transparency), but for reasons that will be discussed below, this rarely happens. Instead, whatever influence SBO networks can exert on international accounting and reporting standards has been exercised by engaging in a dialogue with the bodies creating such standards. Thus, an SBO network's interest is twofold. First, it seeks to ensure that international accounting and reporting are both useful and practical from the perspective of government management. Second, it seeks to reduce the burden of financial reporting.

8.2. The Emergence of the OECD SBO Network

The OECD has supported a network of the senior budget officials (SBOs) of the national governments of its member states since 1979. The initiative for the SBO network came from the OECD Secretariat, but the opportunity to create a network was taken up readily by the budget directors of several

OECD countries. At the time (the late 1970s), most OECD governments were becoming concerned about their growing deficit, and therefore there was heightened interest in using budgeting and financial management functions to constrain burgeoning public expenditure.

Another reason for the creation of the SBO network is that among the different categories of senior officials in OECD member countries, budget officers were among the least integrated in a network of any kind. Unlike senior government economists, they had few links with the larger international scene. This kind of networking was therefore a novelty, and the initial experience of a sometimes embattled budget director interacting with his or her counterparts was very positive. (From time to time an SBO representative jokingly reminds the group that 'a budget officer's only friend can be another budget officer'.)

Technically, the SBO network is a Working Party of the OECD. Each major area of the OECD's work is run by a Committee of member governments, and subordinate to each 'committee' are more specialized 'working parties'. The committee to which the SBO is related was formerly the Public Management Committee (PUMA), and is now the Public Governance Committee (PGC). The idea is that budgeting and financial management is a subset of a broader field called public management. The country representatives on the Committee tend to be from management agencies—although for some governments the management function is part of the ministry of finance.

In practice, however, the OECD SBO has tended to act as a committee in its own right and its subordination to the PGC has been partial at best. There are several reasons for this. First, public expenditure and public service management have been seen as separate fields of interest, a fact that is still strongly reflected in most organizational structures. In many countries, a government-wide perspective of public administration is developed most strongly within finance ministries. Second, the SBO has been the OECD's most successful area of cooperation in public administration and consequently tends to attract more senior participants than the 'parent' committee. This difference in rank makes it difficult for country representatives on the Committee to be very assertive when dealing with the SBO. Furthermore, within governments, the ministries of finance—in which the SBO representatives are senior officials—generally have more clout and prestige than the body responsible for public management. The senior budget officers themselves therefore are not disposed to be deferential to the Committee where the management agency provides the country representative.

8.2.1. *Broadening the Agenda*

The SBO serves as a forum for budget directors to compare budgeting and public expenditure practices with the intention of learning from each other. However, with the passage of years, their agenda has broadened from 'technical' budgeting matters to considering the role of budgeting and financial management in creating incentives for political decision-making and management across the public sector. Topics of growing interest include, for example, performance-oriented budgeting and reporting, top-down budgeting, contracting out, and the structuring of conditional grants.

This broadening of the agenda was partly the result of convergence among countries in the core concepts and processes of budgeting, which followed a period of intensifying international integration. More importantly, over the 27 years following the establishment of the SBO network, budgeting has gone from a rather technical in-house function, to the platform for public sector reform.

After the failure of a number of bottom-up approaches for constraining budgets, 'top-down' budgeting—the setting of a firm *ex ante* limit to the funds available for the national annual expenditure programme—emerged as the only practical solution for countries seeking to avert or resolve a fiscal crisis, and it gradually became regarded as best practice across the OECD. This development changed the role of the budget office: whereas previously it had provided a service, it now took a strategic, government-wide perspective. Furthermore, with the emergence of ideas of New Public Management, the budget process came to be seen as a key instrument for systemic change. These developments progressively raised the importance of budget offices in public management, creating greater incentives for national governments to share ideas in these areas. This, in turn, raised the level of interest in a network like the OECD SBO.

8.3. The Workings of the OECD SBO Network

8.3.1. *Membership*

There are five categories of participation in the OECD SBO network: country representatives, country observers, observers, guests, and OECD staff. Each group has a different status and mode of participation.

COUNTRY REPRESENTATIVES

Each of the 30 OECD member countries has an official representative to the SBO. This is typically the budget director or a deputy secretary or secretary (deputy minister) of the ministry of finance. While the delegation leader/official country representative is always from the finance ministry, some delegations regularly include representatives from other agencies. In the case of the USA, for instance, the delegation leader is usually from the Office of Management and Budget, but senior representatives from the General Accounting Office (now General Accountability Office) and the Congressional Budget Office also attend.

The annual SBO meeting is in most cases attended by the listed representative (as is the case with 25 out of the 30 countries). Usually, this meeting takes place in Paris, but in recent years, four countries (the USA, Italy, Spain, and Australia) have acted as hosts. In a minority of cases, the official representative was a more junior officer, and in the unusual case that no one from the head office was available, the country seat was filled by an embassy representative. Delegation sizes range between two and five people. When larger delegations attend the meeting, only the two or three most senior officials sit at the table.

COUNTRY OBSERVERS

Over the SBO's history, OECD membership has expanded. Relatively new members are Poland, the Czech Republic, the Slovak Republic, Slovenia, Hungary, Mexico, and Korea. Following EU enlargement, it is expected that all the new EU members will soon join the OECD. This is likely to lead to the OECD admitting a number of other countries, with a view to maintaining a balance between European and non-European members. Newcomers are likely to be drawn from the larger 'transitional economies', though both China and Russia may be excluded.

Where a country has an interest in joining the OECD, or at least in participating in some of its activities, there is provision for it to have official observer status on particular committees and working parties, subject to the agreement of existing members. The SBO has a number of such observers, including Chile and Brazil. Once they become familiar with the way the SBO works, these observers tend to behave, and are treated by the chair, as if they were full members.

INTERNATIONAL ORGANIZATION OBSERVERS

Observer status is also accorded to representatives of the International Monetary Fund, the World Bank, and the European Union. Other organizations occasionally request and are granted attendance when a particular topic is of interest to them. The association between the OECD Secretariat and the IMF and World Bank is a close one, but within the SBO there is a clear policy—enforced by successive chairs—to ensure these organizations do not behave as if they enjoyed the status of country members. This reflects a strongly held view that the SBO (like the OECD as a whole) is to be led by the member states. It is also a useful way of ensuring that IMF and World Bank representatives do not take up too much airtime. They are accustomed to using a range of international forums to publicize certain messages, initiatives, and products, and country representatives tend to show little tolerance when their meetings are turned into marketing events.

This sense of reserve in relation to the IMF and World Bank also sheds light on the culture of budget officials. These tend to be bright but practical men and women who see themselves as dealing with the reality of both politics and public service in a constant and tangible way. This leads them to take a suspicious stance on theory and doctrine, and they often perceive the Fund and Bank as both excessively theoretical and doctrinaire. (They may regard the economic policy experts in their own ministries in the same way.)

GUESTS

In addition to the official country observers for the SBO, it is possible for other countries to be invited to attend meetings in the capacity of unofficial observers. In recent years, meetings have been attended by representatives from China, Russia, South Africa, Thailand, and Israel. These countries, sometimes represented at a political level, tend not to involve themselves actively in the meetings. Their involvement is usually confined to an introduction on the part of the chair, and the opportunity to briefly set out their country's interest in the proceedings. (A Chinese delegation attended one of the symposia on accrual accounting, and was reportedly astonished to witness the level of division and diversity of viewpoints on the issue. Their previous experience with the IMF and World Bank had led them to believe that a single method was accepted as best practice in all developed countries.)

OECD STAFF

The meetings are chaired by a country representative, not by the OECD Secretariat, and the senior hierarchy of the OECD is involved only during a short welcome and introduction at the beginning of the meeting, and perhaps during a farewell speech at the end. Sometimes, senior OECD officers also take the opportunity to elicit the support or understanding of the SBO members for some internal OECD matter. Similar to the marketing efforts of the IMF and World Bank, these interventions are not welcomed, and trigger resentment if they go on for too long. (Another aspect of the culture of budget officials is that they are hardened against special pleading. After all, they spend much of their working lives turning down people who are trying to persuade them to support this or that item of expenditure.)

Typically, OECD staff from the division servicing the meeting are present throughout the two-day meetings, and work very closely with the chair, providing detailed briefing notes on the agenda and the issues and people involved, and alerting them to any political issues. Despite the very substantial input staff members provide to any papers at the meeting, it is considered inappropriate for the Secretariat staff to dominate the proceedings. Their presentations are kept as short as possible, and they tend to involve themselves in the round-table debate only when invited by the chair or when specific questions arise relating to the Secretariat and its work. Other OECD staff, both from the Governance Directorate and other interested directorates, such as the Economics or Development Division or the central OECD administration, are free to attend meetings that are of interest to them, but have no speaking rights unless this has been pre-arranged as part of the agenda.

8.3.2. Communication and Resources

Support for the SBO network comes from the Budgeting and Expenditures Division of the OECD's Governance Directorate. The division maintains an up-to-date mailing list of the official SBO representatives. In addition to the correspondence regarding the setting up and reporting on the annual SBO meeting, a newsletter is circulated to all representatives every month or so, keeping them updated on the work programme, informing them of meetings of expert groups, and occasionally seeking their participation in specific activities, either in the context of an expert group on a specific topic or in the context of an SBO outreach activity.

Most of the group-wide communication takes place electronically. Virtual meetings do not take place (for some, trips to Paris have a certain appeal), and while Electronic Discussion Groups have been tried, they have rarely been used in practice.

Where new initiatives are being launched, the Secretariat will first initiate personal contact with key people in the member countries who are considered most likely to be interested. Strong informal communication and relationships between the Secretariat and the most active SBO representatives are very important in maintaining the productive but practical style of SBO operations.

The core SBO activities are supported by the Budgeting and Expenditures Division, drawing on OECD funds. This involves professional support of the SBO work programme (roughly five person years), administrative support (two person years), and the costs of venue and meeting support for meetings held in Paris (on average six events a year). There is also a limited budget to fund expert papers and presenters for the annual SBO meeting. Participating ministries meet their own travel and accommodation costs, and if they choose to host an SBO meeting, they normally contribute 50 per cent or more towards the cost of the meeting, as well as providing venues and offering hospitality to their visitors.

In addition, there is a provision for one or more individual countries to contribute funds, temporary staff, or both, to a technical study in an area of interest to them, provided the study is relevant to the overall SBO work programme. Member governments also meet the costs of any papers they prepare or the costs that arise from the participation of their public servants as speakers or presenters.

Finally, some governments provide and pay for a secondment programme, whereby staff spend a period of two or three years working on the SBO programme within the Budgeting and Expenditures Division in Paris. There may be two or three such secondees in the division at any one time. This programme further strengthens the informal networks that exist between the member countries and the Secretariat. For the country providing the seconded staff, the motivation is usually staff development, but in some cases, it also reflects a desire to benefit from OECD involvement in certain areas of business.

8.3.3. Network Dynamics

The OECD Secretariat exerts the largest influence on setting the agenda of the SBO's work, but it does so on the basis of verbal and written comments put before the SBO meetings each year. The Secretariat is also influenced to some degree by priorities set within the OECD, and quite strongly by the views of the sitting SBO chair. In recent years, chairs have come from Germany, the Netherlands, the USA, and Australia. Typically, the position of chair can be assumed if the candidate, or at least his or her country, has been active in the SBO over a number of years, has gained the informal support of an inner circle of members, and has been invited to take up the job by the Secretariat. The candidate must also be at a career stage where he or she can devote time to issues of international cooperation. The nomination is normally accepted by other SBO members without a debate or competing claims. The chairs serve for three or four years.

While the Secretariat appears to have a free hand with regard to setting the agenda, member states with concerns about the papers and presentations for the meetings have no hesitation in letting the chair and Secretariat know. More than one or two complaints are generally seen as a major loss of confidence. For this reason, the Secretariat works very hard behind the scenes to ensure the work programme is in line with the wishes of a majority of states. Individual countries worry less about the work programme as a whole than they do about particular items. Interest in a particular item can arise because a country has recently been presented with a problem, or because a country has recently implemented a major reform programme.

During the late 1980s and early 1990s, there was a heavy emphasis in the SBO, as in public management networks generally, on the innovative ideas associated with New Public Management (NPM) especially as practised in Australia, Britain, and New Zealand. Budget officials had a particular interest in performance-oriented budgeting and reporting, the use of non-departmental government agencies, contracting out, accrual accounting, and taking a government-wide perspective—often referred to as 'best practices'.[2] After the turn of the millennium, a new set of reformers emerged, including Belgium, France, the Netherlands, and Portugal, which led to a shift in the debate. With budget departments now able to

[2] Under the New Public Management perspective, public management is seen as a 'nexus of contracts'. This led to the rationalization of organizational structures by separating such dimensions as policy and delivery, contracting out, the greater use of market forces, and the formalization of 'outputs and outcomes' to link budgets with management. These innovations were readily taken up in many national budgeting processes. In general, their justification was purely theoretical—'faith-based policies' as one budget director described them. In practice, the new management policies proved more complex, and in the 2000s there was an increasing interest among SBO members in generating more empirical work on how such innovations (e.g. performance budgeting) have actually worked out when real countries have applied them.

see results on the ground, there was a reaction against the evangelistic 'a priori-ism' of NPM, leading to a more nuanced debate, and greater demands for fashionable micro-economic interventions to be empirically verified.

The network at times witnessed lively debates on particular issues, for example on the move by a small minority of countries towards full accrual accounting, which provoked trenchant opposition from some larger countries on both technical and political grounds. Yet, this kind of controversy strengthened rather than weakened the network. When countries were not finding the network very useful, they tended to express this by lowering the level of their representation, or by not attending at all. The rank and number of attendees is therefore seen as a mark of quality for the workings of the network overall, and one which the Secretariat watches closely.

Given the nature of the network and the fact that it does not involve itself too closely with formal standard-setting, there are few incentives for schisms or coalitions. Expert groups are supported only by countries that are interested in the topic; some representatives are close to each other because of regional affinity, language, or system of government, but the group as a whole supports a very open culture and care is taken, often through the chair, to make new members feel included and to guard against the formation of blocs. Interestingly, this culture was much less evident, for example, in meetings of chairs of parliamentary budget committees. Those present at an early meeting of that group were startled when the Danish representative launched a vituperative attack on his Swedish counterpart. This would not happen in the SBO network.

8.3.4. *Successes and Limitations*

The major success of the SBO has been building a safe environment in which the budget officials of different countries can learn from each other, develop a common coinage of language and concepts, test out ideas, pursue particular interests, agree on principles, and install informal, and increasingly formal, peer review mechanisms to monitor each other's budgeting and financial processes. This atmosphere has been achieved without the network losing its professional edge and degenerating into an excuse to visit an interesting place—a fate that has been known to befall other international networks.

The SBO's success is due in large part to the fact that the network is consensus-based, has not been too ambitious, and—while working steadily toward improving the working practices of its member states—has been sensitive to the fact that it takes time for ideas and attitudes to change. Had the SBO set out, for instance, to report on and judge members' fiscal stance, or to institute compulsory reviews, or to pursue an aggressive standard-setting programme, it would have been a very different and much more politicized body, and therefore may not have endured.

For example, it was only in 1999 that the Secretariat produced its first peer review of a national budgeting system, and since then there have been one or two such reviews per year, establishing them as a key part of the SBO agenda. These reviews are conducted by the Secretariat, some-times with a country representative as part of the team. They are presented during SBO meetings, following which two countries that have been nominated as peer reviewers offer additional comments; the reviewed country then has an opportunity to respond. The final review is published in the *OECD Journal on Budgeting*.

These reviews concern the institutional arrangements for budgeting and financial management, rather than fiscal policies. They do, how-ever, provide the opportunity for challenging questions. In general, the atmosphere in the SBO has been such that these examinations have been conducted in a frank but supportive style on both sides. The only excep-tion to this was the 1999 review of Canada, where offence was caused not by any serious misjudgement contained in the review, but by sensitivities between the Treasury Board/Department of Finance on the one hand and the Privy Council Office (PCO) on the other. The Secretariat apparently failed to consult with the PCO during the review process.

In the context of the peer reviews, there are no formal sanctions for uncooperative behaviour. Such measures are generally unnecessary because the loose network structure allows countries to withdraw their participation if they choose. The most common form of what could be termed uncooperative behaviour is that of misrepresenting one's coun-try experience, that is, by making it look better than it is. This can occur, for example, when filling in a cross-country survey. Some countries seem more prone to this than others. In such cases, a confrontational approach is avoided. The offending country tends to be challenged by other members in an indirect fashion (for instance, by means of a seem-ingly innocent request for clarification), through conversations during coffee breaks, and sometimes by the Secretariat going back to (gently) seek further verification of the information provided.

In sum, the OECD SBO is not an appropriate forum for doing 'hard' international financial management business, either in setting rigorous standards or in delivering strong messages to fiscally opaque or irresponsible countries. The IMF once sought to use the debate on the SBO review of the US budgeting system as an opportunity to ask the US representative some hard questions about its deficit. This idea was rejected on the grounds that this constituted an inappropriate use of the SBO.

How can we summarize the reasons for the OECD SBO's relative success as an effective network? One set of reasons pertains to the nature of the network's policy area. This area of activity lends itself to comparison and cooperation because budgeting and financial management can share a common international technology that facilitates constructive discussion and comparison across countries. In addition, important interests are at stake for the member countries, particularly as policy on budgeting and financial management systems has become increasingly important to OECD governments.

The second set of reasons pertains to the qualities of the network itself. The network's medium-term work planning system was flexible enough to accommodate quick responses to new areas of interest on the part of member states. This ensured that the network could remain relevant and useful to its participants, even as their interests and priorities changed over time. Also, the Secretariat was staffed by people who understood budget offices and practices and who were able to maintain an interesting and sometimes challenging flow of papers and speakers.

Third, the group developed a professional and inclusive culture, and while it dealt with some sensitive issues (for instance, on the question of whether tax expenditures should be reflected in government accounts), the network did not seek to confront individual countries. Fourth, the network gradually developed its own traditions and acquired sufficient gravitas to avoid being hijacked by individual members. Indeed, the network was 'owned' by its member countries, a principle respected by the OECD Secretariat. Finally, leadership by a small but changing number of countries also helped—it played a low-key but effective role in helping the network develop.

8.3.5. Creation of Allied Networks

A recent development associated with the SBO has been the spinning off of allied networks on public sector accounting policy and parliamentary budget committees. These bodies were created by the Secretariat with the blessing and under the umbrella of the SBO, but they were effectively independent and functioned purely on the basis of an annual meeting, for which the Secretariat organized papers and speakers. The annual meeting of the accounting group takes the form of a major symposium of 100 or more people but is run less formally than a standard OECD meeting. The meetings of chairs of parliamentary budget committees were hosted by different countries and followed the usual format of intergovernmental meetings.

The stimulus for the creation of the accounting group was the desire on the part of some countries to introduce accrual budgeting and reporting into the public sector. This topic had been raised within SBO meetings, resulting in a polarization between enthusiastic reformers (among whom New Zealand, Australia, and later the UK were prominent) and a number of countries sceptical about any such move beyond the desirability of using accrual accounting to recognize certain liabilities such as public service pension schemes. (The USA was particularly sceptical of the benefits of moving towards budgeting on an accruals basis.) But as time went by, some use of accrual accounting became less an arcane debate than a reality, so much so that all governments were employing this method in one way or another. When the Secretariat decided to run a separate symposium on accrual accounting, not only did the level of attendance greatly exceed expectations but also what was originally seen as a one-off event became an annual one.

The origin of the network made up of the chairs of Parliamentary Budget Committees can be traced back to the interest of the President of the Senate Budget Committee in France in promoting the introduction of major reforms into the French governmental system. In a meeting with the OECD Secretariat on modern budget legislation, it was proposed that the Senate would host a meeting of all the chairs of parliamentary budget committees in the OECD. As a result of this proposal, a very successful meeting was held at the Palais du Luxembourg with about 20 of the 30 parliaments represented. In the following two years, the US Congress and the Italian parliament each hosted similar meetings. Attendance at the meeting in Rome was disappointing and since then (2003) the network has been in abeyance.

8.3.6. Competitor Networks

In aspects of public management such as Human Resource Management and 'e-government', the OECD networks have come to realize that the networks associated with the European Union were engaging the active participation of more than half of the OECD's membership. Where the EU and OECD activities overlapped, European countries would maintain representation in the activities of both organizations, but their most senior people would only attend the meetings of the network considered most significant. As a result, the seniority of membership declined during the late 1990s and early 2000s in the OECD Human Resources Management Working Party, for example, resulting in the loss of clout and continuity of country involvement.

Competition with the EU networks and institutions did not, however, impact adversely on the SBO. The European Commission did not support a directly analogous network, and while its network interacted very closely with the finance ministries of EU member countries, its work programme focused on specific EU matters such as the Maastricht Treaty and the wide range of financial reporting requirements which arise from EU membership.

But only the OECD SBO offers the opportunity to discuss budgeting from a constitutional perspective (i.e. its function for the legislature) and from a strategic management perspective (meaning its role in strengthening public service). Consequently, the interest of European countries in the SBO has not diminished as EU financial institutions have deepened. Indeed, as the Maastricht Treaty ran into trouble, interesting discussions took place in the SBO with regard to the incentives of that treaty and its structural similarity to the failed Gramm-Rudman Act in the USA.

8.4. Exporting the SBO Model: The Collaborative African Budget Reform Initiative (CABRI)[3]

An important development in the last six years has been a policy of 'outreach' by the OECD's SBO, which aims to nurture the development of other SBOs in different parts of the developing world. This policy has been supported by a number of individual members and by the organization itself, particularly as recognition grows that sound national budgeting, financial management, and accountability architecture and systems are crucial in supporting good government. Under this partnership, policy networks have been initiated or supported in Latin America, Asia, Africa, Central and Eastern Europe, and the Middle East. The proximate objective of this programme is not advocacy of particular fiscal policies, but rather

---

[3] This section was prepared by Mickie Schoch with input from Alta Fölscher. Both were actively involved in the establishment of the network while working in the South African National Treasury.

encouraging other groups of budget officials to adapt the SBO experience to build a capacity and supportive culture for their cooperation, peer review, and standard setting in this important area of public administration. This section describes an attempt by a group of sub-Saharan African countries to build such a network, following the example and enlisting the support of the OECD SBO.

8.4.1. Emergence of the Network

The OECD as an organization has traditionally taken little interest in Africa, apart from its role through the Development Assistance Committee, which provides services to the development agencies of member countries, some of which provide aid to Africa. In the new millennium, this began to change as the organization contemplated enlarging its membership and providing more services to non-members. In the early 2000s, the OECD provided technical assistance to the New Partnership for Africa's Development (NEPAD) to set up a peer review system, called the African peer review mechanism (for details, see Khadija Bah's Chapter 6 in this book). The mechanism was modelled after the OECD's own peer review system, which for years had helped the organization undertake peer reviews of members' economic policies. Thus, NEPAD and the African Union (AU) became the focus of OECD support to Africa, and a strategy was adopted by the OECD to help with the development of professional networks in public administration and in budgeting and public expenditure. As part of these efforts, the OECD SBO was enlisted to help. The SBO had three things to offer: long experience in managing a government network, an integrated, government-wide perspective on budgeting and public management, and experience in running programmes relevant to both British and continental systems of government.

Demand for OECD assistance in network-building came from two sources. The Pan African Ministers for Public Administration requested OECD participation at a meeting in Stellenbosch, South Africa in 2004, and later sought assistance from the OECD in the practicalities of networking. In response, the OECD produced a practical guide on supporting the SBO network and participated in workshops. Public management was soon accepted by the African Union as a technical committee. However, after the first meeting under AU auspices, the OECD's interest in the area of public administration lapsed. At about the same time, officials working at the National Treasury of the Republic of South Africa (RSA)—some of whom were familiar with the operations of the OECD SBO—came up with the idea of setting up an SBO oriented mainly towards the South African Development Community (SADC).[4] They believed SADC countries could benefit from learning about the experiences of countries grappling with similar issues.

In addition, the South African Treasury was disappointed with its experience with study tours and was looking for alternatives. The National Treasury received a number of study tours from countries across Africa and further afield to study South Africa's public financial management reforms. However, National Treasury staff did not consider these study tours to be very successful and were unsure of how applicable South Africa's experiences were to other countries in the region. In addition, the staff recognized that South Africa could also learn from other countries, for instance, with respect to carrying out a Public Expenditure Review, but the study tours tended to be a one-way affair. After several visits took place between RSA officials and the Ministries of Finance from Mozambique and Uganda in 2002–03, the idea of holding a meeting between senior budget officials in selected African countries took hold.

The South African Minister of Finance, Trevor Manuel, thought of CABRI as a useful way of promoting good governance in Africa while serving as an example of Africans taking governance reform into their own hands. Subsequently, Minister Manuel continued to promote CABRI in international forums and in the Commission for Africa report. From the outset, it was clear that CABRI reflected the viewpoint of African officials, who often have to deal with prescriptions from international institutions and donors, and which are not always suitable to the country in question or have been inadequately prioritized. Participation and attendance in the network would have been much lower if CABRI had been perceived to be a donor-driven event.

8.4.2. *The Workings of the CABRI Network*

On 14 May 2008 CABRI was officially launched at a meeting of African Ministers of Finance in Maputo, Mozambique. Prior to this, several seminars and meetings had been held to develop the Memorandum of Understanding for the new network. CABRI has been invited by international organizations to comment on the Public Expenditure and Financial Accountability (PEFA) indicators and the OECD DAC's

---

[4] The first official to mention such an idea was Alta Fölscher.

Evaluation of General Budget Support. At this stage, it is not yet clear whether CABRI will take up such invitations.

The first question when setting up the network was the issue of membership. There was no clear strategy on which countries to invite to CABRI's first Budget Reform Seminar in December 2004. The organizers did not know the respective budget directors by name, and it was not yet clear whether it should be an all-African initiative, a sub-Saharan one, or one limited to Southern and Eastern Africa. In the end, the first Budget Reform Seminar, held in Pretoria, was attended by Angola, Botswana, Kenya, Lesotho, Malawi, Mauritius, Mozambique, Namibia, Nigeria, Rwanda, South Africa, Senegal, Tanzania, Uganda, Zambia, and Zimbabwe. Most participants held senior positions within their ministries. The network's Inaugural Meeting in 2005, held in Maputo, was attended by officials from Ethiopia, Kenya, Lesotho, Malawi, Mauritius, Mozambique, Namibia, Nigeria, South Africa, Tanzania, Uganda, and Zambia. Most participants held quite senior positions within their ministries. The second Budget Reform Seminar, held in Nairobi in 2005, was attended by Angola, Botswana, Ethiopia, Guinea, Kenya, Lesotho, Malawi, Mauritius, Mozambique, Namibia, Nigeria, Rwanda, South Africa, Senegal, Tanzania, Uganda, and Zimbabwe. Again, the proportion of senior officials remained high.

Donors also attended the meetings. These included the Deutsche Gesellschaft für Technische Zusammenarbeit (GTZ), Development Cooperation Ireland (DCI), and the European Commission (EC). However, CABRI's members remain committed to maintain a balance that prevents the network from becoming a platform for international institutions and donors to promote their agendas.

Establishing initial contact was difficult. Surprisingly, very few senior budget officials knew their counterparts in neighbouring countries, and there was no international institution with a central database. Letters were written to the Embassies or High Commissions of African countries asking for the names of the officials responsible for budgeting practices and procedures in each country. The Director General of the South African Treasury then drafted a letter of invitation to ensure the attendance of suitably senior officials.

Contact in the network is maintained through meetings, the CABRI website, and email communications. In the case of specific CABRI activities, communication has been coordinated by the RSA. However, countries are also beginning to establish links with each other on an

213

informal basis. A CABRI Secretariat has been created and is based in South Africa's National Treasury.

The RSA supported all of the network's activities in Nairobi and Maputo and made a significant contribution in terms of staff time and travel costs for preparatory meetings. Due to resource constraints, the Ministries of Finance of Kenya and Mozambique were able to contribute only minimally. The South Africans did not see this as a problem, but they have been careful not to overstate their role. The RSA felt it important to ensure that CABRI was not perceived as a South Africa-dominated forum. In Kenya and Mozambique, GTZ provided some logistical support.

South Africa, Mozambique, and Uganda constituted the original troika for the network. Kenya was very active during the first seminar and was thus taken on board. Kenya currently chairs the CABRI Management Team. The CABRI experience highlights the importance of the energy and vision of the three founding countries—South Africa, Uganda, and Mozambique—and the leadership of Neil Cole of the South African National Treasury.

To date, the main financial supporter of the CABRI has been the European Commission, though DCI, the US Treasury, the Swedish International Development Agency (SIDA), and GTZ have also provided some funding. GTZ is helping fund the CABRI Secretariat, and several other donors have indicated a willingness to contribute financially to the initiative.

At this early stage, it is not yet possible to discern tensions or divisions within the group. During the Nairobi meeting in 2005, there was disagreement over the question of offering membership to staff from the national Ministries of Planning. The tension was introduced by the participant from the Nigerian Planning Commission. However, the official in question did not attend the Maputo seminar and the issue appears to have been resolved.

To date, CABRI has not yet witnessed the emergence of any competing institutions or networks. Initially, there were concerns about the lack of participation from francophone African countries and fears that these countries might establish a separate network. This now seems unlikely, and the West African countries attending the seminars have indicated that they will actively encourage countries from their region to attend future CABRI meetings. That said, the United Nations Economic Commission for Africa (UNECA) believes that it has some competence in the area of public financial management reforms in Africa. It has also been important to engage NEPAD, but CABRI participants elected for the network are keen to maintain their independence from the Partnership. A more structured form of engagement with NEPAD may well be devised in the future.

8.4.3. Conclusions

At this stage, it is too early to draw any substantive conclusions on the impact of the CABRI network. The major achievement so far has been the creation of the network itself—the establishment of a platform where senior budget officials from the continent can share their experiences of what works and what does not in an environment of openness and frank exchange. Participants have developed a sense of pride in the post-seminar publications. Moreover, CABRI has been invited to participate in several international settings, and it will be interesting to see whether the network can influence meetings or specific agenda points within other international institutions and agencies.

On the other hand, considerable challenges remain. Unfortunately, there is usually little time for participants to prepare for CABRI activities, although countries have put a substantial effort into drafting country studies and completing pilot questionnaires. Another challenge is attracting francophone countries into the network, before it develops into an exclusive English-speaking club. A third challenge is managing the tensions between planners and budgeters, a battle which in the OECD countries was won by the budget officials. Also, if the network is to be effective, donors and international institutions must refrain from taking every public opportunity to deliver their message. Instead, they should sit back and let the local budget officers run the network. Finally, if the network is to survive in the long term, member countries must have a tangible stake in the proceedings, even if it is just a question of meeting their own attendance costs.

8.5. Exporting the SBO Model: The Central Eastern and South Eastern Europe (CESEE) Senior Budget Officials Network[5]

While budget officials in Africa were busy emulating the OECD SBO model, officials in the transition economies of Eastern Europe were

[5] This analysis is from Dirk-Jan Kraan who organized the network from its first meeting in The Hague. His account picks up from the second meeting of the network.

considering a similar initiative. This section describes the efforts of these countries to create their own budget officials' network.

8.5.1. *Emergence of the Network*

The CESEE was a Dutch initiative, the idea of Budget Director of the Netherlands Helmer Vossers, who sought to organize an event when his government held the EU presidency. The Dutch government enjoys close relations with several East European countries by virtue of its leadership position in the constituency at the International Monetary Fund that brings together the Netherlands with nearly a dozen countries from the Balkans and Eastern Europe.[6] Participants at the first event, held in The Hague in 2004, included the budget directors (often called assistant ministers) of some 22 Central, Eastern, and South-Eastern European countries (out of a possible 26). The OECD Secretariat helped by identifying all the relevant budget officials.

8.5.2. *The Workings of the CESEE Network*

A second meeting of the CESEE network was held in Ljubljana, Slovenia, in February 2006. The same participants were invited. From this point onwards, contact with participants shifted to regular email communication. At the second meeting, participation was high, but lower than in The Hague, with 19 of the 26 CESEE countries in attendance. Russia, Albania, and Georgia cancelled at the last moment. Belarus, Malta, and Moldova said early on that they would not be able to attend. Serbia never responded to the invitation. The high level of participation at the meeting can be at least partly explained by the fact that the participants' travel costs were reimbursed by donors. However, in 2006, the participants were required to meet their own hotel costs. The atmosphere at the Ljubljana meeting was lively. Country reviews of the budget systems of Croatia and Georgia took place (though an embarrassing moment occurred when Georgia failed to attend the meeting because of transit visa problems). The social programme was a success. A third meeting took place in Vilnius, Lithuania in 2007 and a fourth meeting in Bucharest, Romania, April 2008.

[6] The IMF constituency includes the Netherlands, the Ukraine, Armenia, Bosnia and Herzegovina, Bulgaria, Croatia, Cyprus, Georgia, Israel, Macedonia, Moldova, and Romania. The Netherlands, which holds the largest voting share within the constituency, holds the position of Executive Director.

Institutional support came from various quarters. The first meeting was funded by the Dutch government, including airfare and hotel costs. The second meeting was funded by GTZ and the Swedish and Slovenian governments. Airfares were covered by the donors, but hotel costs were covered by the participants. The OECD has provided Secretariat services for all meetings. The CESEE SBO is run much like the OECD SBO—the OECD provides the programme, and the host country is responsible for the local organization and the social programme. This stands in contrast with the CABRI and other regional networks, which are basically run by a single member country, such as South Africa in the case of CABRI.

Naturally, the host countries (the Netherlands, Slovenia, and Lithuania) have been the most active participants of the network. CESEE countries that belong to the European Union are also active, a reflection of their desire to see their non-EU neighbours make progress. The countries that participate the least are those with a problematic reputation in terms of democratic governance (Belarus, Moldova, Russia, Armenia, Azerbaijan, and Serbia), which either fail to attend or say little during the meetings. Yet, there have been no major tensions or divisions within the network so far.

Competitor networks may yet emerge. In 2005, the World Bank organized a meeting with a very similar purpose for Eastern and South-eastern European countries, as well as for Asian countries in the region. A similar meeting was convened in 2006. This has led to talks between the OECD and the World Bank, with the OECD hoping to persuade the Bank to support the SBO network rather than a rival network.

8.5.3. Conclusions

With only four meetings of the network held so far, it is difficult to judge the success of this fledgling network at this point. The biggest success so far is the gradual shifting of responsibility for the network from the Dutch sponsor to the countries of Central and Eastern Europe. The first meeting was entirely organized and funded by the Dutch government, but the initiative has now been taken over by countries in the region (first Slovenia and then Lithuania). This suggests that the network may have a future as a regionally owned initiative.

However, the CESEE countries do not fully own the network, which remains a cooperative project between the OECD and the region. Perhaps this will remain the case for a number of years, but then the sustained support of the OECD may also contribute to success in the longer run.

Another important limitation is that given the very different nature of their budgeting procedures, countries with weak or non-existent democratic governance will never be able to participate fully as active members.

8.6. Overall Conclusion

The OECD now supports regional SBO networks in Africa, Asia, Eastern Europe, Latin America, and in the Middle East/North Africa. Why has the OECD SBO influenced network-building in the developing world? First, the original SBO has a long track record, and its members see it as a valuable asset. Over its 27-year history the SBO has attracted support from all OECD countries, at increasingly senior levels. A number of member countries credit the SBO as having been an important source of ideas and advice, assisting them in making major changes in their public administrative system.

Second, the network has developed a way of doing business which is professional but relaxed, and which members have come to value. The group's modus operandi has allowed it to open up new activities and networks with very little fuss and formality. There also appears, at least in recent years, to be a high level of trust between the committee members and the OECD Secretariat which supports the network and carries out their work programme. As the level of mutual confidence within the network has increased, the SBO has been able to undertake more ambitious and sensitive exercises, such as independent peer reviews of individual members' national budgeting and management systems. It has also been able to avoid losing out to rival networks.

The two non-OECD networks of budget officials discussed in this chapter—CABRI and CESEE networks—are still in their infancy. For the members of these networks, active participation may translate into strengthened domestic capacity in public financial management. These networks will allow budget officials to meet their counterparts in different countries, colleagues who are dealing with problems similar to their own, giving them the confidence to re-examine their own practices. Over time, if and when the SBO network builds up sufficient confidence to move towards comparative research, common norms, and peer review, they will be able to offer stronger advice to their political leaders on the basis of international comparisons and standards.

In addition, one of the greatest benefits to be derived from developing-country SBO networks lies in the fact that this kind of networking can strengthen developing countries' capacity to interact with donors and international financial institutions. Networking can allow these countries to learn from each other and thus understand better what donors are advocating, as well as the alternatives. Moreover, sharing their experience with 'best practices' and the results of comparative research projects will allow them to appreciate how specific working practices play out in practice in a real political setting.

This last point is particularly important. It was an unfortunate coincidence that the initial popularity of NPM in developed countries coincided with a move in the international-development community to focus more attention on governance in developing countries. The simplicity of NPM-based solutions had great appeal to those seeking to improve governance in developing countries, and suddenly the new ideas were leveraged by the power of persuasion exerted by those allocating major development resources. This was unfortunate, because what works in developed countries is not a good guide to what will work in a developing country. Moreover, transferring these 'best practices' to the developing world is based on the assumption that these policies are already commonplace in the developed world and have proven to be effective. In the case of NPM, neither assumption was true. For this reason, the SBO networks have a potentially important role in challenging the 'a priori-ism' of donors' public management policies and in helping countries conduct their own comparative research projects in this area.

An important factor in understanding the significance of SBO meetings is that the attending officials have no other place where they can meet and discuss matters of common interest in an informal atmosphere. These meetings have no policy relevance; nothing has to be negotiated or decided. In this respect, the SBO meetings are very different from meetings that take place between developing countries on the one hand, and the IMF or the World Bank on the other. For this reason, SBO networks will continue to exist and prosper as long as the OECD or some powerful country in the region is willing to bear the burden of providing Secretariat services.

8.7. Policy-Relevant Lessons

SBO networks succeed when they deal with institutions and processes rather than with policies. The reason is that major policy changes in international governance need to be founded on processes of mutual confidence building, cooperation, and professional value building. As a result, the members' sense of ownership of the network is crucial. As Mickie Schooch has pointed out above, a key lesson from the CABRI experience is that donors should be very careful not to undermine the sense of ownership on the part of the network's African members and should refrain from using their position as the principal funding bodies to push particular policy initiatives, no matter how worthy they might be.

Our examination of the SBO networks did not seek to answer the question of whether international cooperation should occur in the framework of formal inter-governmental bodies or of informal networks. Instead, it has attempted to show that these two mechanisms for international cooperation perform important but distinctly different functions, and that combining these functions (for instance, when an international institution uses an SBO network for its development business) may be detrimental.

In the context of budgeting, the SBO networks are best understood not as international rule-setters but as self-managed, professional communities which, if well led, can create a supportive and stimulating environment in which participants develop the personal and institutional capacity to improve in one of the most challenging functions of modern government. The space the SBO networks create cannot be replicated by training bodies, since such bodies would inevitably fail to win the respect of busy government officials.

Nor can the equivalent context be created through donor-driven seminars, since interaction between senior government officials from developing countries on the one hand and donors on the other is inevitably influenced by wider development debates and disputes. Such debates can lead to posturing and politicization, which in turn prevents the development of a culture of honest disclosure, admission of failings, and supportive peer review. Such a culture is necessary to nurture the growing self-confidence that comes from a process of mutual learning. It is this process which makes SBO networks such an effective builder of capacity. A secondary but important strength of SBO networks lies in the fact that the capacity-building that results from the networking—largely through the personal relationships they help foster among officials—help these officials become more effective and influential decision-makers in formal inter-governmental institutions, as well as within their own governments.

9

The Centre for Latin American Monetary Studies and its Central Bankers' Networks

Kenneth G. Coates[1]

9.1. Introduction

This chapter discusses the origins and evolution of a group of networks of central bank officials nested within a formal inter-governmental organization, the Mexico City-based Centre for Latin American Monetary Studies (CEMLA). Created before the rise of the East Asian central bankers' networks discussed by Helen Nesadurai in this book, the Latin American networks are supported by a formal institution with its own legal personality, statutes, governance bodies, and executive structures. While the official mandate of the CEMLA is capacity-building, research, information dissemination, and technical assistance, it also coordinates four networks of senior central bank officials who meet regularly to discuss matters of mutual interest and to respond to emergencies in the international and regional financial environments.

9.2. The Emergence of the Latin American Central Bankers' Networks

In Latin America, truly independent central banking is a relatively recent phenomenon. The region has traditionally exhibited what Coates and

---

[1] The opinions expressed in this paper are the personal views of the author, and in no way should be construed as an official position of CEMLA or any of its members.

Rivera call 'fiscal dominance'—the tendency of central bankers to be politically aligned with the incumbent government and subjected, either de jure or de facto, to the Ministry of Finance.[2] Yet, even under these circumstances, central bankers took comfort in the thought that theirs was primarily a 'technical' activity which gave them a modicum of independence from the political process. In line with this view, central bankers cultivated a kind of mystique around central banking. Until the advent of inflation targeting, central bankers maintained this mystique by minimizing public appearances, and where unavoidable, communicating with the general public in the most inscrutable terms.

Since there is only one central bank per country, central bankers can only compare notes either with their predecessors at home or their counterparts abroad, and they invariably choose to do the latter. Ministers of finance and foreign relations are in a similar position, but the nature of central banking has contributed to a greater sense of camaraderie among central bankers. Perhaps this is because monetary management is one step more removed from politics compared to the budget process, or perhaps because central bankers do not view each other as competitors in the same way that foreign or finance ministers do. In addition, monetary policy is a field for educated technocrats, one where political appointees feel conspicuously out of their depth. For all these reasons, networking is an activity that has always come naturally to central bankers.

9.2.1. CEMLA: The Networks' Institutional Anchor

The CEMLA was established in 1952; its origins can be traced back to an initiative presented in 1949 by Mexico's central bank, the Banco de México. There were seven founding members, including the central banks of Chile, Colombia, Cuba, Ecuador, Guatemala, and Honduras. The Centre was incorporated in Mexico City under private law as a non-profit civil association funded by member dues. The UN Economic Commission for Latin America (ECLA) joined as a collaborating member. CEMLA's founders chose this mode of legal incorporation not only because the Bank of Mexico was at the time a mixed (public and private) capital institution, but also because this legal status allowed the founders to avoid official government funding and international treaty ratification, thereby denying ministries of finance and foreign affairs an opening to interfere.

---

[2] See K. G. Coates and Edwin Rivera, 'Fiscal Dominance and Foreign Debt: Five Decades of Latin American Experience', *Money Affairs*, XVII: 2 (July–December 2004).

CEMLA was, in essence, a private club, and it functioned as such under its statutes and structure.

Since its inception, all Latin American and 10 Caribbean central banks have joined the Centre as associate members. The current associate membership stands at 30. In addition, there are 20 collaborating (non-voting) members, including non-regional central banks, regional bank supervisory authorities, and other financial entities.

The CEMLA was created to provide training, research, and information for monetary authorities and other financial entities in the Latin American and Caribbean region, and to facilitate knowledge exchange and dissemination. The logic behind its creation was threefold. First, the founders believed that Latin America could not solve its economic problems by applying the same policies and instruments employed by more advanced economies, and therefore it had to devise its own. Second, university education in the advanced economies (where many Latin American central bankers did their graduate work) rarely focused on monetary and financial problems from a regional viewpoint. And third, the cost of sending personnel from the region to be trained abroad was exceedingly high.

The driving force behind the CEMLA was the Bank of Mexico. For 35 of the CEMLA's 53 years of existence, its Director General was a Bank of Mexico official. The Bank of Mexico also provided most of the Centre's staff and extraordinary budget contributions in the form of personal income-tax rebates for employees and rent-free premises for the CEMLA's headquarters in Mexico City. During its initial phase, the Centre's activities focused mostly on Mexico's sphere of influence, which tended to exclude South America. In more recent years, the Banco de México came to accept greater participation by other members, and the institution has gradually evolved toward a more balanced regional organization.

Today, the Central Bank of Brazil is one of CEMLA's main supporting members. This was not always the case, as Brazilian authorities were not familiar with CEMLA services, and the language barrier between Brazil and the rest of Latin America did not help. More importantly, there was a sense of political rivalry between Mexico and Brazil, which for a time made Brazil feel like an outsider. The Central Bank of Argentina has from time to time played a leadership role at the Centre, and it has played an active role in recent efforts to strengthen the institution. Venezuela is also a major contributor, and it tends to be the largest consumer of CEMLA services among the Big Four (Mexico, Brazil, Argentina, and Venezuela).

The central banks of Chile and Colombia have been consistent supporters of the Centre throughout its existence, as have the central banks of Peru and Uruguay since their accession.

CEMLA is a member-funded institution, with dues set and paid annually following approval of a programme of activities and its budget. Associate members supply about 80 per cent of budgeted dues, with collaborating members providing the balance of the $2.5 million annual budget. In recent years, the Centre has been able to leverage its activities budget by attracting external funding at a ratio of approximately 2 to 1.

CEMLA's regular activities contain a substantial degree of cross-subsidization. Member dues are assigned roughly in proportion to IMF quotas, so that the larger economies in the region (Argentina, Brazil, Mexico, and Venezuela) provide about half of the annual budget. At the same time, CEMLA services are offered on an equal basis to all. As CEMLA services tend to cater to central banks with relatively basic training needs, and given that the level of sophistication of the central banks varies widely across the region, smaller economies and relatively unsophisticated central banks tend to benefit most from CEMLA and receive an indirect subsidy from the larger members.[3]

Under CEMLA's statutes, the Assembly is the institution's highest decision-making body. While all members may attend and participate in Assembly discussions, only associate members (the 30 regional central banks) may vote. Member representation is exercised by the head of delegation to the Assembly, who is usually the central bank governor. The Assembly meets twice a year to conduct CEMLA business, which includes electing a Board of Governors every two years and a Director General every five years. The Board also approves the annual programme of activities and budget and recommends approval of the annual dues to the Assembly.

The Director General is the chief executive officer at CEMLA, with responsibility for overall policy and execution. Administrative functions are delegated to a Deputy-Director General, who is appointed by the Board from a shortlist provided by the Director General. CEMLA has a total staff of 46, distributed among four departments: programmes, training, information services, and administration and finance.

[3] This situation led to a 2001 reform of the statutes, so that voting power was weighted by budget contributions, and the Board of Governors was enlarged to accommodate the 'Big Four' on a permanent basis and remaining associates on a rotating basis. Simultaneously, the organization has upgraded the level of its activities and implemented advanced technical assistance programmes, so as to provide more events and services of interest to its entire membership.

9.2.2. The Central Bankers' Networks

Nested within CEMLA are several informal networks. Like the Senior Budget Officials' network of the OECD (see Alex Matheson's chapter in this book), the CEMLA supports the meetings of central bank governors and other central bank specialists. The networks began as part of the CEMLA's educational and training mission, but in the mid-1960s it became apparent that this flexible structure could also serve as a platform for other activities. The Centre had intermittently organized meetings of technical-area specialists from central banks for the purpose of exchanging country experiences. In 1963, the Centre established a permanent Secretariat for annual meetings of central bank governors from the region, in order to 'reinforce the spirit of cooperation and friendship at the highest level, broaden their familiarity with problems faced by other countries, exchange experiences, provide for the appreciation of aspects of common interest and contemplate the possibility of joint action'. These meetings began in 1964 on an annual basis, but in view 'of the importance of financial cooperation among Latin American countries', by 1965 the governors were already meeting on a semi-annual basis.

Through these meetings, CEMLA provided a regional forum for the discussion of financial matters and initiatives among central banks at the highest level in a semi-formal environment. Many ideas were floated and some came to fruition, such as the development of a mechanism for the bilateral net settlement of foreign exchange through the Latin American Integration Association (LAIA, or ALADI in Spanish), the Latin American Export Bank (BLADEX), and the Latin American Reserve Fund (FLAR).

9.3. The Workings of the CEMLA Networks

CEMLA organizes meetings of the central bank governors twice a year, and on extraordinary occasions should the need arise. The first meeting of the year is usually a two-day event held in May. The second meeting coincides with the IMF and World Bank annual meetings (generally in late September), and is normally shorter (one day). The CEMLA Assembly and Board of Governors also hold sessions on both of these occasions.

CEMLA acts as Secretariat for the governors' meetings and takes on logistical functions such as arranging the venue, convening the participants, distributing the agenda and documents, providing simultaneous translation, and coordinating the programme of events with the host institution, as well as setting the agenda for discussion and inviting guest speakers. The latter responsibilities are undertaken in consultation with members via the Alternates Committee.

There are three distinct categories of governors' meetings.

9.3.1. *Central Bank Governors of the American Continent*

This is the oldest governors' meeting (held since 1963). It brings together the heads of central banks from North, South, and Central America and the Caribbean. The USA is represented by the Federal Reserve Board. The Bank of Spain has observer status, as long as the meetings coincide with others at which Spain is a full-fledged participant.

This meeting annually convenes governors as part of the governors' meetings in May for the express purposes of 'debating matters of common concern, broadening their understanding of monetary and lending conditions in their respective countries, reinforcing the spirit of cooperation among their institutions and developing closer personal contacts among themselves'. The meeting is intended to foster a lively exchange of opinions, and the delivery of pre-formulated presentations is discouraged. An annotated outline of the several programmed topics is usually prepared and circulated beforehand to set the stage for the lead speakers and allow other participants to prepare themselves prior to the general discussion. Any formal motions are referred to the CEMLA Assembly, where minutes of the proceedings can be kept and votes can be taken.

The meetings are quite exclusive—governors are permitted one adviser each, and he or she is encouraged not to participate in the proceedings. Special guests, either individuals or institutional representatives, are not allowed. On very exceptional occasions, a special session can be convened to invite a special guest to discuss a particularly urgent or important matter, on the condition that his or her participation be restricted to that session. Publicity regarding the events is kept to a bare minimum, and confidentiality of the proceedings is the rule. Submitted documents can be published by CEMLA only with authorization of the meeting and the authors.

9.3.2. *Central Bank Governors of Latin America and Spain*

Perhaps to make the exchange of opinions more lively, CEMLA was entrusted with the organization of a meeting restricted to Latin American governors and their counterpart from Spain. The meeting is held twice a year, once in May and once in September. Non-Latin American CEMLA governors may attend as observers only if the meeting coincides with the meeting of the Governors of the American Continent in May or with the CEMLA Assembly (May and September). Extraordinary meetings can also be called to discuss urgent issues. This forum is the most flexible instrument for reaching regional consensus on urgent issues, as the non-Latin American governors are automatically excluded.

Under normal circumstances, these meetings function very much like the American Continent meetings, and in fact are indistinguishable from them. The only significant difference, aside from periodicity and attendance, is a more liberal policy on special guests. Governors from collaborating member central banks outside the region and senior officials from international financial institutions frequently attend the May meetings, often as lead speakers on specific topics of interest.

For decades, the CEMLA May meetings have been a permanent fixture on the regional public financial circuit, attracting a high level of attendance and participation by governors. While there is unavoidable overlap with the topics discussed at the meetings organized by the World Bank, International Monetary Fund, and Bank for International Settlements, network members value the control they enjoy over the agenda and the regional focus of the discussions.

The format of the discussions has become more flexible over time; the use of visual aids is now routine. Of the original rules of procedure, only the emphasis on confidentiality and the absence of media remain. The main topics discussed are the international and regional economic and financial near-term scenarios, issues of international financial architecture, monetary and exchange rate policies, macroeconomic and financial stability, governance trends in central banking, and specific country experiences, usually following a balance of payments or banking-sector crisis.

9.3.3. IMF and IBRD Governors from Latin America, Spain and the Philippines

While the distinction between the first two meetings has tended to blur over time, the third type of governors' meeting remains separate and distinct. It convenes once a year during the IMF and World Bank annual meetings, usually before the meetings of the G24 and International Monetary and Financial Committee (IMFC). Since the governors of the Bretton Woods institutions are either central bank governors or ministers of finance, both are involved in the meeting. The membership of this network reflects the composition of the three 'Latin American' constituencies on the Executive Boards of the Bank and Fund, which include Spain, the Philippines, and Caribbean nations.

The agenda of these meetings reflects the main issues under current review at the Bretton Woods institutions, which are presented by the three Executive Directors from each institution. A general discussion of the topics usually follows. While these are normally informative sessions, they can sometimes lead to the hammering out of common positions among the regional representatives on the IMFC and Development Committees, and to the designation of regional spokespersons in the plenary sessions. The meeting is also used every two years to announce the new Executive Directors under the current rotation schemes.

9.3.4. Meetings of Central Bank Senior Staff

While central bank governors attending CEMLA meetings are usually accompanied by delegations that include senior staff members, the Centre also organizes periodic meetings for managerial staff. These meetings cover specialized areas, including foreign reserves management, open market operations, institutional communications, monetary policy, payments systems, human resources, legal and security issues, international relations, and internal auditing.

These meetings bring together practitioners with similar specialities for the purposes of experience-sharing, the dissemination of new techniques, and the discussion and adoption of standards and best practices in their respective fields. In some cases, they flag issues that are then brought to the attention of the governors (e.g. the application of international financial information standards to central bank financial statements). In other cases, the governors may refer a given topic for deeper analysis by the specialized group. The focus of this network, by and large, tends to be inward. Given the technical nature of their activities, it is only the monetary policy and international relations advisers who encounter wider issues within the international financial architecture that the governors may then take up in the appropriate international forum.

What is missing from this structure is a second tier of international policy discussion at a level immediately below that of governor, one that can be convened regularly to focus on an agenda of reform advocacy. Officials at this level combine both detailed policy knowledge and sufficient seniority to speak with freedom and authority. It is not that these individuals do not exist, but rather that their positions are difficult to identify within each hierarchy and do not correspond to each other across the structure of individual central banks. If each institution was asked to send the most trusted adviser to discuss a matter of the utmost delicacy in international finance, one would meet individuals occupying a dozen or so different positions from governor down. Since this would only occur in a scenario of urgency or emergency, such a meeting would be difficult to convene on a periodic basis.

9.3.5. Rival Organizations and Networks

At the regional level, there is no organization that competes directly with CEMLA in the services it provides, both in terms of technical support to central banks and as a secretariat for the governors' networks. However, the Inter-American Development Bank (IADB) and the ECLA at times organize events in the field of international finance, especially with respect to financial stability and monetary policy. The fact that IADB ownership tends to remain with finance ministries and that ECLA responds more to foreign ministries, though, creates a natural barrier to further integration with CEMLA.

CEMLA's competition is mainly at the international and sub-regional levels. While it would be difficult for an international organization to provide regional advocacy services for emerging economies, networks such as the G24 seek to provide them on a global level. CEMLA faces the most intense competition in the area of capacity-building, especially as large international financial institutions such as the IMF, World Bank, and BIS experience 'mission creep'. CEMLA's response has been to increase the quality and relevance of its programming and to associate rather than to compete with these well-resourced institutions.

Within the CEMLA's geographical area, the tendency towards sub-regional trade integration (Mercosur, Caricom, the Andean Pact, and Central America) has given rise to parallel moves in the direction of economic convergence, and macroeconomic and monetary coordination could eventually assume an important role. These regional groupings have established their own sequence of internal meetings where CEMLA is still conspicuously absent. If monetary integration were ever to become a feasible prospect at the regional level for Latin America, CEMLA should be considered the prime candidate to provide the basic institutional framework for the process.

9.4. Conclusions

9.4.1. *Achievements: The Debt Crisis of the 1980s*

While individual Latin American countries have experienced severe balance of payments crises in recent years (Mexico in 1995, Brazil in 1999, and Argentina in 2001, to name some of the major ones), their origins and timing were sufficiently different to allow the international financial community to deal with them on a case-by-case basis. Although each separate episode affected the region and brought under scrutiny the existing mechanisms to address them, one cannot compare them to the systemic threat that was the debt crisis of the 1980s. During that crisis, a high level of coordination among commercial bank lenders, debtor governments, lender country governments, and the Bretton Woods institutions became necessary. In that context, the CEMLA governors' meetings contributed to an orderly resolution of the crisis.

This contribution came in various forms. First, regular meetings of country debt negotiating teams (usually combining central bank and ministry of finance staff) were convened to share their experiences at the negotiating table with the Bank Advisory Committees (syndicated commercial lenders) and to exchange information, including the terms of the most recent restructuring agreements. In addition, the governors' meetings, which were attended by officials from the US Federal Reserve, served as a forum to advocate for the more active participation of creditor-country governments.

Third, members of the CEMLA networks who sat on the executive boards of the World Bank and IMF lobbied colleagues and staff at both institutions to end the initial 'hands-off' approach taken by the Bank and Fund, leading to the extension of sector- and structural-adjustment loans by the World Bank and other quick-disbursing facilities at the IMF as balance-of-payments support. Finally, governors from the region acted as spokespersons at Development and Interim Committee meetings and in the plenary sessions of the IMF/World Bank annual meetings. The CEMLA networks gave them a place to coordinate their positions and to focus on the elements most likely to alleviate their position as debtors.

Two factors facilitated the work of the CEMLA networks. In contrast to the fiery rhetoric of the region's foreign ministries, which called through the Cartagena Consensus for a debtors' cartel, the discourse of the finance ministers and central bank governors who sat in the CEMLA networks sounded much more moderate and attractive to the creditors.

In addition, the convergence of other significant debtor countries from around the world, such as Nigeria, South Korea, Turkey, and Yugoslavia, impressed upon bank creditors, their governments, and their supervisory agencies the need to abandon the case-by-case approach and implement a general framework in which all parties shared in the burden of adjustment. Taken together, these elements created the impression of an organized front, which must have had an impact. Thus were born the Baker (1985) and Brady Plans (1988), in which the US Treasury and the Federal Reserve played the lead role in bringing (and banging) heads together among banks, international financial institutions, and national supervisory agencies.

9.4.2. Strengths and Weaknesses

A main strength of the CEMLA networks is that they are embedded within a more formal institutional structure. There is a division of labour between the network and the formal organization—the exchange of knowledge and norm diffusion is performed by the organization, while consensus-building and policy coordination take place through the informal networks. There is, however, a feedback mechanism from the informal network to the institution. Any tensions or conflicts that arise in the networks are deflected towards the formal institution, where the statutes provide procedures and mechanisms to resolve disputes about matters such as the relative weight given to different components of the programme of activities, the absolute and relative structure of member dues and voting power, the succession to the key executive positions, and the reform of the statutes themselves. The governors' meetings remain for the most part uncontaminated by these issues, which are usually processed by the Board of Governors and referred to the Assembly for ratification. At the Board, there has traditionally been a strong emphasis on consensus-based decision-making and avoiding formal voting.

On the other hand, CEMLA networks also face several shortcomings that reflect its own structure, the nature of central banking, its relationship with other spheres of influence, and difficulties of policy coordination at the regional level. The networks are an unwieldy instrument for consensus-building if one considers that they bring together up to 30 associate members representing economies of very different sizes, organization, and economic integration. The larger economies of the region, as systemically significant members of other organizations and networks, often find it practical to forge common positions through bilateral consultations rather than through the network. In addition, it is not always easy to identify within the structure of central banks those persons with sufficient seniority and institutional weight to contribute to and participate in periodic meetings of a sensitive nature.

Third, central banks prefer to keep a low profile and are not quick to question the status quo nationally or internationally. There is a strong 'don't rock the boat' mentality, a natural reaction for institutions accustomed to maximizing under constraints and charged, *inter alia*, with maintaining stability. As a result, it takes a crisis of very significant proportions to galvanize central bankers into consultation and action. One does not get the impression that their main goal is the reform of the international financial architecture, though the subject is often on the agenda. Rather, they react when confronted with strong external shocks.

Experience has shown that the most effective interventions have occurred when central banks have acted in concert with ministries of finance and even with ministries of foreign affairs. This, of course, injects a measure of domestic politics and rivalry into matters, which can make them very complicated unless there is a strong supra-cabinet authority that can impose national teamwork. Also, while domestic politics may occasionally present obstacles to the smooth functioning of a regional network, it is more likely that regional politics play an even larger role.

In summary, we can conclude that while the CEMLA networks are a recognized vehicle for regional dialogue and cooperation, the networks are not permanently in use as agents of change in the international financial system. Rather, members resort to them under conditions of stress. Their efficient functioning in this capacity depends on good teamwork within and among countries, and political signals at the highest national and regional levels of decision-making are required to make this teamwork possible.

9.4.3. *Commentary by Richard Webb*

Former President of the Central Bank of Peru (2001–2003)

I thought this chapter on CEMLA an excellent choice for research into the role of developing-country networks in global financial governance. CEMLA is surely the dean of regional central bank networks in the developing world, and in that role probably stands only below the International Bank for Settlements in its length of service, member comfort and sense of belonging, and volume and quality of practical activities. At the same time, the very strength and longevity of CEMLA as an institution make it a useful test of the real bite that can be achieved by networking experiments in global finance.

I have been a privileged witness of CEMLA's work over four decades, as the course of my professional life drew me into and then out of central banking during three separate periods, in the 1960s, the 1980s, and the new millennium, and that experience is the main source for the following observations on Kenneth Coates' paper. For the most part I agree with his account, and in particular with his nuts-and-bolts analysis of the what and how of CEMLA's contribution. I share his view that in the case of the CEMLA networking story, the devil is in the details, in particular, the details of formal and informal institutional life. Just how much of a contribution was made by CEMLA is harder to determine, especially since what was achieved over that long period varied a great deal over time and across countries.

In terms of prestige and practical contribution, especially through training programmes, informal contacts, and formal meetings to discuss specific administrative and operational issues, CEMLA's best days were probably its early days, from the 1950s and into the 1970s. At the time, there were fewer external information and training resources on the scene, relevant research was scarce and foreign travel rare, while central bankers were relatively unsophisticated in economics and finance. The opportunity to travel to a CEMLA course or to meetings organized by CEMLA carried a prestige and mystique that today has been transferred to study in Wharton or Chicago, or attendance at meetings organized by international organizations. In addition, communication in all forms, access to information, and in-house research have all multiplied in the central banking world, reducing the scarcity value of CEMLA events. CEMLA training programmes are now reserved for more junior or second-tier staff members. For central bank senior managers and Board members, the bonding and networking side-effects of CEMLA's more formal offerings diminished steadily through the 1970s and 1980s, and, in my judgement, are now minor.

I believe that what CEMLA did achieve, especially over its first three decades, had much to do with language and cultural affinity within the region. In the 1960s, for instance, many central bankers did not speak English. There was an element of 'us' as distinct from the gringos at CEMLA events, the Spanish–Portuguese divide was never more than a very low wall, while Asia and Africa were distant planets. Cultural ease favoured bonding and open communication, especially at the more normally reserved senior policymaking level often occupied by non-professionals. In contrast, by the 1990s openness and bonding had become much more a matter of shared professional backgrounds.

The widely shared debt crisis of the 1980s escalated the potential value of networking, and in that sense provides a good test of the extent to which CEMLA's activities had created a capacity for using relationships, shared knowledge, and frequent communication as instruments to deal with the common problem. At this point in the story, my recollection of events is less favourable than Coates' account. It seems plausible that by 1983 a great deal of networking opportunity was indeed in place for collective lobbying and coordination by debtors, and certainly some exchange of information took place, CEMLA did facilitate contact with the US Fed and Treasury authorities, and the Cartagena Consensus did help to precipitate the Baker Plan, but the dominant policy line taken was to shun any form or appearance of collective action. In the psychology of debt resolution, both debtor and creditor persuade themselves of particular arguments for special treatment, and that the risk of contamination is minimal. In practice, CEMLA's potential for encouraging or organizing collective action was shunned by the dominant authorities. And that failure, I believe, helped to seal CEMLA's fate. Networking and capacity-building by Latin American central banks is now more a globalized than a regional business.

Conclusion: Networks of Influence?

Leonardo Martinez-Diaz and Ngaire Woods

Government networks have become a prominent feature of international relations and global economic governance, and they look poised to stay. In a world facing growing transnational problems that require greater international coordination and harmonization, yet one dominated by governments reluctant to cede power to supra-national organizations, networks will retain their appeal. At the same time, inter-governmental networking has also ceased to be the exclusive province of the richest and most powerful countries and is becoming a widespread practice among developing countries, including of both low- and middle-income countries.

How will developing countries fare in an increasingly networked world order? This book has tried to address this broad question by asking two smaller ones: Are networks exacerbating the inequalities of power already present in the world economy by giving the most powerful states another vehicle to exert their influence, or are they helping relatively weak states exert influence and build capacity of their own? And under what conditions might developing countries benefit from building their own networks?

At the outset we identified five distinct functions of government networks, recognizing that the effectiveness of networks will vary across functions: agenda-setting, consensus-building, policy coordination, knowledge creation and exchange, and norm-setting and diffusion. Some networks focus on 'advocacy', aiming to mobilize support for a certain cause, policy, or standard of behaviour, within but also outside the network. Meanwhile, 'self-help' or 'problem-sharing' networks focus on improving the quality of policymaking in member countries by building capacity through learning and coordination.

To guide the analysis and conclusions drawn in respect of each case we posed four conjectures in our introduction:

1. Government networks are a response to a real or perceived failure of formal, hierarchical institutions to deliver particular public or club goods;

2. The largest contributors of resources to a network will try to use the influence they derive from their contributions to 'capture' the network and steer its activities toward their own interests, possibly at the expense of other members. This should be particularly true when low-income countries are involved, as they are usually unable to cover the costs of the network's creation or of their own participation;

3. Even with unequal resource contributions, networks provide developing countries with greater voice and influence than international organizations. The absence of formal hierarchy, the low costs of exit, and the absence of formal voting mechanisms should allow states to interact on a more egalitarian basis than in international organizations and to 'punch above their weight';

4. Because of their much lower relative costs, greater flexibility, and more equal interactions among members, government networks are more attractive alternatives to international organizations and will eventually replace them.

This chapter outlines our findings and answers to these conjectures and to the overarching questions of the study. We first identify what we believe are the main insights to be drawn from each case study. Then, we connect these insights to the central questions of this book and discuss the implications.

1. Insights from the Cases

Of the eight networks studied in this book, some have been particularly effective as advocacy networks, setting or influencing the international agenda or mobilizing support for specific policies or standards of behaviour. Others have been more effective as self-help or problem-sharing networks, helping officials understand and grapple with policy challenges at the national and international level.

Below we present findings from four networks that have served essentially as advocacy networks—the G20 Finance Ministers and Central Bank Governors, the Commission for Africa, the ECOSOC Ad Hoc Groups, and Africa's 'G4'. The first three are 'mixed networks', with memberships that include both developed and developing countries. Subsequently, we present the findings from networks that have served less as advocacy forums and more as self-help and problem-sharing networks—the East Asian finance networks, the HIPC Finance Ministers' Network, the CEMLA networks of Latin American central bankers, and the network of OECD Senior Budget Officials and its non-OECD spin-offs.

1.1. *Group of 20 Finance Ministers and Central Bank Governors*

The first two chapters of this book covered the G20, which is arguably the most important mixed network dealing with international financial matters. Since its launch in 1999, the network has retained a healthy attendance and has produced a steady stream of communiqués and other documents. Some analysts see the G20 as a precursor to what could become an L20—a network of heads of state that would replace the G7/8 and change the contours of global economic governance.

As Rubio-Marquez and Martinez-Diaz show, this network has been most successful in knowledge exchange, building consensus on certain issues, and to a limited extent, in diffusing norms (financial standards). The G20 has helped build consensus around broad ideas that could then be pursued through more detailed commitments in international organizations. In particular, the G20 helped to build agreement on a framework for debt restructuring (collective action clauses and voluntary standards) and pushed for IMF quota reform. Key to these successes have been the network's membership, which includes officials from the G7 and key emerging economies and its agenda, which included issues the G7 was having difficulty dealing with alone.

The G20 was less successful in agenda-setting, knowledge creation, and policy coordination. Here, several constraints limited the network. The absence of a stable secretariat and staff constrained the generation of new knowledge and capacity-building efforts, even as it kept the network free from the bureaucratic agendas of international organizations. The heterogeneity of G20 members and their interests was an important limitation to meaningful policy coordination; policies for stimulating economic growth, for example, were left to individual countries to implement on their own. And once it exhausted its original mandate of financial crisis prevention and resolution, the G20 found it increasingly difficult to design an agenda that was at once relevant to all the members, politically acceptable, and narrow enough to be tractable.

The G20 case confirms the conjecture that networks emerge as a response to a failure or gap in existing institutions. The network emerged because there was no sufficiently autonomous and flexible forum for bringing together the most advanced economies and the 'systemically significant' emerging economies, whose cooperation was deemed necessary to achieve and preserve global financial stability. Existing forums and institutions, including the BIS and the International Monetary and Financial Committee, were seen as having the wrong membership, allowing for insufficient flexibility, or providing insufficient independence from Fund staff.

Were resources used to 'capture' the network? Not in this case. Despite the diversity of the G20's members, resource asymmetries were not severe enough to give some members dominance over the network. Every one of the G20's members could fully finance the costs of participating in the network. To be sure, Canada and Australia volunteered more resources from their own finance ministries to support the network's knowledge-exchange and capacity-building efforts, but these resources were not significant enough to give these countries any special influence. And when it came to hosting the network, holding the presidency, and supporting the secretariat annually, all members were well positioned to take on the task. No country or group of countries had a lock on these functions, especially after 2002, when the presidency began to shift regularly to non-G7 countries.

However, this does not mean that developing countries were able to exercise more influence than in international organizations. G7 influence—at least judging by the contents of the G20 communiqués—has been pervasive, and developing countries have been reluctant to challenge the G7 position, even when they have significant reservations. This may be due to a 'chilling effect' in which developing-country governments prefer to fight policy battles in formal organizations rather than expend political capital in the network. Developing countries became more active and outspoken as the network matured, but on the issues in which the G7 had strong preferences, the position of the dominant economies always prevailed.

The debate about the relationship between the G20, its developing-country members, and the existing institutions is an important one. On one side of the debate are proponents of the G20 who see it as an expansion of the G7, which successfully brought major emerging-market countries to the table. Tough critics of the G20 argue that the G7 created the network successfully to dilute pressure to reform the IMF. By creating an informal network in which discussions over the international financial architecture could take place without authoritative effect, the G7 was able to forestall any move by non-G7 countries collectively to advocate for a more radical reform. Informal networks which bring powerful and less powerful countries together can clearly be interpreted either as facilitating cooperation or co-optation.

Is the G20 a superior alternative and a potential replacement for international organizations? Not likely. Without a bureaucratic machinery of its own, the G20 has always depended on formal international organizations (especially the IMF, the World Bank, and the Bank for International Settlements), as well as other networks (the Financial Stability Forum and the Basel committees), to follow through and implement most of its recommendations. Also, the fact that developing countries seem to avoid fighting political battles in the network and conserve their political capital for battles in the executive boards of international organizations suggests that the G20 still sees those institutions as indispensable.

1.2. The Commission for Africa

In his chapter, Myles Wickstead describes the Commission for Africa as a 'network of networks'. The Commission—a brainchild of the British government—was tasked with forging a consensus on policy toward Africa and with using its well-connected members to mobilize governments and international bodies into action. The Commission was above all an advocacy network, and it largely succeeded in this function. It produced a clear and well-publicized report which served as an advocacy platform on key issues, particularly debt, trade, and aid. Subsequent advocacy by the network (and the networks represented on the Commission) underpinned some of the G8 commitments at Gleneagles. Equally, some of the report's conclusions framed positions taken in the IMF/World Bank meetings in September 2005, which resulted in international support for the debt package proposed by the Commission. The influence of the network also extended to NEPAD, the African Union, and the United Nations Economic Commission for Africa. The network's main functions were therefore knowledge-creation, consensus-building, and agenda-setting.

The Commission's successes include pushing the G8 to agree to deeper debt relief. Its advocacy may also have undergirded the G8's Gleneagles commitments to double aid to Africa, though those commitments have not been achieved. On trade, as Wickstead concedes, the Commission did not manage to shift existing attitudes or commitments. The Commission worked best as a network among its African members, but among several G8 countries, the Commission was seen as a British manoeuvre to circumvent the standard G8 preparatory process. Ultimately, the network could not overcome the unwillingness of G8 countries to coordinate their policies on Africa.

At least three factors seem to have contributed to the CfA's successes. The membership of the network comprised very senior and well-connected people of whom the media, governments, and international organizations took notice. Second, the network's agenda was well-aligned with the concerns of the G8, and the network enjoyed high-level access to the British government when the UK held the presidency of the G8. Third, the Commission's Secretariat was able to prepare a clear, well-argued and carefully costed set of proposals. Unlike the G20, whose secretariat shifts from year to year, the CfA benefited from a well-resourced personnel base. Finally, the informality of the process allowed commissioners to exchange views freely and reach consensus.

The failures of the Commission—in effecting the actual delivery of further aid and in shifting trade policy goals—reflected several constraints. The Commission was effective insofar as its advocacy spoke to items on which the G8 was prepared to deliver, but it seems not to have shifted G8 policies beyond debt relief, nor provided a forum within which powerful donor countries would genuinely engage. Tensions among G8 members were heightened by the composition of the Commission, which included three UK government ministers, and had no representatives from Russia, Germany, Italy, or Japan. This limited the CfA's influence and legitimacy among the G8, as well as its capacity to push the G8 as a whole to act on their collective targets. That said, unlike the G20, the Commission probably had more indirect influence through the personal networks of the commissioners and through its engagement from the outset with the media and non-governmental organizations.

The CfA case study confirms our first conjecture. Like the G20, the Commission filled an institutional gap. It aspired to generate new ideas—in a forum in which African leaders and decision-makers were full partners—about how Africa's growth and development could best be promoted. Existing institutions had largely failed to deliver on this. The World Bank, the IMF, and UN agencies had long been producing policy recommendations for African governments, but they had not succeeded in creating a vision in which African leaders felt they had ownership. In addition, existing institutions had a clear stake in preserving elements of the status quo in debt, aid, and trade. The CfA network was seen as an important way to sidestep the position in which existing formal institutions seemed locked. For developing countries and their development partners, the Commission provided a flexible vehicle to change participation in the debate and to involve African leaders directly.

Our second conjecture was also confirmed. The UK government, which largely bankrolled the CfA network, clearly exerted more influence than other members (the Secretariat was headed and staffed by British civil servants, and there were three UK ministers on the Commission). However, as mentioned above, the perception of excessive UK influence in the network exacerbated tensions among G8 members and undermined the Commission's capacity to mobilize the G8 in favour of the policies it advocated.

Was the Commission trying to replace the international organizations that failed to deliver on Africa? Clearly, the CfA could not replace any formal organizations. Despite its relatively well-developed Secretariat, the network had neither policy-implementation capacity nor a system for monitoring the implementation of the positions agreed in the network. To some degree, this is a limitation of all networks. However, there have been efforts to build in some form of monitoring of the commitments made by the G8 and others. In 2006, British Prime Minister Tony Blair announced the creation of the Africa Progress Panel (APP), an independent monitoring mechanism chaired by former UN Secretary-General Kofi Annan and comprising eight members, most of whom were closely involved with the work of the Commission for Africa. The APP is likely to have much in common with the CfA, not least because it will also operate as a network of networks. Like the Commission, the APP will lack implementation capacity. Its creators hope will have the credibility and authority to exert and sustain moral pressure to ensure continuing progress in Africa.

1.3. *The ECOSOC Ad Hoc Advisory Groups*

The Ad Hoc Advisory Groups (AHAGs) were created by the ECOSOC of the United Nations in 2002 to assist the United Nations in its efforts to promote peace, human security, and economic development in countries emerging from conflict. In his account, Prantl describes the groups as a hybrid of network and institution. They have some degree of formal

241

authority, membership, and leadership, yet no formal decision-making power and considerable flexibility as to procedure and function.

The Ad Hoc Advisory Groups are in essence advocacy networks. As advocates of 'forgotten' countries, the AHAGs supported the cause of small and very poor countries such as Guinea-Bissau and Burundi, countries that risk being neglected by the international community. The groups have also served to highlight problems of coherence where different parts of the United Nations system deal separately with issues of security and development and to highlight the need for more cooperation within and across agencies working towards security and economic development in these countries.

In respect of our first conjecture, the AHAGs emerged as a solution to several failings of formal institutions. Governments had become unwilling to engage in peace-building and post-conflict reconstruction, scared off by the experiences of Somalia and Rwanda. Second, the 'international architecture' for dealing with states emerging from conflict was fragmented and incoherent. A plethora of different UN agencies joined state and non-state donors in peace-building and post-conflict reconstruction with little coherence or coordination. Furthermore, where commitments were made, they were often not monitored or sustained. Finally, to the extent that development assistance was being planned and implemented, the international system was failing to give voice to the government, officials, and people of the recipient country itself.

Resource asymmetries, while clearly an issue because of the very different levels of wealth of the AHAG members, did not have a big impact on power and influence within the groups. This is because the groups were financed not by member governments, but by an international organization—most of the funding came from the UN's Department of Economic and Social Affairs and its Department of Political Affairs. UN funding helped protect the groups against any attempts by individual members to capture their activities. It should be noted, however, that resources were always scarce and a real constraint on the groups' activities. The close symbiosis between the groups and an international organization (the UN) illustrates how networks can complement, rather than replace, formal institutions.

The AHAGs did succeed in giving small, developing countries more voice and influence than would have otherwise been the case. The ad hoc group on Guinea-Bissau provided a vehicle for coordinating government policy and donors' financial contributions, which were channelled through the Economic Emergency Management Fund. In the case of

Burundi, the ad hoc advisory group operated more as an intermediary and champion for the country's interests in donor meetings, looking after the needs of the country before turning over the mandate of the ad hoc group to the Peace-building Commission. Crucial to the success of the ad hoc groups was the membership of each group, which ensured links to the relevant UN organs. The groups also helped to ensure a continuous flow of information between the field and headquarters of several international agencies.

The shortcomings of the AHAGs were not only related to a lack of resources. The groups failed to address how best to bridge humanitarian assistance needs with longer-term development support, and they failed to collaborate with regional and sub-regional institutions. Finally, although the groups came up with innovative ways to meet the emergency needs of countries, in practice, they had no capacity to push donors to live up to commitments.

1.4. *Africa's G4*

Khadija Bah presents an analysis of the network responsible for Africa's New Partnership for African Development (NEPAD). The NEPAD was forged from three different African plans for political and economic renaissance across the continent. President Thabo Mbeki of South Africa had begun to construct a new agenda for Africa. Algerian President Abdelaziz Bouteflika envisioned a Conference on Security, Stability, Development, and Cooperation in Africa (CSSDCA), and Senegalese President Abdoulaye Wade had proposed an 'OMEGA Plan' for the reinvigoration of Africa's infrastructure, education, health, and agriculture. These leaders, together with Olusengu Obasanjo of Nigeria, formed an intimate, personality-driven, four-man network, which Bah calls 'Africa's G4'.

Like the Commission for Africa, the G4 was above all an advocacy network, with agenda-setting as its chief function. African leaders had been challenged by the G8 to come up with a workable plan for a new compact between donor countries and their African development partners. The NEPAD was the G4's answer to this challenge. It presented the G8 with a workable plan to re-engage the continent, this time in partnership with African leaders.

In contrast to other networks, the emergence of the G4 was not so much a response to a failure of international organizations, but an effort to coordinate competing national efforts to formulate a vision for African economic development. More broadly, however, the G4 was motivated by a lack of confidence in existing institutions. The Organization of African Unity was seen as weak and ineffectual, until it was finally dissolved in 2002, replaced by a new, but untested, African Union. The United Nations Economic Commission for Africa was seen as lacking in African ownership. The G4 leapt into this gap, drawing together their respective plans into an overarching project.

The successes of the G4 are attributable to the leadership of the four Presidents—each with their own vision for progress in Africa, political agenda, and interest in giving voice to that vision. The members of the G4 were respectively linked to other regional and global organizations: Mbeki was Chair of the Non-Aligned Movement, Obasanjo was Chair of the G77, and Bouteflika was Chair of the Organization of African Unity. Their joint project, NEPAD, was also linked to other initiatives, including the Commission for Africa. Resources and 'capture' were not a significant issue in this network; most interactions between the four presidents, their personal representatives, and their offices would take place through conference calls or in the sidelines of international meetings.

The G4 illustrates the limits of a personality-driven network driven above all by individuals rather than institutions. According to Bah, these qualities gave the network visibility and prestige, but they also undermined its legitimacy in the eyes of many who did not see the G4 as rightfully speaking for a whole continent. Also, the G4's distancing from regional institutions weakened the prospects for follow-through and cooperation on a regional basis. As Bah puts it, '... the NEPAD was a top-down, G4-driven initiative, with little or no consultation with wider OAU leadership and African society'. This point suggests that the G4 network could have been more effective had it enjoyed a closer relationship with international organizations, especially the OAU.

1.5. East Asian Finance Networks

In the Asia-Pacific region, seven distinct but overlapping networks exist among finance ministers, central bankers, and their officials. Among these, Nesadurai argues that the ASEAN + 3 group and the EMEAP have been the most effective. Above all, these have been self-help or problem-sharing networks, although they have occasionally delved into advocacy activities. In particular, the networks have produced substantive proposals for preventing and managing financial crises. The strongest functions of this network have been knowledge production and exchange, as well as agenda-setting.

The successes of East Asia's finance networks have emerged from two specifically regional networks: one comprising finance ministers and the other comprising central bank officials. The Chiang Mai Initiative pursued by the ASEAN + 3 group of finance ministers has been a success. It has developed bilateral swap arrangements among its members and an increasingly multilateralized mechanism for mutual support. Meanwhile, the EMEAP launched a bond fund investing contributions by EMEAP members in domestic currency bonds issued in the region. It has been accompanied by a further ASEAN + 3 initiative—the Asian Bond Market Initiative—which helps members to develop the national infrastructure needed to support efficient bond markets.

Nesadurai argues that the success of the East Asian networks lies in part in their composition and in part in their working procedures. Leadership by Japan and China has been crucial for providing the resources for swap arrangements, funding research, and taking the initiative in negotiating the swap arrangements. In all these ways Japan and China have played a key role. At the same time, the success of the networks lies in their egalitarianism and the strong embrace of genuine consensus in their workings: no decision is agreed while any member continues to withhold support of it. Power is not exercised to coerce members into agreement. A simple explanation for this seeming contradiction between strong leadership and egalitarianism lies in the counter-balancing effects of Japan and China each vying for influence, yet wedded to the advantages of greater regional financial and monetary cooperation.

A further success of the East Asian networks has been in capacity-building and in this smaller countries have been able to take the lead in areas in which they have technical expertise. One example of capacity-building has been in designing regional bond funds which could invest in domestic-currency denominated bonds. Common standards were required to make the fund work, and this drew officials into jointly designing, executing, and promoting the regional bond fund and thereby sharing (and jointly acquiring) valuable knowledge (including from the BIS, ADB, and private sector) so as to advance common solutions. This is just one of the examples Nesadurai gives to highlight the extent to which networks in the region develop shared and trusted analytical tools (for ASEAN + 3 surveillance) and practical policy-oriented research grounded in practical experience.

How do our four conjectures play out in this case? The East Asian finance networks certainly emerged due to the failure of international agencies to meet the needs of regional governments. In the wake of the

1997 financial crisis, the governments of the region had little confidence in existing institutions, including APEC and the international financial institutions. At the heart of the problem was the US dominance of existing institutions. While Asian countries wanted to pursue regional solutions after the financial crisis, the US government pushed strongly for line that kept the IMF at the centre. This led to the creation (within APEC) of the US-sponsored Manila Framework Group in November 1997, comprising 14 of the 21 APEC members. The Manila Framework Group was envisioned as a way to support and strengthen the IMF's role within the region through regional surveillance. However, with little buy-in from countries in the region, the initiative was dissolved in 2004.

The second conjecture is about resources. China and Japan have played a key role in providing resources to the East Asian finance networks. However, this does not seem to have led to domination or capture by China and Japan. The networks have enjoyed a high degree of egalitarianism, in part due to the counter-balancing effects of two large resource-providers and in part due to their commitment to a consensus-driven process.

The third conjecture is about voice and influence. For developing countries, the successful East Asian networks highlight the useful inward-facing functions networks can play, such as in enhancing capacity, as well as the outward-facing role they can play in cementing international cooperation within the region and thereby enhancing the bargaining power and influence of Asian countries in other forums. They seem to have enhanced both international voice and regional capacity.

Finally, in respect of the prospects for replacing existing institutions, developments in Asia suggest that what began as a group of networks is rapidly consolidating into more institutionalized arrangements, perhaps leading to a de facto Asian Monetary Fund. Put simply, networks are not replacing institutions. Rather, networks have become the seeds for new institutions.

1.6. *The HIPC Finance Ministers*

The Heavily Indebted Poor Countries' (HIPCs') Finance Ministers' Network was established in 1999 as a forum for Finance Ministers from countries that could become eligible for the IMF–World Bank HIPC Debt Relief Initiative, which was announced in 1996. The network has served as a forum within which the indebted countries have had frank discussions among themselves, and sometimes with representatives of like-minded donors and the Bretton Woods Institutions about prospects for debt relief.

It has been particularly effective in fostering learning, the exchange of information, and advocacy.

In terms of self-help, the network permitted HIPC Finance Ministers and their officials to exchange information and views on the progress of debt relief, poverty reduction, and new financing. It also allowed HIPC officials to formulate autonomously their collective positions on international debt and development financing issues. This has had implications for the advocacy functions of the network, which has served as a mechanism for HIPC Finance Ministers better to exercise voice in the international system. It has helped HIPCs to access enhanced debt relief and better quality new financing.

The HIPC Finance Ministers' Network has had no formal organizational authority to arbitrate and resolve disputes, nor a hierarchy for decision-making. Nevertheless, the network has proven remarkably successful in leveraging the influence of the smallest and poorest heavily indebted countries in global institutions, and with the wider international community, as well as fostering learning and cooperation among HIPCs.

With respect to our first conjecture, the network emerged to fill serious gaps in the existing institutions. There was no forum in which HIPC Ministers could exchange information with their peers on how to respond to IMF–World Bank ideas about their debt relief needs and to creditor proposals for debt relief, nor to consider how best to negotiate with these groups. Existing institutions were either dominated by donors or by developing countries with different interests. Furthermore, discussions in the pre-existing institutions were hampered by formal procedures and speech-making, and the lack of formal voting power or voice by indebted countries. Finally, the structure of debt relief negotiations was locked into a case-by-case approach, which meant that individual indebted countries had no access to the experience of others.

In terms of resources, the HIPC Finance Ministers' Network benefited from supportive donors who funded meetings of the Ministers but were kept at arms' length by the Secretariat, which was staffed by a non-governmental group. The network seems to have avoided domination by any one resource-provider. In his commentary on the HIPC Finance Ministers' Network, Gerald Helleiner largely agrees with the assessment presented by Matthew Martin, describing the network as a focused and flexibly structured 'direct mutual support system', distinctive because it is largely unfiltered by and independent of aid donors, international institutions, other networks or private sources of finance, each with agendas of their own.

Did the group enhance the voice or influence of the HIPC Ministers? Here the findings are weaker. Martin argues that the network strengthened positions taken in international negotiations. However, as Helleiner reflects, a stronger 'voice' in the international arena is of little avail if traditional power relationships or bureaucratic structures continue to determine outcomes that take little account of what is being expressed. Helleiner suggests that such networks could further strengthen influence in two ways. First, armed with better information about donors and their programmes in other countries, HIPCs might push more confidently and effectively for more attractive modes of aid financing, in Helleiner's words, for 'grants rather than loans, budget support rather than project finance, less stringent and inappropriate conditionality, etc.—and mechanisms that more adequately support local ownership of programmes. Equally, the HIPC Finance Ministers' Network can provide a collective springboard for engaging more with like-minded donor governments in order to press for change in international institutions. Could the network replace international institutions? Clearly not. The network exists to strengthen the hand of otherwise weak officials negotiating within formal institutions.

1.7. Senior Budget Officials' Networks

The network comprised by the Senior Budget Officials' Working Party of the OECD was established in 1979 as a forum for developed-country budget officials to exchange information about budgeting practices and to learn from each other. The OECD SBO has been a very effective network at knowledge production and exchange, norm diffusion, and gradual consensus-building. While this is clearly not a developing-country network, its story is instructive because, as one of the OECD's more successful technical working groups, it is seen today by developing and transition economies as a model to be emulated when building their own networks of budget officials.

Like other networks studied here, the OECD SBO was created to fill an institutional gap. It was established by civil servants looking for national solutions to national problems in an area where formal international organizations were neither active nor well-suited to deal with the political sensitivities of public-expenditure management. It was also driven by the fact that budget officials found few opportunities to network productively with other government officials in their own countries. As Matheson quips, 'a budget officer's only friend can be another budget officer'.

The SBO's success is due to several aspects of the network. The network is nested within a formal international organization (the OECD) that supports it logistically, financially, and intellectually. Thanks to the OECD staff who are paid to consult with the network's members and brainstorm about the network's agenda, the SBO's agenda has remained fresh and relevant to the membership. At the same time, thanks to the seniority of the network's participants, the network has remained autonomous from its institutional host. Indeed, the SBO illustrates well how a network can establish a mutual symbiosis with an international organization, benefiting from its support but neither replacing it nor compromising its own autonomy in the process.

Another ingredient for its success is that the network is a peer group that can be considered an epistemic community, as it is composed of officials from advanced economies, drawn from the same government agencies, facing similar policy problems, and sharing a common professional culture and common technical language and technology. The participants also shared a common political agenda—to strengthen their own position at home by networking with their counterparts abroad.

An approach characterized by gradualism also helped. The network moved slowly, avoiding premature commitments or peer review processes that members would have found overly intrusive and might have scared off network participants. Over time, this gradualism promoted an environment in which members felt sufficiently comfortable to experiment with more ambitious and sovereignty-sensitive initiatives, such as peer reviews of domestic budget policies. In the OECD SBO, all members shouldered a significant portion of the resources, directly and indirectly through their contributions to the OECD's budget. For this reason, the issue of 'capture' was not relevant in this case.

As in the case of the OECD SBO, the non-OECD spin-offs of CABRI and CESEE were sparked by the absence of meaningful cooperation and exchange on budgetary matters in international or regional organizations. One of the problems in these new 'self-help' or 'problem-sharing' networks in sub-Saharan Africa and Central and Eastern Europe was the lack of resources, as poor countries and even transition economies could not cover the cost of their own participation in the networks. Therefore, a dominant state or leader emerged to provide intellectual and political leadership and to bear much of the financial costs of running the networks. CABRI was largely bankrolled by the South African Treasury, while the CESEE, to a smaller extent, was financed by the Dutch government.

Has this unequal distribution of costs led to capture? CABRI appears to be manoeuvring the donor-capture dilemma well—South Africa plays the central role, but early on Kenya, Uganda, and Mozambique became more active supporters of the network. The South African Treasury also appears to be sensitive to the need to foster a sense of ownership by other network members. The CABRI network appears to be most promising in knowledge production and exchange, with potential for agenda-setting and norm diffusion. Critical to its future will be South Africa's willingness to keep providing financial and intellectual leadership, as well as whether other leaders emerge over time to share some of the costs. The CESEE in Eastern Europe is even newer than CABRI and therefore harder to assess. It suffers from the risk of being perceived as too donor-driven, and it is not yet clear if there is enough interest among the membership to sustain it, especially as the Dutch government begins to reduce its contribution.

Will these networks replace international organizations? This seems unlikely, partly because other organizations are largely absent from this issue area and partly because the networks still have to show that they can survive and flourish. This is not a foregone conclusion. The CESEE, in particular, is hamstrung by its heterogeneous membership; countries with undemocratic governments—whose budgeting practices differ substantially from those of their more democratic counterparts—may find little relevance and value in network participation.

1.8. *Latin American Central Bank Governors' Networks*

In Latin America, four separate but overlapping networks of central bankers started coming together in the 1960s, bringing together governors from the entire Western Hemisphere, from Latin America, from Spain, and from the 'Latin American' constituencies of the executive boards of the World Bank and IMF. Nested within CEMLA—a formal organization devoted to enhancing the technical capacity of the region's monetary authorities—the networks enjoyed logistical and technical support. The CEMLA networks have many promising qualities: senior representation, a long history, support from a formal organization, autonomy from the institutional host, and a regional focus. Yet, the CEMLA networks, while relatively effective in their early history, have been weak and unproductive since the 1980s, especially when compared with their East Asian counterparts.

The Latin American central bankers' networks confirm our conjecture on the origins of networks: they started meeting in 1963, when technical expertise in the region's central banks was modest and when central bankers had few opportunities to compare notes with each other. As we have seen, this motivation became less important as global networks of central bankers thickened and as central banks became more sophisticated and globally connected.

Our second conjecture was also confirmed by this case. The Mexican central bank was the driving force behind the CEMLA and its networks. Based in Mexico City, the CEMLA was largely staffed by the Bank of Mexico and headed by a Mexican official for most of its history. This suggests that Mexican officials had considerable influence over the networks' agenda and work plans. The Mexicans' dominant role in CEMLA probably contributed to undermining their effectiveness by making officials from the other major Latin American economy, Brazil, more reluctant to participate actively in a network perceived to be too dominated by Mexico. This is unfortunate, as the network would have benefited from the leadership of both countries, just as Chinese and Japanese leadership has been crucial for the APT and EMEAP networks in East Asia.

Coates argues that during the debt crisis of the early 1980s, the CEMLA networks helped Latin American governments strengthen their position during negotiations with creditors and international financial institutions by providing a forum where they could exchange information, coordinate positions, and lobby each other. This is consistent with our conjecture that networks can help developing countries exert more influence in international financial matters.

However, as Richard Webb points out, that capacity was limited by the authorities' fear that they might be forming a bloc, something they perceived as deleterious to their negotiating position. Since the debt crisis, it is not clear that the networks have accomplished much beyond information sharing and possibly some consensus-building. Knowledge and expertise in the region's national central banks has improved dramatically, reducing the need for networking. Today, the CEMLA networks have become another entry in the long list of networks and meetings to which Latin American central bankers now have access, and not a particularly important one at that. For this reason, it seems implausible that they could ever replace formal international organizations.

2. Networks and International Organizations

This book has explored the emergence of networks in development finance, their relationship with international institutions, the ways they work, and the conditions under which they are most likely to be influential. What are the central insights to be drawn from these cases?

The cases point to a clear relationship between networks and formal international institutions. Typically, networks have been created where formal institutions have failed in terms of responsiveness, representativeness, or effectiveness. The failure of existing institutions adequately to represent countries spurred the creation of East Asian finance networks, while their insufficient responsiveness toward specific groups of countries spurred the creation of the Commission for Africa, the Ad Hoc Groups, and the HIPC Finance Ministers group. The inability of existing regional institutions to effectively facilitate and coordinate national policies spurred the emergence of Africa's 'G4'. In other cases, networks emerged to fill voids where formal institutions were not sufficiently flexible or sensitive to regional concerns. The former concern led to the creation of the G20, and the latter to the creation of the CABRI and CESEE networks and the CEMLA networks.

The cases suggest that the relationship between government networks and international organizations can be of four different types. In some cases, the two are *complementary*: a mutual symbiosis develops between network and organization, with the networks providing the sort of flexible, confidential, and non-bureaucratic exchanges necessary for officials to reach consensus or learn from each other, while the international organizations provide the technical and institutional backing needed to translate the network's ideas into implementable policies. International organizations provide another advantage: as Coates points out in his chapter, networks can sometimes deflect conflictive issues away from themselves—where conflict cannot be arbitrated effectively—and toward formal institutions, where conflict-resolution mechanisms exist. Finally, networks can help global governance adapt to changing conditions more quickly than would otherwise be the case.

Facilitating adaptation of global governance and international organizations is an especially important contribution that networks can make. For example, the G20 was created because the G7 perceived the need to engage emerging economies in a grouping that mirrored the flexible and autonomous structure of the G7. The Commission for Africa was created by the UK Prime Minister to bring together like-minded officials sharing a resolve to find a new approach to Africa, including officials from Africa, as well as private and NGO networks. The ECOSOC Ad Hoc Groups were created to draw together small and effective groups of those sharing a concern for small and otherwise neglected countries. In each of these cases, powerful actors were pushing for a network as a flexible, small, efficient way to build and drive a new agenda, and in the process, the resulting networks helped formal institutions—the IMF, the G7 governments, and the UN—adapt to new challenges.

In other cases, the nature of the relationship between networks and organizations is *competitive*. Here, the networks attempt to provide the same goods as international organizations, as is the case, for example, with the Asian central bankers' networks, which are trying to provide a few of the same public goods currently provided by the IMF. The obstacle, however, is that in contrast to international organizations, networks do not have the authority or processes to arbitrate and resolve disputes among members, and this limits the degree to which networks can provide goods that might generate conflict among members.

For example, the East Asian central bankers' networks have been very useful for building a net of multi-country swap agreements to provide emergency liquidity to the network's members under the Chiang Mai Initiative. But if those agreements are ever invoked, and if conflict arises over the terms of the financing or other aspects of the arrangements, the network will have no way of resolving that conflict with finality, should the members reach an impasse. At the IMF, in contrast, such a conflict would ultimately be resolved through voting in the executive board. In short, there are limits to how far networks can supplant formal institutions, unless they adopt some of the characteristics of formal institutions.

A third kind of relationship between networks and international organizations can be characterized as *rebalancing*. Here, networks serve to strengthen the position of countries that are relatively weak inside international organizations by providing them with an external forum for strategizing, sharing information, and coordinating positions. This kind of relationship can strengthen the influence of developing countries in major institutions, and it comes closest to the title's concept of a 'network of influence'.

For example, the HIPC Finance Ministers and NEPAD G4 networks have facilitated an exchange of views and some coordination in respect of an agenda to present in international negotiations with donors and 'partners'. In doing so, these networks have facilitated collective capacity-builder and consensus-building for negotiations, quietly rebalancing power in negotiations in favour of the less powerful participants.

Finally, networks and formal institutions may operate in *parallel*, having little effect on each other. The CEMLA networks and the networks of budget officials come closest to this category, even though they still have some degree of interaction with other international organizations. This kind of relationship is rare in its pure form, as it would require network activity in an area in which international organizations are totally inactive and a network that has no use for a relationship with formal institutions. While our fourth conjecture was that networks would eventually replace international organizations and give way to a fully networked world order, the cases in this book suggest that government networks are much more likely to flourish alongside international organizations, often complementing them, sometimes competing with them, and occasionally helping to rebalance their internal political dynamics.

3. Building Effective Networks

The case studies in this book also allow us to identify characteristics that make networks effective. The right balance between securing adequate resources while maintaining sufficient autonomy from those providing the resources is crucial. Yet, it is also particularly difficult to attain in mixed- and developing-country networks, where members' capacity to contribute varies widely, and where outside donors or regional leaders may be required to foot all or most of the bill and are therefore tempted to dominate the network.

Second, and closely related, is the issue of leadership and hierarchy within the network. In some networks, the leadership of powerful states has been key for providing resources as well as an agenda and political momentum, and when the resolve of powerful creators has weakened, so too has the momentum of the network. For example, the G20, the CEMLA networks, and the Commission for Africa are all instances where the ongoing leadership of the instigators seems crucial to the ongoing centrality of the network, and where that leadership wanes so too does the network. This contrasts with networks in which leadership plays a less central role, because key leaders counter-balance one another's influence, or because they use procedures for agenda-setting and debate which encourage a more egalitarian approach (such as in the East Asian central bankers' networks), or because the coordination and knowledge-production role is less unequally shared among members (such as among the HIPC Finance Ministers).

The degree to which a network is properly 'nested' in a larger institutional landscape—whether the network has the right linkages to other networks and formal institutions—is also a key characteristic of successful networks. For example, the OECD's Senior Budget Officials network found the OECD a useful nesting place, but developing-country spin-offs are having difficulty forging the right institutional links. The East Asian finance networks have strong connections to each other and to overlapping regional initiatives, while the HIPC Finance Ministers have benefited from non-governmental assistance, which has helped create a member-driven structure. The G20's relationships with the BIS-based networks, with the FSF, and with the World Bank and IMF have been crucial for translating its communiqués into policies. In the case of Africa's 'G4', their partnership with the G8 has locked them into an ostensible compact. But they will be expected to deliver more accountable government even if G8 members defect on their promises of more aid.

At the outset of this study, we expected to find that the size of a network would affect its success. Collective action theory suggests that networks with a smaller number of members will be more likely to succeed than larger networks, even though larger numbers might be of some use in agenda-setting.[1] Size can affect the degree of participation by each member in a network, as well as the depth and quality of the discussion. Free riding is also likely to increase with size.[2] The confidentiality of proceedings also diminishes as membership size grows, making members more reluctant to share sensitive information and to speak frankly, eroding the quality of the exchange within the network.

That said, these conjectures are not borne out by our case studies. Some small networks have been used by powerful actors to push forward issues or build a consensus among a small, effective grouping (such as the G20, and the Ad Hoc Groups). In other cases, the size of the membership network compares favourably to the size of membership in associated international institutions (the IMF, the United Nations ECOSOC). Some of the effective information and knowledge-sharing networks have

[1] Mancur Olson, *The Logic of Collective Action: Public Goods and Theory of Groups* (Harvard University Press, Cambridge: 1st edn. 1965, 2nd edn. 1971).

[2] On the problems of coalition-building as membership size increases, see Amrita Narlikar and John Odell, 'The Strict Distributive Strategy for a Bargaining Coalition: The Like Minded Group in the World Trade Organization, 1998–2001', in John Odell (ed.), *Negotiating Trade: Developing Countries in the WTO and NAFTA* (Cambridge: New York University Press, 2006).

relatively large memberships and their effectiveness seems to have been more a function of the like-mindedness of their members, the extent to which they share similar problems, and define those problems in similar ways.

In conclusion, networking among government officials can enhance the prospects, influence, and negotiating power of weak states in international relations, but the challenges are considerable. Networks of the weak risk never quite getting off the ground and lacking the resources, the leadership, and the institutional linkages to have influence. At the same time, participation in networks of the strong poses a different dilemma for developing countries. Mixed networks promise a place at the table with powerful countries and therefore a possible measure of voice and influence. However, networking with the powerful also poses the risk of participating in a forum in which weaker countries do not enjoy institutional protections and where they can be more easily pressured into endorsing a course of action they do not support.

The rationale and advantages of mixed government networks from the point of view of powerful countries are clear. They provide small, informal forums within which new solutions can be road-tested and a new consensus to back them can be built. But for developing countries the question is: will they have input into the new consensus? Some networks look more like pure power-political arenas in which developing countries have no formal rights of representation or participation; they are simply beholden to those who have invited them and seek their agreement. But other networks are more forums for genuine solution-finding, deliberation, and learning in which the weak can exercise influence through participation.

Our study highlights two critical factors. First, the network's agenda must be designed to ensure that all members see it as relevant to their interests, amenable to practical solutions, and not easily dealt with through existing institutions, either because the institutions lack capacity or because the issue is too sensitive to be dealt with in a formal setting. If the agenda ceases to be universally relevant, tractable, and best dealt with within the network, the group begins to atrophy and decline.

Second, and most importantly, the most powerful players in the network (in terms of their global or regional standing, financial contributions, or political influence) must be willing to foster and tolerate a high degree of ownership by other members, allowing the network to develop inclusive procedures for agenda-setting, deliberation, and decision-making. Because networks have low barriers to exit, those who value the network face high incentives to accommodate all members and foster ownership. This low-cost exit option is at once the networks' greatest strength and greatest weakness, and what gives otherwise weak states a measure of influence they do not enjoy in formal organizations, where the costs of exit are higher.

Index

Figures, notes and tables are indexed in bold.